The Messenger's Motives...

Ethical Problems of the News Media

John L. Hulteng

University of Oregon

Prentice-Hall, Inc., Englewood Cliffs, New Jersey

Library of Congress Cataloging in Publication Data

HULTENG, JOHN L (date)
    The messenger's motives.

    Bibliography: p.
    Includes index.
    1. Journalistic ethics.   I. Title.
PN4756.H8   174′ .9′097   75–25631
ISBN 0–13-577478–0
ISBN 0–13-577460–8 pbk.

© 1976 by **Prentice-Hall, Inc.**, Englewood Cliffs, New Jersey

Printed in the United States of America

10   9   8   7

Prentice-Hall International, Inc., *London*
Prentice-Hall of Australia, Pty. Ltd., *Sydney*
Prentice-Hall of Canada, Ltd., *Toronto*
Prentice-Hall of India Private Limited, *New Delhi*
Prentice-Hall of Japan, Inc., *Tokyo*
Prentice-Hall of Southeast Asia (Pte.) Ltd., *Singapore*

Contents

A Pervasive and Perplexing Issue...

"I think the ethics of our profession are on trial with the American people." Howard H. Hays, Jr., newspaper editor.[1]

A news photographer's lens catches the anguished, unbelieving faces of five small children seated in a police car, watching as firemen carry the body of their mother from her burning home. The picture appears on page one next morning.

A TV anchorman, delivering his nightly newscast, pauses after an item quoting the governor on new plans to deal with industrial pollution, smiles ever so slightly, and adds: ". . . or so he says."

A California winemaker invites three dozen food editors and writers for newspapers, magazines, and broadcast networks to San Francisco to spend an eventful and expense-free weekend inspecting vineyards, tasting vintages, and touring night clubs—all to give the journalists a "better understanding" of the products about which they are going to write or broadcast in the future.

A wire service files from Hollywood a lengthy story on the arrest of the son of a famous actress, now past her peak but still remembered throughout the world. The son has been charged with making pornographic movies involving pre-teenage boys, and the story includes references to reporters' vain attempts to get comment from the actress.

1

These actual instances from the media of mass communication—and countless others every working day—pose ethical questions that must be confronted and somehow answered.

Are there news values in the picture of the five children which warrant its use? Or should it be filed unpublished, on the ground that it represents a morbid exploitation of a moment of shattering grief?

Is the anchorman justified in putting the little twist of opinion at the end of his report on the governor's program because that same politician has been overready with glib and unrealized promises in the past? Or should he leave the editorializing to others who openly hold such a franchise?

Were the junketing food writers legitimately adding to their background, or were they submitting to a velvet-gloved but nonetheless blatant form of bribery?

Would the story about the Hollywood star's son have merited a place on the national wire service if it had involved an unknown with no newsworthy family connections? Is it justifiable to build up the story at the expense of an innocent third party?

The men and women who are in the business of gathering, processing, and reporting the news must face such questions routinely, and come up with answers within hours or minutes as the urgent deadlines of the mass media impose their inexorable demands. Many of the ethical questions that trouble the journalists' working hours (and often haunt their dreams as well) would tax a Solomon. Few are clear cut and uncomplicated. And in reaching these decisions, the journalists—reporters, editors, broadcasters—are pretty much on their own, without detailed ground rules to guide them.

Some other groups in our society are able to turn to sets of principles that have been standardized and codified; lawyers and doctors, for example, study the ethics of their professions along with torts and anatomy. They know that the ethical codes in their fields are universal, and that they are policed by bodies of their peers who have the power to take away the license of a practitioner who departs from the paths of righteousness.

For the journalist, the guideposts are blurred, indistinct, or nonexistent. There are few restraints, internal or external, and neither licenses nor policing agencies. How well or how imperfectly an individual journalist subscribes to ethical standards depends upon what he or she understands to be the working code of the business, and upon how sensitively tuned his or her conscience may be.

An awareness of journalistic ethics is sometimes acquired on a trial-

and-error basis, or soaked up osmotically from fellow workers, or inculcated by means of case studies in journalism classes. But there are not many universal precepts. And, inevitably, there tends to be wide variation in practice.

Ethical lapses, some with widespreading consequences, can be cited in all of the media of mass communication, even though it is probably true that a great many of the men and women who gather and bring us the news *do* have a lively perception of the need for ethical performance, and true also that in much of their work, much of the time, they *are* attempting to respect standards of responsible journalism.

It will be the purpose of this book to explore what few, generalized philosophical charters do exist to guide the journalist through the ethical mine fields that come with the territory; to examine, case by case, examples drawn from current experience which suggest the extremely wide variety of ethical decisions that must be made by someone, somehow, before air time or press time; and to consider how responsibly the men and women of the media are approaching those decisions.

Now let's be quite open about the objective of all this. It isn't simply to set out a description of the state of the art to this point, but to furnish a basis for expansion of understanding of journalism ethics both by those who are practicing or hope to practice in the field, and by those who for the rest of their lives are going to be regular consumers of the end products of the media—the newspapers, magazines, radio and television broadcasts, and cable transmissions.

As Aristotle, one of the early investigators of ethics, told his students: "We are not inquiring merely in order to know what excellence or virtue is, but in order to become good; for otherwise it would profit us nothing."[2]

The hope that has led to the writing of this book is that if the nature of the ethical problems constantly facing journalists can be more clearly understood, there can result: (1) a wider adherence to responsible standards among the men and women of the media, and (2) an enhanced respect for the media among the consuming public.

So this is not a parochial topic, appropriate only for in-house consideration by journalists. The media of mass communication impinge daily, hourly, on the lives of every one of us, sketching out the pictures we get of the world around us, largely determining what topics will be grist for our conversational exchanges with others ("Did you see in the paper last night about . . . ?"), and to a very great extent shaping the opinions and the decisions that we reflect variously in our lives, at the ballot box, around the home circle, in the marketplace.

How responsibly and how ethically we are served by the men and women who produce the contents of the media of mass communication is a matter of real and practical moment to every citizen.

Notes

[1]Editor and copublisher of the *Press* and the *Daily Enterprise* of Riverside, California. *Quoted in Editor and Publisher*, CVII, No. 16 (April 20, 1974), 44.

[2]Joseph Katz, Philip Nochlin, and Robert Stover, eds., *Writers on Ethics* (Princeton: D. Van Nostrand Company, Inc., 1962), p. 6.

Searching for the Context...

"One may say that in the first book of Plato's Republic the principal ethical positions Western men have taken are already clearly stated." — Crane Brinton [1]

2 From Plato to the present the subject of ethics has absorbed the attention of thoughtful persons in all cultures. This has been the case partly because the topic is so fundamental to our simple survival, our ability to get along harmoniously with our fellows in an ever more complex and interdependent society. But it has also been a recurring subject for speculation and analysis partly because it is tantalizingly elusive, difficult to pin down in definitive, concrete terms.

We all make use of the words "ethics" or "principles" or "standards" as everyday conversational coinage. But rarely are we confronted with the necessity to go behind the label terms and provide definitions for them; and when such occasions do arise most of us are hard put to come up with anything but the broadest of generalities ("Oh, you know what I mean, doing the right thing . . . not breaking the rules . . . being fair . . .").

Yet, what is "right"? Whose rules, established by what authority? "Fair" in what context?

If the answers don't come readily to hand, you needn't be disconcerted. You have plenty of company.

Through several thousands of years, legions of philosophers have written libraries full of scrolls and books on the topic of ethics. The theories advanced in these volumes range over a wide spectrum, from religious to behavioristic. Some of these theories are vague and mystical, others are infinitely complex, still others coldly mechanical.

Most of the definitions of ethics that have emerged from the centuries of theorizing tend to be laid out first in broad and general strokes, and then painstakingly explained in voluminous, analytical detail that must be considered in totality to be comprehended.

If you grope through the volumes in search of simple, one-sentence definitions, you are likely to find yourself back with the label terms.

One twentieth-century philosopher, George E. Moore, observes that "we find that many ethical philosophers are disposed to accept as an adequate definition of 'Ethics' the statement that it deals with the question what is good or bad in human conduct."[2]

If you turn from the philosophers to the dictionary you won't be much more precisely enlightened. There you will find that the word "ethics" can be used in a general sense to describe the body of moral principles or values governing or distinctive of a particular culture or group (as in "business ethics"). Or it may be used with respect to an individual as a term expressive of the complex of moral principles held, or rules of conduct followed, by an individual.

In all of these attempts to set down the meaning of the word, there are open-ended, elastic variables, just as in our own homely amateur efforts at definition. What, exactly, do "good" and "bad" mean? What is suggested by "moral principles" or "values distinctive of a culture?" However, unless you are prepared to undertake a short course in philosophy (and don't expect that from this book or this author), you will probably have to get along as best you can with definitional frames of reference that *are* broad and generalized, even though this will pose problems as we attempt to fit into these frames specific cases drawn from journalistic practice.

In Simpler Days...

It perhaps should be noted here that in other eras the terms that now seem to us to be frustratingly vague and lacking in specific meaning would not have been so regarded, at least not by the average person of the time. As Walter Lippmann wrote:

Once all things were phases of a single destiny: the church, the state, the family, the school were means to the same end; the rights and duties of the

6

individual in society, the rules of morality, the themes of art, and the teachings of science were all of them ways of revealing, of adumbrating, of applying the laws laid down in the divine constitution of the universe. In the modern world institutions are more or less independent, each serving its own proximate purpose, and our culture is really a collection of separate interests each sovereign within its own realm.[3]

In this complex present-day society, where a divine constitution is not universally acknowledged, fixing the exact meaning of the generalized terms that still are used to define ethics may be impracticable, except perhaps in totalitarian societies where verities are decreed as universally and as starkly as in the Middle Ages.

The distinguished historian Crane Brinton made an effort to give some specific meaning to the broad ethical labels of "good" and "bad":

Both as to formal philosophical ethical writing and as to folk notions of ethics incorporated in tradition, codes, aphorisms of folk wisdom, the three or four thousand years of our Western recorded history show an unmistakable constant element. Honesty, loyalty, kindness, self-control, industry, cooperativeness are virtues; lying, treachery, cruelty, self-indulgence, laziness, conspicuous and uncontrolled aggressiveness, and selfishness are vices.[4]

The same writer, in another passage, observed that "I shall use the term 'ethics' or 'ethical principles' to refer to the statements men make about what their conduct, or the conduct of others, or of both, *ought to be.*"[5]

All of Brinton's contributions are helpful. His laundry lists of instances add specificity to the generalized terms. And his emphasis on ethical conduct as what *ought to be* underlines a dimension essential to any discussion of ethics. Kant put the same notion somewhat differently:

To be truthful from duty, however, is an entirely different thing from being truthful out of fear of disadvantageous consequences, for in the former case the concept of the action itself contains a law for me, while in the latter I must first look about to see what results for me may be connected with it.[6]

In other words, conduct that is ethical—for example, telling the truth—is embraced not because someone is standing by with whip and lawbook to make sure you don't transgress, but because you have made an inner commitment.

7

So where, to this point, have we come out?

Ethics has to do with conduct—with conduct that is "right" in the view of a given society and time period, with conduct that is "good" out of a sense of duty or conviction rather than from fear of punishment. By common consent, various modes of behavior are viewed as "good" and various others as "bad," even though in today's society there may be wide individual differences as to the appropriate label for a specific action in a specific situation.

This may not be as precise a formulation as some readers might like, but it is perhaps far enough to take the general discussion of the subject of ethics. Let's turn now to consider how the various concepts thus far explored can be applied to the practice of journalism.

Narrowing the Focus

As one of the most erudite explorers in the field of journalistic ethics has pointed out, not many professional journalists have attempted to write about the subject, except to formulate generalized codes. John C. Merrill, author of *The Imperative of Freedom*, observes that:

Perhaps one reason for this is that most editors, publishers, news directors and other journalists simply write the whole subject of ethics off as "relative," giving little or no importance to absolute or universal journalistic principles. A newspaper friend put it succinctly recently when he said that he looked at ethics as "just the individual journalist's way of doing things." Certainly a free journalist has the right to consider ethics in this way, but such a relativistic concept relegates ethics to a kind of "nothingness limbo" where anything any journalist does can be considered ethical.[7]

At another point in his exhaustive analysis of the philosophical underpinnings of journalistic freedom and integrity, Merrill touches on another reason why the topic of ethics has been one that journalists typically have treated in broad, vague terms rather than detailed specifics:

When we leave the subject of basic orientation and allegiances and enter the area of journalistic ethics, we pass from the more solid ground of socio-psychological empiricism into a swampland of philosophical speculation where eerie mists of judgment hang low over a boggy terrain.[8]

Yet Merrill does not hesitate to strike out into this mist-shrouded countryside, and neither should we. The footing may not be solid, but there is a trail of sorts, so let's follow it as best we can.

In journalism, as in society generally, ethics may be viewed either as a group influence, governing the behavior of all or most who are in this field of activity, or as a set of guidelines unique to an individual practitioner.

In the final analysis, whether an individual journalist behaves ethically depends upon the personal code by which he or she gauges rightness of conduct, that is, determines what *ought* to be done as a journalist.

These personal codes are of course beyond our ability to catalog or anatomize, varying as they do from person to person and reflecting many kinds of input, experience, and orientation. What we *can* do, however, is sort through some of the institutionalized influences that may have shaped the personal codes.

Here, as in the earlier general discussion, it is possible to discern central ideas that run far back in time (though not back to Plato, since the press is a relatively recent phenomenon). But the central ideas (for example, the concept that it is the journalist's chief responsibility to report news honestly) have been modified from time to time by the various societal contexts in which the media of mass communication have developed since the invention of the printing press.

William L. Rivers and Wilbur Schramm, in their scholarly and comprehensive *Responsibility in Mass Communication*, note the several basic theories under which the press has functioned since the time mass communication first became possible.

The first journalists were obliged to operate within an authoritarian society. The rulers of the time were absolute, and the interests of the state—embodied in the ruler—were paramount. All institutions functioned within this context. As Rivers and Schramm put it:

The basis for communication ethics in such a system is clear. Stated negatively, there should be no publishing which, in the opinion of the authorites, would injure the state and (consequently) its citizens. More positively, all publishing should contribute to the greatness of the beneficent state, which would as a consequence enable man to grow to his fullest usefulness and happiness. Significantly, one need not decide for himself; there is always an authority to serve as umpire.[9]

Authoritarian regimes survive today in some parts of the world, and where they do the press must contend with an imposed ethical system

9

(almost a contradiction in terms). In many nations, however, as absolutist governments were replaced by democratic forms, the authoritarian theory of the press similarly gave way to another concept, that of libertarianism.

This theory rejected the notion that the press must operate to support and benefit the state, and instead encouraged the free expression of ideas without governmental hindrance.

All voices should be free to be heard in the press and, as various viewpoints contended, the public would be able to discern the truth amid the hubbub. There would be an open marketplace of ideas; government must keep hands off, letting the various shades of truth and error contend for the attention of the community. Underlying this theory was the assumption that the public would make rational decisions if it had access to all ideas and viewpoints.

What ethical code figured in this theory? Again from Rivers and Schramm:

The ethical responsibility of the libertarian communicator might be expressed by John Locke's phrase, "enlightened self-interest." The degree of enlightenment, of course, varies widely with individuals. At one extreme might be a Pulitzer, who wrote that "nothing less than the highest ideals, the most scrupulous anxiety to do right, the most accurate knowledge of the problems it has to meet, and a sincere sense of social responsibility will save journalism." At the other extreme might be placed a statement attributed to William Peter Hamilton of the *Wall Street Journal*: "A newspaper is private enterprise owing nothing whatever to the public, which grants it no franchise. It is therefore affected with no public interest. It is emphatically the property of the owner, who is selling a manufactured product at his own risk." Between these extremes are the positions and practices of most publishers, broadcasters and film makers.[10]

During the last several decades, the libertarian theory has undergone substantial modification. Some writers about the press and society believe that a new theory—that of social responsibility—now influences (or *ought* to influence) the thoughts and behavior of the men and women who work within the media of mass communication.

The social responsibility theory holds that the simple "hands-off" thesis of the libertarians is insufficient as a guideline for the media of today. The libertarian theory was based on the assumption that access to the means of publishing or disseminating information would be available freely to all, or most. Thus it would not matter whether what was published by some journals was distorted or biased, since these would

10

be offset by others slanted in another direction. In the clash of contending viewpoints, the truth would eventually emerge for all to see.

Shrinking Channels

In the period when the libertarian theory was taking form, and particularly at the time that it was embodied in the American Constitution as part of the First Amendment, there may have been at least some plausibility to the assumptions on which it was based. Although there never has been a time when the media were accessible to all, there were in the late eighteenth century relatively numerous channels available, in proportion to the literate population of the time. Newspapers, broadsides, and pamphlets came and went on the journalistic scene; neither substantial capital nor complex technology was needed to launch a new communication venture—the proverbial "shirttail full of type" would serve.

But in today's world the means of mass communication are a good deal less accessible to all than they were at the time of the Revolution. Now there are a very few channels, controlled by relatively few persons. In the United States there are approximately 1,750 daily newspapers, 9,000 weeklies, 930 television stations, 7,100 radio stations, nearly 3,000 cable television systems, and about 8,000 magazines of various kinds, most of them highly specialized. And there are about 220,000,000 Americans.

How many of these 220,000,000 have free access to any of the various channels for the dissemination of ideas and information? How many have the wherewithal to hire space or time on those channels? How many have the vast means that would be required to buy or launch their own communication channels to reach large numbers of their fellows?

Today, in virtually all American cities where there are daily newspapers, there is only one such paper, or perhaps one ownership publishing a morning-evening combination. In only 3 percent of our cities does true head-to-head competition between different owners survive. Attempts to revive competition by starting new large-circulation papers have been ruinously costly (with losses running to many millions yearly) and have almost invariably failed. Only in small towns and suburban communities have new papers emerged on the scene and survived.

In most cities there are no more than two or three television stations, some of them owned by newspaper interests. And to acquire a TV station is, if anything, even more costly than buying a daily newspaper. Radio stations are more numerous but typically are specialized, reaching only one or two segments of a community with target programming of music and news. The opportunity for the average citizen to find on radio an outlet for his views is limited. In time, the realization of the promise of cable systems should provide greater opportunities for public access to the channels of communication, but the full development of multichannel, two-way cable networks may be many years away.[11]

So as a practical matter, the assumption on which the libertarian theory of the press once rested does not hold today. And that is why the concept of social responsibility has taken hold.

This theory of the press contends that since the channels of communication now are so limited, the persons who own those channels, and the persons who gather and process the information that flows out through them, must accept a responsibility to society along with the freedom that they still enjoy from any kind of governmental interference.

In brief, that responsibility is to provide a truthful, balanced, and comprehensive account of the news. Under the libertarian theory, it was possible to tolerate biased, distorted, or one-sided presentations because there were many channels and many voices were being heard over those channels; the distortions would balance out, and reality would be discernible. But the social responsibility theory recognizes that when there is only one game left in town, it must be an honest one.

Unless those few channels that are available to us provide an accurate, complete flow of news and information, how else can we hope to get a true picture of the world around us, and acquire a basis for making the decisions expected of us in a democratic society?

So the proponents of the social responsibility theory would lay obligations on the journalists, as well as reaffirm their rights. (Among the proponents of the responsibility theory was the Hutchins Commission on Freedom of the Press, which issued a landmark report in 1947 after an extensive investigation of the condition of the press at that time.)[12] And from the obligations laid on the press flow ethical implications.

Most observers of the press tend to view these implications as positive. That is, they assume that journalists who subscribe to the theory of social responsibility will direct their efforts toward identifying and then serving the interests of society. The massive power of the media will be employed responsibly, and an accurate picture of reality will be fashioned for the public. Media excesses and abuses will be minimized.

But this is not the only way in which the social responsibility concept is perceived. Some see built into it ominous pitfalls. John C. Merrill warns in *The Imperative of Freedom:*

This "theory" of social responsibility has a good ring to it and has an undeniable attraction for many. . . . . Implicit in this trend toward "social responsibility" is the argument that some group (obviously a judicial or governmental one, ultimately) can and must define or decide *what* is socially responsible. Also, the implication is clear that publishers and journalists acting freely cannot determine what is socially responsible nearly as well as can some "outside" or "impartial" group. If this power elite decides the press is not responsible, not even the First Amendment will keep the publishers from losing this freedom to government, we are told.[13]

Merrill's point cannot be ignored; it poses a real and valid concern. As far back as 1947 the Hutchins Commission report was hinting darkly at the necessity for the press to discipline itself or face the prospect that some external agency would step in—presumably some agency of government.

Yet most proponents of the concept of social responsibility contend that the press can make its own internal adjustments in time to avoid the prospect of intervention from outside. And they argue that in this period of shrinking channels of information, social responsibility is the only valid and acceptable guiding theory for the press. This appears to be the position of the majority of editors and educators, and of many working journalists as well. That does not mean, however, that there follows a simple step from the social responsibility theory to the definition of an ethical framework logically evolving from it. It is not that easy to pin down the basis for contemporary journalistic ethics.

The principles and standards that are influential in the workings of the mass media today stem from many sources and a variety of theories. The concept of social responsibility does indeed influence many of the men and women who own or work in the media of mass communication. But libertarians abound, too, and even some crusty individualists who share the nineteenth-century philosophy that a newspaper is a private enterprise "owing nothing whatever to the public."

As a practical matter some ethical concepts—but only some of them—have roots in press theories. Others have grown up as craft attitudes, folkways of the news business. Still others seem to be almost visceral, instinctive in their origin and persistence.

One of the most thoughtful and respected writers on the standards of journalism, J. Edward Gerald, contends that "the whole of journalism's dependability and usefulness rests in adequate conformance to the articles of faith upon which communication is based and upon rewards and punishments for behavior." And at another point in his excellent overview. *The Social Responsibility of the Press*, Gerald asks: "What are the

13

conventions journalists are taught to respect? What are the rules of their trade? What skills in communication entitle a journalist to the acclaim of his fellows? What errors bring loss of face?"[14]

If we can uncover some answers to these questions we should have a starting point, at least, for the case-by-case exploration of ethical problems that plague the journalist today.

But be warned: the search for these articles of faith, the answers to Gerald's questions, won't be completely productive. The ethical scene in the field of journalism is almost as imprecise and generalized as is the case with the ethics of society as a whole. We can get a view of some wide parameters and some broad principles, but don't expect neat and comprehensive blueprints.

A Very Mixed Bag

One way to acquire a feel for the precepts and principles that journalists seek to observe is to look to their own professions of objectives and statements of policy. The early writers in the field of journalism ethics did just that, combing through the policy platforms set out in newspaper mastheads, and searching the codes adopted by national and state press associations.

One of these writers, Nelson A. Crawford, devoted most of a book, *The Ethics of Journalism*,[15] to quotations from and analysis of such ethical artifacts. He came up with a very mixed bag indeed.

Some of the credos he surveyed were infused with self-conscious rhetoric:

Upon those who practice this profession rests the sacred duty of keeping these mighty means of communication among mankind pure at the source, undefiled of intent, and free of bias.—from the code of Ethics of South Dakota editors.[16]

Others mixed down-to-earth self-interest with their bows to principle:

Beware of the seekers after free publicity. Remember that space in *The Eagle* is worth twenty-five cents a line. What you give away *The Eagle* cannot sell. Don't help press agents cheat the advertising department.—from a statement of policy by the *Brooklyn Eagle*.[17]

And some of the policy positions have a quaint and ⟨
in today's world. For example, the *Christian Science Mon*
staff members: "Never use expressions that suggest nauseating ١ᴜᴖ.
Slang . . . must be excluded from the columns. . . . Verify all quotations,
especially from the *Bible*, whenever time will permit."[18]

However they varied in other respects, all of the early statements of
principle or codes of conduct cited by Crawford in the 1920s tended to
be couched in general terms, leaving the specific application of these
broad strokes to the individual judgments of the men and women who
had to make the decisions and call the shots out on the streets or at the
newsroom desks.

The *Detroit News*, for instance, informed its reporters, and the
world, that:

The paper should be:

Vigorous but not Vicious.

Interesting, but not Sensational.

Fearless, but Fair.
Accurate as far as human effort can obtain accuracy.

Striving ever to gain and impart information.

As bright as possible, but never sacrificing solid information for brilliancy.

Looking for the Uplifting rather than the Depraved things of life.[19]

How to determine the difference between Interesting and Sensational, Fearless and Fair, the editors left to their staff members to work
out as best they could.

Nearly half a century later the Associated Press Managing Editors
Association published a loose-leaf book of guidelines for its members, and
in 1970 issued a supplement to those guidelines dealing specifically with
ethics.[20] As did Nelson Crawford's 1924 compilation, it contained extracts from the policy positions adopted by editors and publishers. The
phrasing in these extracts was more up to date, and sometimes more
specific than the earlier pronouncements, but there was still evident a
reliance on broad, generalized themes.

The APME officers had solicited member newspapers for comments
on their codes, statements of principles, and reportorial rules. As Court-
ney R. Sheldon, editor of the 1970 guidelines supplement, acknowledged:

15

The response was not overwhelming. Meaningful codes of ethics are scarce, and some of the country's most outstanding newspapers had little or nothing in their files. But enough material was received from more than 50 papers to excerpt it and give managing editors some means of measuring their own paper's standards against those which the profession has put into writing.[21]

Some sample excerpts from the APME supplement:

Our theory is that the reader buys the news columns and is entitled to unbiased and impartial news from all sides of the picture just as accurate as we are able to get it.—*Omaha World-Herald*

Our staffers are told to use the golden rule as far as getting the man's side before his reputation is damaged, but if the golden rule doesn't mean anything to them, they should picture themselves in a witness chair before a jury with a hostile lawyer asking just what they had done before destroying a man's reputation.—*Asheville (N.C.) Citizen-Times*

Our business is facts. We have learned to search deeper for facts, to dig for the meaning of facts, to relate facts to each other, to analyze them and put them in perspective. . . . Although total objectivity may be impossible because every story is written by a human being, the duty of every reporter and editor is to strive for as much objectivity as humanly possible . . . personal opinions should be excluded from the news columns . . . presenting both sides of the issue is not hedging but the essence of responsible journalism.—*New York Times*

One of a newspaper's major functions is to be a mirror of the society in which it exists. The reflections of that society may not always be pretty or easy to look at but they won't go away just because we don't want to see them. A community can't change those reflections unless it is aware they exist and is stimulated to alter them.—*St. Paul Pioneer Press* and *St. Paul Dispatch*.[22]

The Newer Media

Comparable statements of principles and codes of ethics for the electronic media—radio and television—have tended to be more detailed and specific. This has been the case in part, at least, because these newer media began operations under circumstances different from those that affected the newspapers and other print media. The electronic media are licensed by government and periodically must submit their operations to scrutiny by the Federal Communications Commission before their licenses are renewed. This has obliged the operators of radio and television to be more conscious of detailed guidelines.[23]

The Television Code, for example, contains 35 separate provisions under the single sectional heading *General Program Standards* (and there are 14 sections in all). Some sample entries:

4. Racial or nationality types shall not be shown on television in such a manner as to ridicule the race or nationality.

9. Law enforcement shall be upheld and, except where essential to the program plot, officers of the law portrayed with respect and dignity.

22. Quiz and similar programs that are presented as contests of knowledge, information, skill or luck must, in fact, be genuine contests and the results must not be controlled by collusion with or between contestants, or any other action which will favor one contestant against any other.

27. Any telecasting designed to "buy" the television audience by requiring it to listen and/or view in hope of reward rather than for the quality of the program, should be avoided.

30. Camera angles shall avoid such views of performers as to emphasize anatomical details indecently.

Many of the provisions of the Television Code and its counterpart, the Radio Code, have to do with the entertainment and service aspects of broadcasting, which is to be expected in light of the fact that both media grew up initially with entertainment and the dissemination of advertising messages as their primary functions.

But both codes also take up the journalistic function of the electronic media and, when they do, the phrasing tends to be much less specific and to resemble the generalized terminology of the statements of principles of the print media.

For example, again from the Television Code, under the sectional heading *Treatment of News and Public Events:*

2. News reporting should be factual, fair and without bias.

6. Commentary and analysis should be clearly identified as such.

7. Pictorial matter should be chosen with care and not presented in a misleading manner.

8. All news interview programs should be governed by accepted standards of ethical journalism, under which the interviewer selects the questions to be asked. Where there is advance agreement

materially restricting an important or newsworthy area of questioning, the interviewer will state on the program that such limitation has been agreed upon. Such disclosure should be made if the person being interviewed requires that questions be submitted in advance or if he participates in editing a recording of the interview prior to its use on the air.

And from the Radio Code section on *News:*

2. *News Reporting.* News reporting shall be factual and objective. Good taste shall prevail in the selection and handling of news. Morbid, sensational, or alarming details not essential to factual reporting should be avoided. News should be broadcast in such a manner as to avoid creation of panic and unnecessary alarm. Broadcasters shall be diligent in their supervision of content, format, and presentation of news broadcasts. Equal diligence should be exercised in selection of editors and reporters who direct news gathering and dissemination, since the station's performance in this vital informational field depends largely upon them.

Pulling It All Together

Attempts have been made for the print media, as was done for radio and television in the two comprehensive code statements, to bring together into a single document the ethical guidelines of the field. Many such efforts have been made by various professional, scholarly, and business associations of editors, educators, or rank-and-file newsmen.

The thrust of such compilations can be conveyed best, perhaps, by setting out here the substance of two of them, the Canons of the American Society of Newspaper Editors, adopted shortly after the founding of that organization in 1922, and the Code of Ethics of the Society of Professional Journalists, Sigma Delta Chi, adopted at the national convention of the organization on Nov. 16, 1973. The ASNE canons were formulated particularly with respect to newspaper journalism; the Society of Professional Journalists' code deals with the journalistic function in all media.

The Canons of Journalism

American Society of Newspaper Editors

The primary function of newspapers is to communicate to the human race what its members do, feel, and think. Journalism, therefore, demands of its practitioners the widest range of intelligence or knowledge and of experience, as well as natural and trained powers of observation and reasoning. To its opportunities as a chronicle are indissolubly linked its obligations as teacher and interpreter.

To the end of finding some means of codifying sound practice and just aspirations of American journalism, these canons are set forth:

I   *Responsibility.*   The right of a newspaper to attract and hold readers is restricted by nothing but considerations of public welfare. The use a newspaper makes of the share of public attention it gains serves to determine its sense of responsibility, which it shares with every member of its staff. A journalist who uses his power for any selfish or otherwise unworthy purpose is faithless to a high trust.

II   *Freedom of the Press.*   Freedom of the press is to be guarded as a vital right of mankind. It is the unquestionable right to discuss whatever is not explicitly forbidden by law, including the wisdom of any restrictive statute.

III   *Independence.*   Freedom from all obligations except that of fidelity to the public interest is vital.
  1.   Promotion of any private interest contrary to the general welfare for whatever reason is not compatible with honest journalism. So-called news communications from private sources should not be published without public notice of their source or else substantiation of their claims to value as news, both in form and substance.
  2.   Partisanship, in editorial comment which knowingly departs from the truth, does violence to the best spirit of American journalism; in the news columns it is subversive of a fundamental principle of the profession.

IV   *Sincerity, Truthfulness, Accuracy.*   Good faith with the reader is the foundation of all journalism worthy of the name.
  1.   By every consideration of good faith a newspaper is constrained to be truthful. It is not to be excused for lack of thoroughness or accuracy within its control, or failure to obtain command of these essential qualities.
  2.   Headlines should be fully warranted by the contents of the article which they surmount.

V   *Impartiality.*   Sound practice makes clear distinction between news reports and expressions of opinion. News reports should be free from opinion or bias of any kind.
  1.   This rule does not apply to so-called special articles

unmistakably devoted to advocacy or characterized by a signature authorizing the writer's own conclusions and interpretation.

VI   *Fair Play.*   A newspaper should not publish official charges affecting reputation or moral character without opportunity given to the accused to be heard; right practice demands the giving of such opportunity in all cases of serious accusation outside judicial proceedings.
1.   A newspaper should not invade private rights or feelings without sure warrant of public right as distinguished from public curiosity.
2.   It is the privilege, as it is the duty, of a newspaper to make prompt and complete correction of its own serious mistakes of fact or opinion, whatever their origin.

VII   *Decency.*   A newspaper cannot escape conviction of insincerity if while professing high moral purpose it supplies incentives to base conduct, such as are to be found in details of crime and vice, publication of which is not demonstrably for the general good. Lacking authority to enforce its canons the journalism here represented can but express the hope that deliberate panderings to vicious instincts will encounter effective public disapproval or yield to the influence of a preponderant professional condemnation.[24]

The Society of Professional Journalists, Sigma Delta Chi

Code of Ethics

The Society of Professional Journalists, Sigma Delta Chi, believes the duty of journalists is to serve the truth.

We believe the agencies of mass communication are carriers of public discussion and information, acting on their Constitutional mandate and freedom to learn and report the facts.

We believe in public enlightenment as the forerunner of justice, and in our Constitutional role to seek the truth as part of the public's right to know the truth.

We believe those responsibilities carry obligations that require journalists to perform with intelligence, objectivity, accuracy, and fairness.

To these ends, we declare acceptance of the standards of practice here set forth:

Responsibility: The public's right to know of events of public importance and interest is the overriding mission of the mass media. The purpose of distributing news and enlightened opinion is to serve the general welfare. Journalists who use their professional status as representatives of the public for selfish or other unworthy motives violate a high trust.

Freedom of the Press: Freedom of the press is to be guarded as an unalienable right of people in a free society. It carries with it the freedom and the responsibility to discuss, question, and challenge actions and utterances of our government and of our public and private institutions. Journalists uphold the right to speak unpopular opinions and the privilege to agree with the majority.

Ethics: Journalists must be free of obligation to any interest other than the people's right to know.

1. Gifts, favors, free travel, special treatment or privileges can compromise the integrity of journalists and their employers. Nothing of value should be accepted.
2. Secondary employment, political involvement, holding public office, and service in community organizations should be avoided if it compromises the integrity of journalists and their employers. Journalists and their employers should conduct their personal lives in a manner which protects them from conflict of interest, real or apparent. Their responsibilities to the public are paramount. That is the nature of their profession.
3. So-called news communications from private sources should not be published or broadcast without substantiation of their claims to news value.
4. Journalists will seek news that serves the public interest, despite the obstacles. They will make constant efforts to assure that the public's business is conducted in public and that public records are open to public inspection.
5. Journalists acknowledge the newsman's ethic of protecting confidential sources of information.

Accuracy and Objectivity: Good faith with the public is the foundation of all worthy journalism.

1. Truth is our ultimate goal.
2. Objectivity in reporting the news is another goal which serves as the mark of an experienced professional. It is a standard of performance toward which we all strive. We honor those who achieve it.
3. There is no excuse for inaccuracies or lack of thoroughness.
4. Newspaper headlines should be fully warranted by the contents of the articles they accompany. Photographs and telecasts should give an accurate picture of an event and not highlight a minor incident out of context.
5. Sound practice makes clear distinction between news reports and

21

expressions of opinion. News reports should be free of opinion or bias and represent all sides of an issue.

6. Partisanship in editorial comment which knowingly departs from the truth violates the spirit of American journalism.

7. Journalists recognize their responsibility for offering informed analysis, comment, and editorial opinion on public events and issues. They accept the obligation to present such material by individuals whose competence, experience, and judgment qualify them for it.

8. Special articles or presentations devoted to advocacy or the writer's own conclusions and interpretations should be labeled as such.

Fair Play: Journalists at all times will show respect for the dignity, privacy, rights, and well-being of people encountered in the course of gathering and presenting the news.

1. The news media should not communicate unofficial charges affecting reputation or moral character without giving the accused a chance to reply.

2. The news media must guard against invading a person's right to privacy.

3. The media should not pander to morbid curiosity about details of vice and crime.

4. It is the duty of news media to make prompt and complete correction of their errors.

5. Journalists should be accountable to the public for their reports and the public should be encouraged to voice its grievances against the media. Open dialogue with our readers, viewers, and listeners should be fostered.

Pledge: Journalists should actively censure and try to prevent violations of these standards, and they should encourage their observance by all newspeople. Adherence to this code of ethics is intended to preserve the bond of mutual trust and respect between American journalists and the American people.[25]

Some of the Answers

This chapter's review of the publicly proclaimed credos of editors, publishers, broadcasters, press associations, and professional societies does not, of course, leave us with a complete grasp of the ethics of the news gathering and disseminating business. What men and women say does not necessarily correspond to what they do, or even to what they believe.

Lip service allegiance to lofty principles is an almost universal self-protective ploy.

As we have noted earlier, the guidelines that actually do govern the behavior of the men and women in the journalistic media have various roots, some of them traceable, others far below the surface. We cannot hope to uncover all of them. Ethics in application must, of necessity, be individual.

But it is fair to conclude that we are now able to identify—if, admittedly, only in broad, general terms—the principles that a great many journalists have put on the record as the ground rules that *ought to govern* their conduct. And we thus have at least partial answers to the key questions posed several pages back by Dr. Gerald: "What are the conventions journalists are taught to respect? What are the rules of their trade? What skills in communication entitle a journalist to the acclaim of his fellows? What errors bring loss of face?"

Just as historian Crane Brinton was able to identify strains of behavior that through the generations had been universally acknowledged as right conduct, so can we now attempt the same sort of distillation for the special field of journalism.

Through the original collection of codes assembled by Crawford, through the fragmented quotes from editors, through the radio and television codes, and through the compilations of professional societies, run some consistent and repeated themes. They crop up again and again. They are, as best we can discern them, the ethical values of the journalist.

As one who has spent many years in journalism as a working newsman or a close observer from the academic sidelines, I would sum up those themes and values in these terms:

—Journalists must observe a responsibility to the public welfare; their impressive power should be employed for the general good, not for private advantage.

—Journalists should provide a news report that is sincere, true, and accurate; accounts should be thorough, balanced, and complete.

—Journalists must be impartial; they should function as the public's representatives, not as the mouthpieces of partisan groups or special interests.

Journalists must be fair; they must give space or air time to the several sides of a dispute; private rights should not be invaded; corrections of errors should be prompt and wholehearted.

—Journalists should respect the canons of decency, insofar as those canons can be identified in a society with changing values.

23

Some of these principles derive from press theory, as we have seen. Some of them have grown up in an evolutionary fashion, as the media have developed through the generations. Some can be traced to the more general ethical values of society as a whole.

They are, now that we have them distilled from all of the foregoing discussion, still very general in nature. But if they are taken together with the various amplifications and elaborations that we have also surveyed in passing, they do provide us with some frame of reference, some meaningful context within which to begin a case-study examination of practical ethical problems that confront journalists every hour of every working day. By looking in detail at the ways in which newsmen and newswomen have applied—or failed to apply—these broad principles to concrete instances, we can gain some understanding of the ubiquity and the centrality of ethics in journalism.

So, for most of the remainder of this book, let's get down to those concrete cases.

Notes

1Crane Brinton, *A History of Western Morals* (New York: Harcourt, Brace and Company, 1959), p. 8

2"The Indefinability of Good" in *Writers on Ethics*, ed. Joseph Katz, Philip Nochlin, and Robert Stover (Princeton: D. Van Nostrand Company, Inc., 1962), p. 504.

3Walter Lippmann, *A Preface to Morals* (New York: The Macmillan Company, 1929), p. 112.

4Brinton, *A History of Western Morals*, p. 417.

5*Ibid.*, p. 5.

6Immanuel Kant, "Foundations of the Metaphysics of Morals," in *Writers on Ethics*, p. 52.

7John C. Merrill, *The Imperative of Freedom: A Philosophy of Journalistic Autonomy* (New York: Hastings House, Publishers, Inc., 1974), p. 172. Copyright © 1974 by John Calhoun Merrill, excerpted by permission of Hastings House, Publishers.

8*Ibid.*, p. 163.

9William L. Rivers and Wilbur Schramm, *Responsibility in Mass Communication* (New York: Harper & Row, Publishers, 1969), p. 33.

10*Ibid.*, p. 40.

11In *The Information Machines, Their Impact on Men and the Media* (New York: Harper & Row, Publishers, 1971), press analyst and critic Ben H. Bagdikian suggests that the full-scale "Wired city," with communication consoles in every home and 100 or more two-way cable channels available for everything from information retrieval to grocery shopping, may be a reality by the beginning of the twenty-first century. Other writers pick earlier dates.

12Commission on Freedom of the Press, *A Free and Responsible Press* (Chicago: University of Chicago Press, 1963).

[13]Merrill, *The Imperative of Freedom*, p. 91. Copyright © 1974 by John Calhoun Merrill, by permission of Hastings House, Publishers.

[14]J. Edward Gerald, *The Social Responsibility of the Press* (Minneapolis: University of Minnesota Press, 1963), pp. 149–50.

[15]Nelson A. Crawford, *The Ethics of Journalism* (New York: Alfred A. Knopf, 1924).

[16]*Ibid.*, p. 196.

[17]*Ibid.*, p. 212.

[18]*Ibid.*, pp. 214–15.

[19]*Ibid.*, p. 224.

[20]Associated Press Managing Editors Association, *Guidelines* (New York, 1969), and *1970 Supplement—APME Guidelines*.

[21]*1970 Supplement—APME Guidelines*, p. 8A.

[22]*Ibid.*, pp. 8A, 9A.

[23]The Television Code and the Radio Code were compiled and produced by the members of the respective divisions of the National Association of Broadcasters. Copies of the full texts of the two codes may be obtained from the NAB.

[24]The *Canons* are published annually as an appendix to the *Proceedings* of the annual meeting of the ASNE.

[25]Published in the *Quill*, LXI, No. 12 (December 1973), 27.

How Many Masters?...

"Ethics are vital to the successful businessman," the merchant told his son. "For example, an old customer paid his account today with a hundred-dollar bill. Later I discovered that he had given me two hundreds, stuck together. Immediately, a question of ethics arose: Should I tell my partner?" — Jackie Kannan[1]

3 A recurring note in the various codes and statements of principle surveyed in chapter 2 had to do with the independence of the journalist. Recall the American Society of Newspaper Editors' canons: "Freedom from all obligations except that of fidelity to the public interest is vital." Or the code of ethics of the Society of Professional Journalists: "Journalists must be free of obligation to any interest other than the people's right to know."

This theme is as universal as any of those set out in the numerous guidelines endorsed by those who own or work in the business of gathering and disseminating the news. Yet in practice the ethic of independence is respected with widely varying degrees of fidelity. Cases abound, from those that are clearly violative of the principle involved, to the borderline or toss-up variety. In this chapter we'll look at some of those cases and their implications.

It is the boast of journalists generally that truly blatant corruption is rare in their field. The discovery in recent years that a reporter for a major Eastern daily was blackmailing prominent citizens in the community by threatening to publish adverse stories about them was a nine-days' wonder in the trade press because it was so unusual and out of character. Newsmen are fond of arguing that cases of bribe-taking judges or malpracticing doctors crop up far more often than do instances of comparable wrongdoing among reporters or editors.

One of the ablest of journalism educators, Curtis D. MacDougall, himself a former editor, wrote in his excellent analysis *The Press and Its Problems:*

Of absolute venality there is little or none in American newspaper journalism. By comparison with newspapermen of virtually every other nation in the world, the American editor is bribe-proof.[2]

This is a defensible assertion. But it is a limited one, as Dr. MacDougall no doubt intended it to be. For in the vast reaches of landscape short of the ultimate "absolute venality," there is a good deal of room for maneuver. And the men and women of the press—or at least a substantial number of them—do a good deal of maneuvering in various sectors of that territory.

Easy Calls, and Tough Ones

A member of Congress, Rep. Charles S. Gubser (R.-Calif.) once asserted that:

there is no greater group of free loaders in the world than the press. They will take anything they can get.[3]

That was partly hyperbole, of course. But there was feeling behind it, and at least some truth.

In the course of the journalist's daily work, whether as a reporter assigned to the courthouse beat or as the managing editor of the *Washington Post*, there are numerous situations in which favors of various kinds are proffered, thus posing the potentialities for conflict of interest.

The reporter whose job it is to cover the police station gets to know the desk sergeants well in the course of time; there will inevitably be shared coffee breaks, maybe a beer together after work. Who buys the coffee or the brew for whom is relatively unimportant; the newsman's integrity is hardly at stake.

However, let's up the ante a bit. Suppose the district attorney, an ambitious young man who has high hopes of a political future, takes a sudden liking to the same reporter. He invites the reporter to his lake place for a weekend of fishing; at Christmas he sends two fifths of Chivas Regal around to the reporter's home, with a cheery card; he regularly feeds the reporter tips that result in bylined exclusive stories. And then the election campaign comes along, and in the DA's eyes it is time for the reporter to provide some *quid* for all that *quo.*

That last is not a hypothetical, but an actual, instance. In this case, the reporter didn't come through with the slanted puff stories that the candidate had hoped for; he also quit accepting the compromising favors, and presumably learned a sound lesson.

The lesson is one that a distinguished editor, J. Russell Wiggins of the *Washington Post*, read out years ago in an article addressed to his colleagues and to journalism educators:

Newspapers do not differ greatly from the bench. They sit in daily judgment upon the events of the community and are required to make decisions involving more discretion and fewer rules than guide the lawyers on the bench. The length with which they treat an event and the manner in which they treat it requires of the press complete impartiality. Each person benefited or harmed by a news story or a bit of publicity is a "litigant" in the court of the press. He is suing for his share of the vital columns that convey to the people a presentation of the world of the day. It is as improper for a newspaperman to accept from any litigant in his kind of court cash considerations, gratuities or favors as it would be improper for a judge to accept such inducements in his domain.[4]

Yet, improper or not, it does happen. Sometimes the matter may be trivial, and no hazard to integrity is involved. In other cases, the appearances are dubious, or even downright shady.

A Pulitzer Prize for investigative reporting went one year to some Midwestern reporters who discovered that half a hundred Illinois newsmen had for years been on the state payroll, at the same time that they had supposedly been providing impartial coverage of state government. Their total take up to the time the whistle was blown was $480,000.

Another set of investigative reporters for the *Providence* (R.I.) *Journal* didn't win a prize but they did expose the fact that half the sportswriters on New England newspapers also held jobs as "consultants" to various race tracks in the area at retainers ranging up to $5,000 or more a year. Both the Illinois state officials and the New England race track owners apparently felt they were making sound investments in good public relations. The result certainly *wasn't* good journalism.

Occasionally the conflict of interest bugbear will work its way into the newsroom unnoticed. The four members of the women's page staff on an Oregon daily were invited to come once a week to the hairdressing salon at the largest local department store for a free wash and set, no strings attached. The women checked with the paper's managing editor, who inquired whether it was truly a no-strings offer. Apparently so. He gave them a green light. Everything went well for a time, and the staff had never looked so well groomed, until the hairdressers from the department store began showing up occasionally at the newsroom with a "suggestion" for a feature interview on some new techniques or just-introduced products. At that point the whole arrangement was abruptly canceled.

Part-Time Spooks

In other instances, the problem surfaces abruptly and dramatically.

Late in 1973, the *Washington Star-News* broke the story that 35 American newsmen were on a secret payroll of the Central Intelligence Agency as undercover informants. Five of them were described as working for "general circulation news organizations."

Once the story was out, the CIA officials indicated that they would drop the five from their secret payrolls; nothing was said about the 30 others, many of them part-time free-lance writers working abroad. According to the *Star-News* report, the arrangement with the reporters had been going on for some time, and there had been even more journalists on the secret payroll during the Cold War period of the 1950s.

What was most intriguing about the episode was the reluctance of the press generally to follow it up, to investigate all of its ramifications. During the same period, reporters were having no trouble digging up all sorts of top-secret material on government figures, but seemed strangely unable, or unwilling, to ferret out the names of their fellow scribes who had moonlighted as CIA spooks. (In the earlier cited cases of the Illinois

Statehouse reporters and the New England sports writers, names had been named.)

Stuart H. Loory, a former Washington correspondent for the *Los Angeles Times*, decided to look into this paradoxical situation. He reported later that he was repeatedly urged by fellow newsmen to abandon the story; the then CIA director was reluctant to discuss it at all, privately or publicly.

Loory's conclusions as to the ethical sensitivity of his journalistic colleagues were both disconcerting and discouraging:

Some journalists feel it is bad form to criticize a colleague who has made only a few bucks moonlighting. They are also uneasy that the whole tangled web of relationships between reporters and intelligence agents so beneficial to reporters will come undone.

The CIA established its network of informants in the news business with the consent of some editors, publishers, and other news executives. In some cases they specifically condoned the arrangements. In others, they tacitly permitted them.

The lack of reaction to the *Star-News* story is an indication that the news business—reporters, editors, publishers and other executives alike—did not probe the specifics of the CIA infiltration for fear of what might be learned, and published.

If the crisis of confidence faced by the news business—along with government—is to be overcome, journalists must be willing to focus on themselves the same spotlight that they so relentlessly train on others.[5]

There is some evidence that the unexposed CIA moonlighters did not represent an isolated case of cover-up by journalists of the untidy activities in their own back yards.

A passage in *The Press*, a book compiled by the editors of the *Wall Street Journal* from articles on press practices carried from time to time in that publication, notes that:

blackouts of news involving newspapers are quite common; hardly a working journalist could deny that one of the gravest weaknesses in coverage exhibited by the American press is its coverage of itself. This became apparent in Philadelphia recently when Harry Karafin, a prize-winning investigative reporter for the *Inquirer* and a staffer for nearly 30 years, was arrested on charges of blackmail and extortion. *Philadelphia* magazine, not a local newspaper, printed the first blast at Karafin in its April issue.

From then until the reporter's arrest earlier this month, the rival

Philadelphia *Bulletin* carried not a word on the case—even though the *Inquirer* itself (which claims it had repeatedly pursued tips about Mr. Karafin's activities but could not prove anything) fired him shortly before the magazine exposé and carried the whole story afterward.

More often newspapers try to cover up when unfavorable news breaks about their own operations. A few years ago the *Clarion-Ledger* and *Daily News*, jointly owned papers in Jackson, Mississippi, were hauled into court by U.S. officials on charges dealing with violations of Federal laws governing overtime pay. The court action resulted in a permanent injunction barring the papers from continuing the offending practices. Not a word of all this appeared in the Jackson papers; staffers were even ordered to stay away from the court, and they did.[6]

In fairness, it should be noted that in a great many conflict of interest situations, even where dirty linen is involved, editors and broadcasters do not hesitate to take prompt corrective action.

The *Newark* (N.J.) *Star-Ledger* removed the chief of its state capitol bureau and reassigned him to the Newark office after it was disclosed that he had accepted a position as secretary to a new lobbying organization opposed to automobile exhaust inspections. Said Mort Pye, the editor of the *Star-Ledger*, "It is absolutely against the policy of the paper to permit a member of the editorial staff to engage in any such activity."[7]

The Radio Television News Directors Association adopted a policy under which it will no longer "accept or solicit any commercial sponsorship or underwriting of any conference-related function." The action followed a CBS "60 Minutes" program which included a segment on a party put on by the Chrysler Corporation at the RTNDA 1973 convention.[8]

The American Society of Newspaper Editors took similar action several years earlier, after the scramble by auto companies and other corporations to stage ever more lavish cocktail parties and buffets at the annual ASNE convention had become too much to swallow, literally or figuratively.

On May 30, 1973 (the week following a *New York* magazine article on how sportswriters at New York daily newspapers receive thousands of dollars' worth of free tickets to Madison Square Garden sports events), the *New York Times* posted this memo: "We are of this day putting into effect a new policy with regard to complimentary tickets to sports events. From now on we will accept none."[9]

Sometimes editors even anticipate problems before they arise. When Barry Bingham, chairman of the board of the *Louisville Courier-Journal* and *Times*, planned to invest some money in a new restaurant in Louisville, he first extracted a pledge from the operators of the restaurant that the firm would never advertise in the papers, so there could be no question of conflict of interests.[10]

In some instances there may be two sides (or more) to a conflict of interest case.

During the Watergate scandal investigations, one witness, Jeb Stuart Magruder, testified that in 1972 the Committee to Re-Elect the President had paid $20,000 to a syndicated columnist, Victor Lasky, whose columns were carried on numerous editorial pages around the nation. When this came to light the National Conference of Editorial Writers took strong exception. The NCEW executive board unanimously passed a resolution charging Lasky with having "abused his position as an editorial page columnist," and another one criticizing the syndicate, North American Newspaper Alliance, for not taking sufficiently energetic action after the matter was revealed.[11]

Lasky, however, distributed a statement to editors who subscribed to his column, noting the NCEW claim "that I was paid by the committee to 'write speeches and articles for Republicans.' What I actually was paid for was to write speeches and articles for my then neighbor Mrs. John N. Mitchell. The material I prepared for Mrs. Mitchell was non-political. The articles had to do with such things as women's rights, of which Mrs. Mitchell was an advocate. . . . My arrangement lasted for several months, ending when Mrs. Mitchell left the political scene. I had no further connection with the Committee to Re-Elect the President." Unsatisfied, the NCEW referred the matter to the National News Council, a body set up to investigate complaints against the media. The council reviewed the case in public hearing and upheld the charge of the NCEW that Lasky's actions had been unethical. The council findings urged syndicates to adopt guidelines on conflict of interest for columnists.

Caesar's Many Wives

The conflict of interest problem in various forms has plagued the news media for generations. As editor Charles Long of the *Quill* once pointed out:

There's nothing new about the "freebie game." It is being played all the time and shows up in hundreds of different places and with varying sets of rules. Freebies—meaning token as well as expensive gifts, tickets to events large and small, junkets to simple and exotic places—have been floating in and about newsroom operations for as long as there has been a way of saying thanks for good publicity.[12]

As we have earlier noted, in many cases the considerations involved are so minor and the motive so clearly not ulterior that the journalist's integrity is not really in jeopardy. Yet that may not be justification enough. The journalist, like Caesar's wife, ought to be altogether above suspicion.

Ralph Otwell, managing editor of the *Chicago Sun-Times*, once put the problem thus:

But in the performance of our journalistic jobs there is more than a conscience to be served; it is not enough to know down deep inside that you are not being bought or influenced, that the "freebie" has not dulled your critical senses or lulled your watchful vigilance. The conflict of interest might not be felt on the inside . . . but it may be imagined or perceived on the outside. And there is the rub . . . the point where self-image and self-confidence end and public confidence begins.

The so-called "appearance of impropriety" is a condition which we in the media invoke against politicians, judges and even preachers—it is one which we must be on guard against also.[13]

One journalistic area—sportswriting and sportscasting—illustrates the many shades of the appearance-of-evil problem well. Here there are instances that seem open and shut, and others that are closer, more uncertain calls.

Consider, for example, a practice that has been widespread for generations—the assignment of sportswriters as official scorers at baseball games. In the minor leagues this may involve no compensation for the local sportswriter, and in fact may constitute a kind of onerous extra chore he undertakes as a gesture of good will. After all, the official scorer (who determines whether a given play constitutes, say, a base hit or an error on the shortstop) can easily make enemies among the players and managers and thus make his job more difficult.

In the major leagues, however, there is a fee paid to the official scorer, usually $35 or $50 a game. Obviously, major sums aren't involved; a sportswriter who scores local games through a whole season may net somewhere from $500 to $1,000. Still, he is being paid by a representative of the news activity that he is covering. Is there a conflict of interest involved?

Most sports editors think not. The *Bulletin of the American Society of Newspaper Editors* surveyed members of ASNE on the practice. Of responding editors, 62 percent said they permitted their sports reporters to serve as scorers and saw no problem. The other 38 percent indicated that they had a rule against such activity.

Those editors who permitted the practice said they felt that there was no genuine conflict of interest involved, and that the sportswriters were the best-qualified people to call the close plays from their lofty perches over home plate.

But some others disagreed. Tim Kelly, executive sports editor of the *Philadelphia Inquirer*, told the *ASNE Bulletin* editors:

Aside from the obvious aversion to having our writer paid by the people he's covering, we also feel that having a writer as official scorer can put him in unnecessary awkward positions with players he may have credited with an error or not given a "save" or taken a base hit away from.

And Paul Poorman, managing editor of the *Detroit News*, responded simply: "It is not an appropriate activity for a newspaperman."[14]

Drawing Lines

Serving as official scorer may indeed represent no more than a border-line conflict of interest problem. But sportswriters and sportscasters may also be party to other practices that stray more definitely into shady territory.

Most big league baseball and football teams will willingly provide various kinds of subsidization to writers who want to cover preseason practice camps. This may involve living quarters at the practice camp site, free meals, even transportation to and from the location. Most editors long ago recognized that this sort of thing wouldn't do and now make sure that their writers pay their own way. But some editors on small papers, with modest expense accounts, still aren't above accepting a helping hand from the team management. ("How else could we get our man down to Florida? We just wouldn't have any spring practice coverage, that's all.")

The insistent temptations posed to the impartiality of the sportswriters are not limited to the preseason period, by any means. Bill Surface, a former sportswriter himself, examined some of the problems in an article in *Columbia Journalism Review*.[15]

He described how some sports reporters routinely accept free drinks, meals, and other favors from team officials while covering games away from home. Others are hired by teams or leagues to write chapters for "authorized" histories of the sport, or to rewrite their regular game stories into a page for a stadium program.[16]

The relationship that develops between sportswriters and their sources results, Surface claims, in a brand of sportswriting that is "so partial and so predictable that, on many occasions, it resembles more the work of a master of ceremonies than that of a journalist."[17]

In the electronic media it has been customary for years for professional sports teams to have veto rights over the selection of play-by-play or color announcers on radio and television stations—or even to pay their salaries outright. The team's owners can then make sure that the games will be described on the air with a consistent "home team" slant. College teams have begun to emulate the professional system, offering exclusive broadcasting rights in exchange for a voice in the hiring and firing of sportscasters.

There can be little argument about the existence of conflict of interest problems in cases such as these. And it may be that the only way to end such conflicts is to divorce the sportswriters and sportscasters completely from any dependence on the news sources they are theoretically supposed to cover without fear or favor.

Jack Mann, sports editor of *Newsday*, holds that view. In an article entitled "Whose Bread I Eat, His Song I Sing," he asserted:

One way to eliminate both payola and junkets would be to pay salaries and provide expense accounts that would make both unnecessary. Some newspapers have tried it, and it works. It gives a man pride and a man with pride is more likely to hustle. A man who hustles is less likely to bat out the hackneyed nonsense which still, after a generation of improvement, clutters up most of the sports pages.[18]

Another method of reducing or eliminating the problem might involve rotating sports reporting or sportscasting assignments so that a given writer would not become too close to his beat to give it impartial coverage. An obvious drawback: such rotation would end the advantages stemming from the reporter's familiarity with his sources and access to well-cultivated pipelines.

So far as the electronic media are concerned, the strong show business strain that runs through the industry, and the well-entrenched influence of advertisers on the content and production of sponsored shows, both constitute roadblocks to substantial reform.

A-Junketing We'll Go...

If sports reporting constitutes a problem area so far as journalistic ethics and the "appearance of impropriety" are concerned, it is not the only one, by a long shot. The junket, which Surface and Mann cited as one of the temptations held out to the sports reporters, is readily available to other journalistic departments as well.

The editors of food pages, for example, are the targets of food companies hopeful that their products will show up frequently in the recipes and feature stories that fill in between the big grocery ads. Richard Karp, a Washington free-lance writer, made a study of the situation with the support of a grant from the Fund for Investigative Journalism. His report, published in *Columbia Journalism Review*, noted that:

The big payoffs to food editors ... are the numerous junkets each year that masquerade as food tours, conferences, and contests. The German, Portuguese, and Italian trade commissions each year take groups of food editors on "wine tours" of their countries. The Swedes and the Danes take the ladies on "carte blanche" food tours of Scandinavia. The R. T. French Mustard Company flies the women to Acapulco for a "conference" and to Catskill Mountain resorts for a "Winter Weekend."

Executive House Hotels, Inc., of Chicago flies them to Aruba, and Quaker Oats brings them to the Windy City for a tour of their plants and lots of wining and dining. Pepsi-Cola hosts posh New York nightclub parties where everyone goes home with a new camera or similar gift. Pillsbury hold its popular annual "Bake-off" contest in various cities around the country—last year it was in Honolulu. Christian Brothers Wines each fall celebrates the harvest by giving food editors lavish dinners in New York and San Francisco. ... In addition, dozens of smaller companies and scores of trade associations representing everyone from California raisin distributors to Maryland poultry breeders offer the women an array of junkets the year around.[19]

Do the junkets pose a conflict of interest? Will the food writers who are thus favored be inclined to give some extra space to French's mustard, or Pillsbury products, when the occasion comes around?

Some publications forbid their writers to be exposed to temptation in this fashion, but not all have such a policy. And even those that do, have some problems making it stick. The *Philadelphia Inquirer*, according to Karp's report, permits food writers for the paper to go on company-sponsored excursions but the newspaper itself insists on paying the expenses. Elaine Tait, the *Inquirer* food editor, spent a weekend touring the New York State wine country in the care of the Taylor Wine Company. As Karp recounts it:

According to *Inquirer* policy, Miss Tait said, "the newspaper paid all my expenses. . . . But I should tell you that there was no transportation cost because Taylor took me up in their private plane." Asked if she wrote up the trip, Miss Tait said, "Well, I don't accept a trip and then not write an article about it."[20]

What about the reader who turns to the food section for helpful tips on what products offer best value, or what recipes promise to brighten the family mealtime? Is she being served a journalistic full measure? Or are the editors and writers who have enjoyed the fringe-benefit junkets giving her slanted coverage? Does the food writer really find out enough new and useful things about raisins or Maryland chickens to justify the trip—and the subsidy?

Perhaps in response to surveys such as Karp's, or possibly reflecting an industry-wide concern about ethical values, a Newspaper Food Writers and Editors Association was formed in 1973, and a little more than a year later the organization adopted (by a vote of 57 to 7) a code of ethics "encouraging" its members to shun freebies whenever they were proffered. One provision of the code:

Gifts, favors, free travel or lodging, special treatment or privileges can compromise the integrity and diminish the credibility of food editors and writers as well as their employers. Such offers should be avoided.[21]

A somewhat better case, at least on the surface, can be made for the travel writer who goes a-junketing. After all, how can a travel writer cover his or her beat while sitting behind a typewriter in Dubuque or Minneapolis? And yet a publication cannot reasonably be expected to foot the bills to send one of its staff members roaming the world just to provide "local" coverage of a relatively minor news area. So some editors who draw the line at junkets for other members of the staff take a more indulgent view where the travel writers are concerned.

But is the ethical question involved any less pertinent?

A travel writer who has been the guest of an airline and a new Hawaiian hotel is not likely to make any unfriendly observations about either when back in front of the office typewriter or the studio microphone. Yet some editors, according to a *Columbia Journalism Review* report by Stanford Sesser, not only wink at but actually foster the conflict-of-interest situations that compromise the integrity of their travel writers:

> The way newspapers handle travel writing assignments provides part of the explanation for what finally appears in print. In some newsrooms editors accept for themselves the most appealing free trips and distribute the rest of the invitations among favored reporters. Other papers use the position of travel editor as a reward to a staff member who in addition takes on less glamorous duties. . . .
>
> Most newspapers insist that their travel writers work out as many free deals as possible, and a surprising number won't reimburse them for extra expenses.[22]

As with the case of subsidy abuses affecting sportswriters, the surest way to do away with the ethical compromises is to sever the dependency ties. Sesser cites the *Los Angeles Times* as an example. That paper provides a $20,000-a-year expense account to its travel editor, Jerry Hulse, and insists that he accept not a cent's worth of subsidy from outsiders. As a result, Hulse is able to make such unvarnished, heretical assessments as his description of Atlantic City, New Jersey, as "the Skid Row Riviera. The nicest thing about visiting Atlantic City is the drive out of town. Visiting Atlantic City is like taking your vacation in military boot camp."[23]

And after paying his own way to Hawaii for the dedication of a new Hilton Hotel, Hulse wrote a lengthy column describing the four-day party the hotel put on for reporters and others, and confined his only comment on the hotel to a single paragraph: "There is a certain sameness to all Hilton openings, of course. Good plumbing and dry martinis."[24]

It is one thing, to be sure, for the wealthy *Los Angeles Times* to assert such independence. Smaller papers or local radio or TV stations face a tougher choice; they simply could not afford to send their own staff members on distant assignment if the whole tab had to be covered by the publication or station involved. For them, the dilemma remains: accept the free ride and the appearance of impropriety that goes with it, or do without any staff-written coverage of the travel beat at a time when more Americans are spending more time and money on travel than ever in our history. An increasing number of publications and stations—in many cases prodded by their staffs—are making the hard decision on the side of ethics rather than expediency.

A Word from the Defense

Some journalists undertake to defend the venerable convention of the junket, despite the pejorative connotations it has acquired. And they are able to make some solid points, even though the case overall may not be altogether convincing.

The *Masthead*, quarterly publication of the National Conference of Editorial Writers, published a symposium of commentary from its members on the question of where to draw the line. The editors took the title of the article—"Does It Begin with a Cigar?"—from an anecdote about Senator Paul Douglas of Illinois, who recalled that he had once asked a policeman how some of his colleagues got started on the downward path to corruption. The policeman replied: "It generally began with a cigar."

Here, from the symposium in the *Masthead*, are a few sample excerpts reflecting a somewhat different side of the junket debate:

When the invitation came to me out of the blue to join a group of American editors who were to visit South Africa early this year as guests of the republic's government, I promptly responded (with the approval and encouragement of my publisher) that I was interested and probably available.

One question, however, came to mind and I put it with blunt directness to the South African public affairs officers: "Has your country ever sought or received U.S. foreign aid?" The answer came back with equal bluntness: "We have never requested nor received any foreign aid from any government." . . .

I was relieved on the foreign aid score because we are more critical of U.S. foreign aid policies than approving. And I am frank to admit that I don't know whether I could have reconciled the attractiveness of the opportunity to visit South Africa with my conscience if the element of U.S. assistance funds had been involved. I guess I'm just glad it wasn't. . . .

I make no apologies for having accepted South Africa's generous hospitality. . . . I went and wrote with that I considered the objective attitude and frank reporting expected of a newspaperman under any circumstances—paying visitor or nonpaying guest. That, in my opinion, is the key consideration in the course of accepting and enjoying any hospitality large or small.—Paul McKalip, editor of the editorial page, *Tucson* (Ariz.) *Daily Citizen*[25]

(Would it be fair to ask Mr. McKalip whether the question about U.S. aid was the *only* one he would want answered before accepting the invitation? And the next time a debate about South African racial policies came up in the U.N.—and in the news—would his readers wonder whether Mr. McKalip's editorial analysis of the issue was truly disinterested?)

Another bit from the *Masthead* symposium:

Only a downright purist, with the usual lack of peripheral vision associated with extremism, could propose that editorial writers accept no trips, junkets, hospitality from anyone.

On the smaller papers we are offered fewer free holidays and are inclined to accept a higher percentage, therefore. How else are we to capture the glamor and romance promised by our calling?

I traveled for the State Department for eight weeks in the hardship-filled hinterlands of Jamaica, Ecuador, Martinique and (hardships for real) British Guiana. I worked, but not as hard as I wanted . . . .

I wanted the trip, could not have gone otherwise, and felt I could make some contributions to others' understanding of the U.S. South. I also received a stipend. . . .

I would take a no strings deal, or an invitation from an outfit that knows in advance it risks criticism as well as commendations.

In short, it depends. It depends on the newspaper guy and on the host.—Sylvan Meyer, then editor of the *Gainsville* (Ga.) *Daily Times*[26]

And one more view:

There are two dangers inherent in the acceptance of offers to go on junkets. The first is the possibility of being indoctrinated or brainwashed, being led to see only what our hosts want us to see, and putting them in the most favorable possible light. The second is the gratitude of a guest reluctant to report anything unfavorable about a host, or more bluntly, quid pro quo.

We have no hard and fast rules about junkets, but try to judge each invitation on its own merits, using as criteria whether it is a legitimate matter of news-editorial interest, and whether it would unduly influence the objectivity of the reporter or editor. . . .

Ideally, each paper should pay its own reporter's or editor's way. But since we're not all the New York *Times*, if we followed that rule strictly we would miss out on experiences that would enable us to do our jobs better.—Eric W. Allen, Jr., editor, *Medford* (Oreg.) *Mail Tribune*[27]

On one pan of the scales must go the possibility that the junket may open up opportunities for coverage or the acquisition of insight that would be of genuine benefit to the journalist and to the readers or viewers served; and on the other pan must go the hazards noted by Mr. Allen above. Which way the scales dip may, however, be determined by a third factor—the personal integrity of the journalist involved. That may be more important than whether the consideration at stake is indeed only a cigar or eight weeks in Jamaica and Ecuador.[28]

On a 1974 CBS *60 Minutes* program, reporter Mike Wallace examined the phenomenon of the junketing journalist. In the process he acknowledged that some notable newsmen—among them Walter Cronkite—had gone a-junketing and hadn't been bought. But he asked whether even the suspicion that journalists might be influenced by favors is not enough to damage press credibility—bringing us back full circle to Caesar's wife.[29]

(Incidentally, it was a signal tribute to the integrity of the CBS news department that this particular program zeroed in on a conflict of interest episode involving its own network. One segment of the *60 Minutes* film showed a TV critic from the *Pittsburgh Post-Gazette* checking into a New York hotel and opening an envelope handed to him. Inside were two $10 bills. He, along with numerous other TV writers, had been brought to New York to preview some new network shows and CBS had picked up the whole tab—transportation, hotel, meals, and even the $20 "mad money." The producer of the show said that although network executives knew of the segment, no pressure was put on him to cut it out.)[30]

Litmus Tests

This chapter has by no means canvassed all the various conflict of interest soft spots in the journalistic media. Among the many others that might be explored, had we no other fish to fry:

42

—The sticky situations that arise when editors, publishers, reporters, or broadcasters run for or win public office, or sit on boards of community agencies, about which their media are presumably reporting the news without slant.

—The real estate sections of newspapers, in which thinly disguised puff stories about local real estate developments are used, as one editor put it, as "shinplaster to keep the ads from bumping."[31]

—The fashion reporting scene, in newspapers, magazines, and broadcasting, where the dress-designing firms pay the expenses of reporters coming to New York or Paris to cover the new openings, and where the leading press agent for the fashion industry, Eleanor Lambert, can publicly boast: "I own every fashion editor in America."[32]

—The numerous contests and awards offered each year by various commercial or other special-interest groups as inducements to reporters to crank out stories that will put their organizations or products in the public eye. (Examples: the Cigar Institute award for the best photograph of a prominent news figure puffing on a cigar; the American Furniture Mart Awards for reporting on home furnishings; the American Meat Institute awards for reporting about food.[33]

It isn't necessary, however, to catalog *all* the problem areas in order to be satisfied that problems do exist with respect to "the appearance of impropriety" in all of the media.

What is important is that those in the news business, and those who may be planning to get into it, recognize how ubiquitously and how insidiously a conflict of interest situation can develop, and recognize also how to cope with it.

In the judgment of one press critic, Ben H. Bagdikian, a good many working journalists *are* aware of the conflict of interest soft spots but tend to look the other way, or at least do not take any positive steps to deal with the problems:

Special sections like real estate, business and finance, travel, and food, for example, are almost always industry-oriented, their editorial content handled outside the tenets of ethical news. Most professional journalists regard these sections as the least ethical and professional in printed journalism, with blurring between commercial promotion and news that would be considered corrupt in the rest of the news columns.[34]

Yet this "see no evil" attitude shouldn't have to continue. Ethics and ethical decisions are personal matters, but in a professional field the way in which they are approached affects all of those who work in that field. Every journalist has an obligation to his or her colleagues, whatever the beat involved.

There are some internal tests of conscience a journalist can apply, as one might use litmus paper to detect the presence of an unwanted chemical. The first test is whether you can honestly conclude that the favor or consideration involved—whether it is a cup of coffee, a cigar, a weekend in Miami, or a tour of the Middle East as a guest of the Arab League—will be likely to tinge your impartiality when you turn to journalistic assignments that have to do with the source of the favor.

And the second test—more difficult—is whether, even if you know in your heart that you won't be bought by the proffer, the audience you serve will be equally sure of your integrity. Will the mere fact of your having accepted the trifling freebie, or taken the "fact-finding" junket, be enough to place you under suspicion in the eyes of your readers, listeners, or viewers?

Admittedly, these aren't simple tests to apply. They put to exacting trial the conscience of the individual journalist. But, if you choose to enter the media fields, you ought to bear in mind that no one has promised you a rose garden.

Let's close this aspect of the discussion of ethics with a comment from Louis M. Lyons, former curator of the Nieman Foundation for Journalism of Harvard University:

I don't know that we can prove that journalism is a profession. But the important thing is that the men in it act as if it were. The professional attitude is simply the feeling of responsibility toward the news, the obligation to the readers that the reader is their only client.[37]

Notes

1Quoted in "Getting the Business," *Catholic Digest*, April 1974, p. 76.

2Curtis D. MacDougall, *The Press and Its Problems* (Dubuque: William C. Brown Company, Publishers, 1964), p. 234.

3Quoted in J. R. Wiggins, "Gifts, Favors and Gratuities," *Bulletin of the American Society of Newspaper Editors*, No. 411 (August 1, 1958), p. 1.

4*Ibid.*, pp. 2–3.

5Stuart H. Loory, "The CIA's Use of the Press: a 'Mighty Wurlitzer'," reprinted from the *Columbia Journalism Review*, XIII, No. 13 (September/October 1974), © 9–18.

6A. Kent MacDougall, ed., reprinted from *The Press: A Critical Look from the Inside* (Princeton: Dow Jones Books, 1972), pp. 144–45. Copyright © Dow Jones Books, 1967. Excerpted by permission of Dow Jones Books.

7*Editor & Publisher*, CVII, No. 7 (February 16, 1974), 34.

8*Quill*, LXII, No. 3 (March 1974), 11.

9Charles Long, "Games Newspeople Play," *Quill*, LXI, No. 8 (August 1973), 16.

10"Publisher Not Allowed to Advertise in Newspapers," *Editor & Publisher*, CVII, No. 12 (March 23, 1974), 29.

11"National News Council Studying Victor Lasky Column Complaint," *Editor & Publisher*, CVII, No. 8 (May 4, 1974), 29.

12Long, "Games Newspeople Play," p. 16.

13Ralph Otwell, "Can a Reporter Be Bought for a Ham on Rye?", *Editor & Publisher*, CVII, No. 17 (April 27, 1974), 40.

14"To Score or Not to Score . . . ," a symposium, *Bulletin of the American Society of Newspaper Editors*, No. 577 (April 1974), pp. 6–8.

15Bill Surface, "The Shame of the Sports Beat," *Columbia Journalism Review*, X, No. 5 (January/February 1972), © 48–55.

16*Ibid.*, pp. 51–52.

17*Ibid.*, p. 49.

18Jack Mann, "Whose Bread I Eat, His Song I Sing," *Bulletin of the American Society of Newspaper Editors*, No. 446 (October 1, 1961), pp. 1–3.

19Richard Karp, "Newspaper Food Pages: Credibility for Sale," reprinted from the *Columbia Journalism Review*, X, No. 4 (November/December 1971), © 36–44.

20*Ibid.*, p. 42

21"Food Editors, Writers OK Code; 'A Great Victory,' Says Clark," *Associated Press Managing Editors News*, No. 82 (April 1975), 3.

22Stanford N. Sesser, "The Fantasy World of Travel Sections," reprinted from the *Columbia Journalism Review*, IX, No. 1 (Spring, 1970), © 44–47.

23*Ibid.*, p. 47.

24*Ibid.*

25"Does It Begin with a Cigar?", a symposium, *Masthead*, XVII, No. 4 (Fall, 1965), 5–15.

26*Ibid.*, p. 12.

27*Ibid.*, p. 6.

28The "freebie" issue took an unusual twist when it was introduced into labor-management relations as a collective bargaining topic in mid-1974.

The American Newspaper Guild, the union representing news and other employes, asserted the claim that codes of ethics ought to be subject to bargaining, in the same fashion as salaries and hours. The union leaders' rationale was that the adoption of a code of ethics by a news organization in effect changes working conditions; for example, a ban on "freebies," specifying dismissal as the penalty for continuing to accept such goodies, would alter job security. The management spokesman for the two papers involved, the *Madison* (Wis.) *Capital Times* and the *Pottstown* (Pa.) *Mercury*, contended that ethical values are so important to the constitutional role of a newspaper that they cannot be haggled over at a bargaining table.

Some of the journalists who were caught in the middle found the situation awkward, at least. One of them, John Stallard of the *Capital Times*, said that "I do not consider free passes, tickets, or any other handouts of influence a tradition of the industry or part of my working conditions." And in a TV news interview he was even more outspoken:

> The Guild, in this challenge of the code of ethics, is presenting an image of itself as a house full of whores. I don't want to indicate to the public that I am one of these whores.

Other observers pointed out that the ultimate enforcement agency for provisions of any collective bargaining agreement is an arm of the federal government, through the processing of unfair labor practice charges. Should government be made the final arbiter of journalistic ethics? It would seem to be a perilous expedient. See: Dave Offer, "The Guild Enters the Ethics Fray," *Quill*, LXII, No. 10 (October 1974), 18–21, and Ed Cony, "Is Ethics a Bargaining Issue?", *Wall Street Journal*, Nov. 15, 1974, p. 12.

[29]"Junketing Journalists," *Time*, CIII, No. 4 (January 28, 1974), 56.

[30]*Ibid.*

[31]Ferdinand Kuhn, "Blighted Areas of Our Press," *Columbia Journalism Review*, V, No. 2 (Summer, 1966), 5–10.

[32]Dick Leonard, "The Fashion Market—A News World Unto Itself?", *Bulletin of the American Society of Newspaper Editors*, No. 527 (February 1969), p. 12.

[33]See William B. Blankenburg and Richard L. Allen, "The Journalism Contest Thicket: Is It Time for Some Guidelines?", *Associated Press Managing Editors News*, No. 76, September 1974, pp. 1, 8–9. Also: Donald Pfarrer, "Awards: Do They Conflict with a Paper's Mission?", *Associated Press Managing Editors News*, No. 78, November 1974, pp. 7–8.

[34]Ben H. Bagdikian, "Professional Personnel and Organizational Structure in the Mass Media," in *Mass Communication Research: Major Issues and Future Directions*, eds. W. Philips Davison and Frederick T. C. Yu (New York: Praeger Publishers, Inc., 1974), p. 130.

[35]Quoted in Curtis D. MacDougall, *The Press and Its Problems* (Dubuque: William C. Brown Company, Publishers, 1964), p. 4.

Taste and the Journalist...

"Saying that hiding photographers in brothel keepers' cupboards is in the best traditions of journalism is really grotesque" — Winston Churchill, Member of Parliament[1]

4 Any discussion of ethics in journalism must take up—though only briefly—the nature and incidence of tastelessness in the mass media. Why only briefly? Because in matters of taste, one who points fingers and drafts rules is knee-deep in shifting sands. Manners and mores always have been changeable, and never more so than in our present day when the passage of a half dozen years can bring radical alterations in what the generality of society will consider acceptable and proper.

Skim quickly through some of the old newspaper codes collected by Nelson Crawford and cited in chapter 2 ("Never use expressions that suggest nauseating ideas. . . . Slang must be excluded from the columns. . . .") and think back to the shocked fuss that was stirred up throughout the country only a few years ago when the word "virgin" was uttered in a motion picture ("The Moon is Blue"). Then call to mind the subject matter of some of the most successful motion pictures of recent years (blasphemy and masturbation in "The Exorcist," full nudity and simulated copulation in half a dozen other box office hits).

47

Remember that only a couple of decades ago all the news media used a whole repertoire of euphemisms for touchy topics ("assault" for "rape" is a classic example: "The girl was beaten about the head and body, her nose was broken, her eyes blackened, and two ribs cracked. But she had not been assaulted, a police physician reported"). Then look to the news pages today, or to the interview shows on television where the comparative size of apes' and men's penises is calmly and explicitly discussed.

Think of the days when open-air nakedness was confined to the rural childhood swimming hole, or the secluded, leafy nudist colony. And then call to mind the spate of news stories on rock festivals, both picturing and reporting the youthful music and dope enthusiasts cavorting in the nude while sightseers ogled, and even describing couples in intercourse surrounded by unshocked onlookers in an interested circle.

Presumably, the point has been made. To attempt to set down any kind of permanent do's and don'ts for journalists where matters of taste are concerned would be futile. This book wouldn't even make it to the library shelves before its precepts would have been overtaken by the times.

Instead, this chapter will undertake two other, and more modest, objectives. It will call attention to some special instances of lapses in taste in journalism that may be inadvertent or borderline but which nonetheless besmirch the profession and injure individuals and institutions. And it will note some debatable cases that have been superficially classified under the rubric of taste but that actually involve other considerations as well.

Beyond the Pale

There are, of course, some kinds of excesses that would be almost universally condemned, both inside and outside the news business. The old *National Enquirer*, before it decided to go respectable in the late 1960s, used to sell millions of copies weekly, and make a fortune for its owners, by publishing first-person accounts of such outrageous episodes as that of a husband who had murdered his wife, cut off her head, and planted it in her favorite flowerpot.

In this permanently blacklisted category would also be the tactics that called forth the brief quote that appears under the title of this chapter.

48

The episode that so repelled the grandson of the late Sir Winston involved the reporting by two major London newspapers of a sex scandal in which a cabinet minister was a featured figure. The Sunday *News of the World* (circulation 6,000,000 each week) admitted that one of its photographers had arranged to have infrared pictures taken of the cabinet minister, Lord Lambton, romping in bed with two prostitutes. Provisions were also made to get clandestine tape recordings of the boudoir activities to go with the pictures. Then, when the *News of the World* editors had second thoughts about using the material, the intermediary (husband and pimp of one of the prostitutes) took the picture and tape package to a rival paper, *Sunday People* (circulation 4,600,000). The *Sunday People* editors bought the lot from the pimp and apparently were intending to publish them in some form, but the case broke in the courts in the meantime and under British law that ended further press treatment of the matter for the time. It was this performance by two of the largest British papers that Churchill labeled "grotesque." At the least.

Our concern here, however, is not with the blatant cases about which there can be little or no argument. Let's look instead at some instances in which tastelessness slipped onto the journalistic scene simply because someone was too calloused or too indifferent to the sensibilities of others.

Someone Should Have Paused

In early 1960 Richard L. Neuberger, a former newspaperman, was serving as the senior senator from the state of Oregon. He had been ill the previous year, but his death on March 9 came as a surprise and shock to everyone. He had filed as a candidate in the Oregon primary, seeking another term in the Senate. The filing deadline for the primary fell on March 13, the Friday of the week in which the senator died.

Neuberger's wife, Maurine, had served in the Oregon state legislature, as had Senator Neuberger in his earlier political career. At the urging of Oregon political leaders, Mrs. Neuberger decided to file on Friday as a candidate for her husband's seat in the United States Senate.

When news of the filing became known, the Associated Press office at Portland received what it reported as "numerous requests" for the redistribution of a picture of Mrs. Neuberger that had been in the news two years earlier. It showed the wife of the senator in a bathing suit,

49

seated smilingly on a chair while a hairdresser put finishing touches to her hairdo before she was to model in a Democratic fund-raising fashion show in Washington.

The picture was sent out, as the editors requested, and it appeared in several Oregon dailies the next day—which also was the day of Senator Neuberger's funeral.

There can be no argument about the legitimacy of the photograph when it had first been taken; Mrs. Neuberger undoubtedly had no objection, and presumably was glad of the publicity. Nor can anyone fault an editor for remembering a newsworthy picture of a person who has just announced candidacy for high office. But run the smiling bathing suit picture on the day her husband was to be buried? Shouldn't someone, somewhere along the news pipeline, have paused a moment to consider whether this was defensible journalism or a grossly insensitive lapse in taste?

The fact that someone has become a newsworthy figure does not constitute a writ of dehumanization—it does not strip him or her of sensitivity and dignity. Journalists ought to have a lively ethical concern that the pursuit of news not become an excuse for disregarding the feelings of persons who are in the news or associated with those in the news.

Slips That Pass...

Sometimes an instance of tastelessness in the treatment of news appears to have been inadvertent, while in other cases not even that excuse can apply.

In the former category was one feature story that appeared in a small city daily, telling of a marriage in that community. The groom was a man who had come to the state as a captive, literally. He had been mugged and robbed on a San Francisco street and then locked inside an empty railroad boxcar by his assailants. The car moved on north, by slow hitches, and with several stops on sidings. But no one heard the man's calls for help at any of the stops. Seven days later some railroad yard workers in an Oregon community heard faint noises from inside the car and opened it to find the gaunt but still living victim. After he had recovered from the ordeal, he settled down in the community and finally met and married a local girl. That was the substance of the feature story, which was accompanied by a picture of the bridal couple.

The copy editor assigned to write a headline for the story evidently tried to get a hint of the feature angle into the head, which came out:

Unwilling Jonesville Resident Takes Himself a Bride

As it happened, the picture showed the bride to be a pleasant-faced but very plump young lady. The headline and picture in conjunction lent themselves to a meaning not intended by the reporter or the headline writer, but one that caused the young couple painful embarrassment. It was not a major tragedy, to be sure, and unintentional.

That last could not be said for another feature story and picture combination that appeared in another small-town paper.

This story described the successful efforts of a local woman to lose weight. There were pictures showing her "before" (228 pounds) and "after" (124 pounds), illustrating how dramatically she had slimmed down. But the lead paragraph of the story read:

Being a butcher's wife, Helen P——— knew how to trim the fat off a steak or roast. Her biggest job, though, was in trimming 104 pounds of fat off herself. It took 88 weeks to do it. But she did it.

And the headline over the story was:

A Butcher's Wife, She Trimmed off 104 Pounds of Ugly Fat

Any reporter or headline writer tries to be alert to humorous, play-on-words, or topical possibilities in a news situation; exploiting them can turn a drab story into what the news services call a "brite"—a lively and amusing item.

But such exploitation is not defensible if it is at the expense of the sensitivities of an innocent party, or if it treats in flip terms what is basically a tragic situation. The "butcher's wife . . . ugly fat" approach held the subject of that story up to needless ridicule. And in the following instance, a desk man chose the wrong subject for light treatment.

In a California town a migrant worker with a wife and four children committed suicide by slashing his wrists and hanging them over the edge of the bathtub so that his blood drained into the tub. A copy editor put this headline on the story:

At Least He Was Neat About It

The treatment would have been offensive in any setting, even if the story had been published in a distant community; but this appeared in the man's hometown paper, for his widow and four children to read and remember forever.

Consider one more instance arising out of a reporter's efforts to reach for some kind of off-beat angle for his lead.

In this case a sportswriter had an advance story to do on a pair of forthcoming basketball games that would pit the team from a local college (with a dismal season record) against one of the leading collegiate powerhouses in the nation. The theme of the story was the impending slaughter of the locals. And this is how the writer opened:

If you loved My Lai, if you screamed deliriously for another Biafra, if you craved for a new and improved India-Pakistan conflict, then you won't want to miss the two-night production planned for University Court this weekend.

My Lai, of course, was the scene of the infamous Vietnam war episode in which American troops wantonly killed more than 100 civilians in a mindless orgy of violence; Biafra referred to the recently put-down rebellion in an African nation, in which a long blockade had brought about the slow starvation of thousands of children; and the India-Pakistan war was one in which unusual episodes of cruelty and massacre had been reported. All had been in the news recently at the time the sportswriter composed his lead; he had topical touches, certainly. But he had no sense of proportion, no sensitivity, no feeling for the tastelessness of the juxtaposition that he had created with his approach.

The following, quoted from a news item in *Columbia Journalism Review*, requires no elaboration or explanation; it conveys its own lesson in journalistic ethics unaided:

The *New Hampshire Sunday News*, affiliate of the Manchester *Union-Leader*, ran on Sept. 2, 1973, an editorial entitled, incredibly, "Kissinger the Kike?" It criticized attacks on the secretary of state [Henry Kissinger] by "an interlocking cabal of TV networks and newspapers which are themselves owned and operated largely by Jews," among them "the N.Y. *Times*, which is owned by the Jew, Sulzberger." In reply to a letter that complained about the editorial, B. J. McQuaid, the editor, asserted that "the three TV networks, all owned by Jews," had criticized Kissinger. He concluded: "If ordinary Jews of this country were more inclined to criticize the leftist-liberal bias of such news media as the N.Y. *Times*, Washington *Post*, and the big TV networks, they would do much to allay the suspicions and bitterness of many of their fellow citizens." Yes, the date was 1973, not 1933.[2]

Not Only Taste

Let's turn now to consider some situations in which the question of taste is cited as the reason for a news decision, but in which other issues are also present—and are perhaps overriding.

On June 11, 1963, the Associated Press sent from Saigon one of the most startling news photos ever distributed up to that time. It showed a 73-year-old monk, seated in a Saigon street, wreathed in flames. He had poured gasoline over himself and then calmly struck a match. Photographers had been alerted to the episode ahead of time; the monk had planned the suicide as a protest against the regime then in power in South Vietnam. The photograph showed him sitting erect, flames billowing up around him, and with his already-blackened features clearly visible.

Editors around the nation reacted variously to the shocking photograph. Some used it in their papers, some promptly filed it unpublished. Comments, some in protest and some in praise, flowed in to the AP. The American Society of Newspaper Editors polled its members for their views on the photograph and its use. Here are some excerpts from their comments:

Alfred L. Hewitt, *Shreveport* (La.) *Times*—Orange juice and fried monk for breakfast?

That's the way our editors looked at the photo of the self-immolation of the Buddhist monk.

How would it look over the breakfast table? That's the rule of thumb our editors are instructed to use to evaluate questionable or controversial photographs.

For that reason, we passed up that particular shot. Generally, this is our rule for real grisly pictures—those that don't help the digestion of early-morning *Times* readers.

* * *

Turner Catledge, the *New York Times*—The picture of the burning Buddhist monk was unquestionably a dramatic one, and far above the average of news pictures. However, the responsible editors in charge of the New York *Times* "Bull Pen" on the day the picture was serviced decided without dissent to pass it up. Their reasoning was that it was somewhat gruesome. We have tried over the years to follow the old dictum of Adolph Ochs that everything in the New York *Times* should be fit for the breakfast table, and this picture seemed to our editors not to meet the test.

* * *

T. T. Hunt, *Beaumont* (Tex.) *Enterprise*—We didn't use it.

In our eyes, the overriding impact was of a gruesome picturization of a human being burning away his life.

The published picture offers no alternative for the reader. He cannot elect to ignore it.

The choice, then, was between the words and the photograph. Words being more selective, we chose words to tell the story.

The question was solely one of good taste.

But was it one *solely* of taste? The "breakfast table" argument cropped up in the comments of many of the editors who responded to the ASNE survey. It has some substance, certainly. But does it tilt the scales when you consider what other considerations are also involved? Here was an instance of ultimate protest against what this man and many of his fellow religionists believed to be an unbearable situation. Can a journalist ignore such a protest gesture, or muffle its impact?

Moreover, the "breakfast table" thesis, as the editors cited it, had some structural weaknesses. One editor, for example, said he had used the picture in the afternoon paper of his morning-evening combination, but had withheld it from the morning editions.

Many editors indicated that they did or would use the picture, and told why:

John K. Quad, *New Brunswick* (Me.) *Home News*—The picture of the burning monk in Saigon is one of the great pictures of history—particularly photographic history. It would have been a mistake not to have used it.

* * *

Bennett DeLoach, *Tampa Times*—What better way was there to tell readers of the intensity of the religious struggle in South Vietnam? Or to illustrate the futility of it all in a place where the United States is up to its neck in big troubles?

To us the religious strife story was wrapped up more effectively in those pictures than in 10,000 words.

The Tampa editor's comment goes to the heart of the matter—the compelling public interest argument for using the picture, however controversial or disturbing it might prove to be to many readers.

This is not to suggest, however, that it should have been an easy decision for all the editors to reach. The considerations to be weighed were several, and all were rooted in long-standing journalistic practice.

Felix R. McKnight of the *Dallas Times Herald* responded:

The final conclusion was that it was a bit too grisly, even though it was the guts of the Vietnam story. It was a tough decision to make. . . . We play each decision by ear—weighing shock and standards of taste against newsworthiness.

And John F. James of the *Pueblo* (Colo.) *Star-Journal & Chieftain* alluded to another factor:

Proximity, it seems to me, enters into such decisions in a very real way. We would not use a picture of a local person being burned to death in an auto crash. We probably would print a similar picture of an accident far removed from our area, if it met all reproduction standards.

A. A. Smyser of the *Honolulu Star-Bulletin* echoed that view:

We have a policy against using grisly pictures and showing tragic personal moments, particularly of local persons. But we had no hesitation about using this picture.[3]

Rough Justice

The worsening situation in Southeast Asia was to pose other, similar decisions for editors and for television newsmen in the years that followed the fiery suicide of the Saigon monk.

For the first time in our history, the American people were eye-witnesses to an on-going war, in living (and dying) color. If still pictures of violent death posed dilemmas for editors, how about film footage of battle or corpses on TV's dinner-hour network newscasts?

And once again, although taste and ethics were advanced as considerations arguing against use of such films, other factors were also weightily involved. How to balance them all out and determine what was journalistically and also ethically the right course was not easy.

It was particularly difficult in one instance that occurred during the Tet, or lunar New Year, offensive that the Viet Cong and North Vietnamese mounted against South Vietnam in 1968. The city of Hue became a ruined battleground, and Saigon itself was penetrated by the attacking forces.

NBC television crews were in the embattled streets of the capital city one afternoon when troops brought a suspected Viet Cong to the head of the South Vietnam police, Brig. Gen. Nguyen Ngoc Loan, for questioning. The cameras were rolling as the general looked at the suspect's impassive face, apparently decided that he would give no information, and then put a pistol to the man's head and blew out his brains.

A still picture of the summary execution, showing the pistol against the suspect's head and his face twisted in pain as the bullet tore through his skull, was taken by AP photographer Eddie Adams (who won a Pulitzer Prize for the photo) and it later appeared widely on newspaper front pages throughout the United States. The *New York Times* put it on page one, as did the *Washington Post*, filling five columns with it. (See page 57.)

The film footage of the episode was processed in Japan, then transmitted back to New York by satellite, with the strong recommendation of the NBC staff on the scene that it be used on that night's newscast.

But executive producer Robert Northshield, putting together the schedule in the New York control rooms, was shocked by the grisly footage, particularly zoom closeup shots of blood spurting from the fallen corpse. Did the news value of the scene, graphically portraying the terrible nature of war, justify its use, even though it would inevitably offend and sicken many viewers?

This is how he remembers reaching a decision:

The film came in over satellite between 6:20 and 6:30 p.m. before airtime and it was recorded routinely on tape. I saw the pictures then and heard what was said over the pictures [by a newsman on the sound track]. John Chancellor happened to be in the studio that day. He saw it with me. We were both stunned, because the way it came in the general took the gun, shot him in

The moment that South Vietnamese national police Chief Brig. Gen. Nguyen Ngoc Loan executes a Viet Cong officer with a single pistol shot in the head is pictured by Associated Press photographer Eddie Adams, in Saigon Feb. 1. The Viet Cong officer grimaces at the impact of the fatal bullet. Carrying a pistol and wearing civilian clothes, the Viet Cong guerrilla was captured near An Quang Pagoda, identified as an officer, and taken to the police. Wide World Photos.

the head, the man fell down, and we held the picture while Loan reholstered the gun and walked through the frame. You still see the corpse from whom blood is now gushing. So it was too much for me. Now here the interesting point is that those men in Tokyo had been looking at the rawest, roughest film anyone has ever seen. They saw it differently than I did in an air-conditioned control room in New York. It was too rough for me. So I said to Chancellor, "I thought that was awful rough." He could hardly speak. I said I was going to trim it off a little. So when it went on the air you saw less than what I have described. That is, as soon as the man hits the ground we went to black. It had already been established between me and the director that we would go to black after the film, which is unusual for our show. Usually we go right to the Huntley-Brinkley slide. This time we went to black for three seconds and then to the slide. . . . Another member of the NBC staff working on the film later said that he thought some of the closeup should have been shown, for Americans were getting a "too sanitized" picture of the war and they should have "their noses rubbed in" the violence and gore.[4]

A good many analysts of the Vietnam war and U.S. involvement in the conflict were convinced that it was the news media's role in rubbing the American public's nose in the graphic, horrible detail of the war which generated so unprecedented a revulsion, forced President Johnson to quit public life, and kept pressure on his successor until the American commitment was withdrawn.

Thus the issues involved in decisions such as those made by TV producer Northshield, and by the newspaper editors who published the Tet execution picture and others of like impact, were really not ones of taste or ethics, even though these terms were frequently used in debating the decisions.

What was also involved was the basic mission of the press to report the news as fully and as accurately as possible, so that the public would have the information necessary for decision-making in a democratic system. In some circumstances the furtherance of that mission can be advanced as justification for the disregard of considerations of taste or ethics which in other situations would command respect.

Death in Dacca

Let's examine one more journalistic situation in which these several factors—taste, ethics, and basic journalistic functions—were also on the scales.

The picture at the bottom of this page was taken, along with several others, by two Associated Press photographers, Horst Faas and Michel Laurent, shortly after the end of a bitter 1971 war involving India, Pakistan, and a force of East Pakistan guerrillas seeking independence for their sector of that nation. The war ended with a victory for the guerrilla rebels, aided by Indian troops, and East Pakistan became the new state of Bangla Desh.

In the hectic hours following the end of hostilities, the guerrilla forces, the Mukti Bahini, exacted terrible vengeance on persons who had collaborated with the central Pakistani government during the rebellion. Crowds roamed through the streets of Dacca, the former East Pakistan capital city, lynching suspected collaborators.

Faas and Laurent were at Dacca, on assignment by AP, and obtained pictures of some of the victims of the revenge slayings and lynchings. Then, along with other newsmen, they received an invitation to "the first public meeting of Bangla Desh at 1530 hours at the Dacca race track."

A Mukti Bahini soldier thrusts his bayonet into the chest of an execution victim in Dacca, East Pakistan, Dec. 18, while a crowd and other Mukti Bahini soldiers watch. Other victims are strewn around the area. Wide World Photos.

The meeting was a rally, addressed by leaders of the Bengali rebel faction, and attended by crowds there to cheer the founding of the new nation. On the outskirts of the crowd were four prisoners taken by the guerrilla troops, suspected of having supported the Pakistani central regime during the fighting.

Let Photographer Faas pick up the account of what then happened, and how the ghastly pictures came to be made:

While General Abdul Kadar Siddiqui harangued the crowd with a long fanatical speech, I walked around to photograph faces. Michel stayed to picture the general. That was how I discovered the four prisoners, their arms tied behind their backs with ropes, squatting and almost ignored by the crowd and the men in uniform around them. I told Michel about them. Few other correspondents had noticed them.

When the crowd stood up to pray, led by a Mullah, the first notice was taken of the prisoners. Unable to raise their hands with open palms toward heaven—the proper Muslim prayer position—they were abused by two soldiers. One pulled a prisoner's hair, then rifle butts cracked down.

When the prayers had ended, other soldiers joined in the beating and kicking. Then the prisoners were thrown on the ground and jumped on. . . .

Almost ignoring the few Western newsmen who witnessed the hour-long horror, a small band of Mukti Bahini guerrillas tortured, bayonetted and finally butchered the bound prisoners.

My colleague, Michel Laurent, and I were in the center of the pressing crowd of about 5,000 who formed a human wall around the prisoners and their torturers. Cries for death to the prisoners and "Joi Bangla" (Victory to Bangla Desh) punctuated the grisly scene.

Inside that circle, Laurent and I were so close that we often had to dodge the soldiers' rifles, swung with fixed bayonets, and the reeling victims, themselves. We watched and photographed it until the end. We were never more than two steps away.

When the crowd closed in to stomp the victims, we pushed our way outside the nightmarish scene. I was bathed in sweat, even though it was a cool evening. My hands were trembling too much to remove the film from my camera. Michel and I were too numbed to talk. He was pale like the dying men. I probably was, too. Michel walked away. He gave me his film only hours later, when I called on him to write the story of the Dacca massacre.[5]

As with the case of the burning monk, editors disagreed about whether the photographs made by Faas and Laurent ought to be used. Some editors decided that they were too horrible to inflict on the public. Others concluded that these photographs showed the unspeakable face of war in unique and unforgettable fashion, and that the readers and viewers ought to know that face as it really was.

A somewhat different ethical question was raised by some editors, not so much about the pictures themselves as about the role of the photographers in the episode. Should they have attempted to prevent the tortures instead of standing by to photograph them? Were they, by their presence, actually inciting the mob to more and more bloody savagery?

This point had occurred to Faas at the time. Again, from his account:

One photographer suggested that they might carry out the beatings for the benefit of our cameras. I also had this impression at least once. Twice I shouted at a soldier, "Stop it! We don't want to see that."

Both times, the soldier dragged his victim away from me to the other side of the circle only to continue.

After about 15 minutes, most of the newsmen and photographers walked out and into the crowd. Some left obviously sickened. Michel and I and a few others watched from about 20 yards distance. For 10 minutes we saw the violence continuing without any photographer or newsmen taking pictures.

I was then convinced that the events had nothing to do with our presence and would not be influenced by it. Michel and I walked back and were never spoken to or hindered up to the very end.[6]

It may well have been that in this instance, the blood lust of the mob would have been satisfied sooner or later whether or not cameras had been present. But the editors, and Faas, were right to consider the possibility that the photographers could have played an inciter or catalytic role in the chemistry of the situation. Exactly that sort of thing has happened in some other, less terrible news events, as we shall see in examining other cases in later chapters.

Notes

[1] Quoted in "Rivals in the Muck," *Time*, CI, No. 25 (June 18, 1973), 72–73.

[2] Reprinted from the *Columbia Journalism Review*, XII, No. 5 (January/February 1974), © 1.

[3] "A Bonze's Self-Immolation and Photo Judgment," *Bulletin of the American Society of Newspaper Editors*, No. 467 (September 1, 1963), pp. 11–13.

[4] George A. Bailey and Lawrence W. Lichty, "Rough Justice on a Saigon Street: A Gatekeeper Study of NBC's Tet Execution Film," *Journalism Quarterly*, XLVIII, No. 2 (Summer, 1972), 221–29, 238.

[5] Horst Faas, "A 'Political Rally' in Dacca Becomes Scene of Butchery," *Editor & Publisher*, CV, No. 1 (January 1, 1972), 14.

[6] *Ibid.*

The First Gatekeepers...

"In order that any society may function well, its members must acquire the kind of character which makes them want to act in a way they have to act as members of the society or of a special class within it. They have to desire to do what is objectively necessary for them to do. Outer force is replaced by inner compulsion, and by the particular kind of human energy which is channeled into character traits." — Erich Fromm[1]

5 Many of the ethical decisions journalists must make arise very early in the process of gathering and distributing the news.

These decisions typically have to be reached quickly, almost automatically, since time is always an insistent fact of life in the media of mass communication. And they have to be reached by men and women acting individually, guided by their personal and professional consciences and informed by whatever understanding they have acquired of the codes of their business.

Some communication researchers have described journalists as the intellectual gatekeepers of our society. They open the gates of the mass media—the newspaper columns, the air time on radio and television—

and let through to the public information and ideas. Or in some instances they keep the gates closed and block out certain information and certain ideas. How freely and how selectively these gates are maneuvered determines to a great degree the perception the rest of us gain of the scene and events outside the narrow range of our immediate circle.

Virtually everyone has had some personal experience that brought home forcefully the gatekeeper functioning of the media. If you have attended a speech or a public meeting and then later watched the 90-second filmed coverage on the nightly TV newscast, or read the 500-word account in the morning paper, you know that much of what transpired at the meeting, or much of what the speaker said, never got through those media gates.

Most of us understand that the discrepancy between what we saw and heard and what later turned up as the media versions of those same happenings is largely a function of the packaging limitations of those media. The journalist is supposed to be guided by the central ethic of reporting the news fully and accurately; but he also must function within the context of the particular medium for which he is reporting. There is only so much space in the newspaper's news hole (that part of the total space not given over to advertising) and only so much time on the TV newscast after commercials and announcements have been allowed for.

Within these limits the journalist must fit a representative version of the news. He can't get it *all* in; he can't function as a vacuum cleaner. But if he is acting responsibly, the elements that he does report, through whatever medium, will faithfully reflect the essence of the reality.

It is entirely likely that the layman who attended the council meeting with a special concern for one item on the agenda will disagree with the reporter's judgment as to what is the essence of the reality. To the layman, *his* agenda item loomed as all-important and clearly should have been in the news account. The reporter, weighing the respective elements of the news situation in terms of their interest to large circles of viewers or readers, makes his decisions—opens and closes the gates—in the effort to serve the majority of the public best.

Among the considerations that guide him in the operation of those gates are the dimensions of newsworthiness learned by precept or experience (readers *need* to know about consequential matters, events affecting the public interest; readers *like* to learn about exciting, intriguing, out-of-the-ordinary happenings). Among them, also, are considerations for the rights and sensitivities of the people and institutions that are the subjects of the news. Reconciling all of these various considerations, professional and ethical, is not always a simple matter for the reporter.

In fact, it is *rarely* a simple matter. Yet he must manage it somehow, and without dallying, on nearly every assignment.

Consider an instance.

A retired minister in a small town, in his late sixties, was fond of fishing and often drove alone to a nearby lake to spend an afternoon with rod and reel. One day he did not return at the usual time, and his daughter-in-law asked the police to help locate him. They found his car parked on a small side road about halfway to the lake. It was locked and undamaged. A reporter was with the police detail that spotted the car, and observed the initial search which turned up: (1) a half-eaten ham sandwich on the front seat; (2) the minister's fishing tackle in the trunk of the car; (3) a small-caliber revolver in the glove compartment, with one shell fired; and (4) in the back seat of the car a copy of *Penthouse*, a magazine noted for its explicit nudes. The minister himself was not at the scene, nor was there any indication of his whereabouts.

The reporter had a deadline to meet and a story to write for the morning paper. What details should he include, which ones might he leave out—and why?

Did the public's right to know (an imperative in all the codes) require that he report all that the police found, as being possibly significant in explaining the man's disappearance?

Or, out of deference to the sensibilities of the minister (who might well turn up shortly, perhaps back from a hike), should the report omit mention of the girlie magazine?

Should the gun be mentioned, and the fact that one shell had been fired? Should the police officer's speculative comment that the minister had probably picked up some hitchhiker who had robbed him be included?

There are numerous proponents of the "let it all hang out" approach who would contend that the reporter's obligation is to include in his story all that the police search turned up, and the officer's speculation as well, even if some of the detail might injure the reputation of the retired minister. (One nineteenth-century editor observed complacently that whatever the good Lord permitted to occur he would not hesitate to publish.)

But many reporters and editors feel that the "print it all" dictum must be modified in certain circumstances, that ethical ends are best served if both the public's right to know and the individual rights of persons in the news are taken into account. Some of them would undoubtedly feel that this was such a case.

How would *you* have decided to handle the story?

(One reporter who did face the situation put in his story the gun, the sandwich, the fishing tackle, and the condition of the car—but not the magazine, and not the speculative explanation. The minister's body was later found nearby, victim of a hitchhiker who had been carrying the magazine when he was picked up.)

A similar case occurred several years ago in Los Angeles, when a nationally known sports figure, idol of many youngsters, died of a heart attack while in a hotel room with a call girl.

In this instance, a number of reporters covered the story, including representatives of the wire services. All had to resolve some difficult questions.

Should the full details of the death be reported, with the inevitable impact on the sports star's family, his fans, and his standing in sports history? Or should the account simply say that he died of a heart attack, period? How weighty was the public interest in knowing all, including the feet of clay? And how much consideration could be given to the human factors?

(The wire services carried the whole story, with an alert to editors who might want to cut it. Some individual reporters covering the episode left out details; so did many editors using the wire reports. But some publications carried all, including the seamy aspect.)

In mid-1975 Steve Prefontaine, holder of seven American records as a distance runner and a favored Olympic prospect, died in an accident when his car failed to make a tight curve. The news of his death at the age of 24 was a banner front page story in his Oregon home town paper, and the lead item on the national television network sports segments.

The next day an autopsy showed that the runner's blood had contained enough alchohol at the time of the accident for him to be considered legally drunk; he had earlier been attending a party for a Finnish track group he had been instrumental in bringing to this country. As with the death story, the autopsy report was featured as the lead-off item on the television network sports shows; but in the home town paper the autopsy finding was reported as unobtrusively as possible, in the back pages, where many of his grieving young fans would not see it.

In a great many kinds of news stories—more often than the general public supposes—journalists do weigh in the scales the human factors as well as the conventional elements of newsworthiness.

In writing crime stories, for example, it is fairly commonplace for reporters to omit the names of juveniles if they are first offenders. It is reasoned that many youngsters caught in such circumstances may yet straighten out; but if they are publicly stigmatized by being named in an arrest story, the chances are great that they may continue on a path of crime. So the ethic of the "full and complete" story is modified to take individual factors into account.

The rule is not universal, however. Some newspapers and broadcast stations invoke it for offenders who are under 16; others draw the line at 18. Some will omit the name of the accused juvenile if the offense is minor, but include the name if murder or rape is charged, whatever the age of the defendant.

Another virtually universal practice in both print and broadcast media is the omission of the name of the victim in a rape story, in order to spare her further anguish.

In these various instances, compassion for the sensitivity and dignity of persons caught up in the news sways the journalist in making gatekeeper decisions, and properly so.

The record of the media is not all good, however.

A writer in *Nieman Reports*, Ignaz Rothenberg, cited several instances in which journalists had shown little or no sensitivity:

In August, 1953, a 21-year-old West Point cadet died in a fire while on leave at his home in Virginia. A year before, his father, a general, was convicted in a court martial of failing to safeguard his diary that contained military secrets and was relieved of command of troops for six months. Soon afterwards he retired.

The press, reporting the death of the young man, warmed up the case of the general. "Father Was Court-Martialed for Slack Care of Diary" shouted a sub-head of the report in one of the most prominent papers. With the exception of the local press, the fatal accident would most probably not have been mentioned at all but for the father.

What a cruelty to bring up the old story in that hour of grief! Some papers went to great lengths in retelling the abrupt end of the general's career although the case had been legally closed. Whatever the general may do in the future that deserves press publicity, he may be sure that a repetition of that account will accompany the story. . . .

In another case a young woman was charged with forging and cashing a $300 check. The district attorney declined to prosecute "because full restitution had been made and the tearful defendant had no previous record." The newspapers identified her and added that she was the wife of a Naval Laboratory physicist and mother of a 21-month-old infant. Now everyone in the neighborhood knew who she was.[2]

Out of the Past

Almost invariably, when a person is released from prison after serving time for a particularly spectacular or newsworthy crime, the press accounts of the release will include some reference to the original crime. Often the whole record will be dug up and rehearsed once more.

Critics of this convention say that it negates the whole concept of rehabilitation. What chance will the paroled convict have of making a new life if his or her return to society is accompanied by scare headlines and a lurid recounting of all the earlier misdeeds? What chance will there be of finding an honest job? Won't the circumstances just push the parolee back to criminal activity?

But there is another side to the matter. Editors argue that when a convicted criminal is paroled the public is entitled to know that this person is once again back in the community. Moreover, how can the public know how the parole system is working—whether it is being too leniently or too rigidly administered—if the basic facts about its workings are not subjected to public scrutiny through the news report?

Similar arguments have to be sifted through when a person who has sometime in the past been in the news in an unfavorable way re-enters the public scene in some other fashion—say, as a candidate for public office. How much of the old record is fair game for reporters covering the current news development?

When in October 1971 Senator Richard Byrd was mentioned as one of six persons whose names President Nixon was thinking of sending to the American Bar Association to be checked as potential Supreme Court nominees, the fact of his earlier association with the Ku Klux Klan was noted in all the stories dealing with the matter.

One television commentator, ticking off the list, described him this way:

And Senator Richard Byrd, former organizer for the Ku Klux Klan, who more recently severed his connection with that group.

The fact was that Byrd's connection with the Klan had been broken off in 1946, a quarter of a century earlier, and it had been a very brief association even then.

Presumably someone being considered for so significant a post as the nation's highest bench ought to be checked out thoroughly. But fairness still ought to be a guide; when the TV announcer said only that the connection was "more recently severed," he left the clear impression with the viewer that it may have happened only last year.

A much less consequential use of a news figure's past involved a former child movie star.

68

Under the headline: **Ex-Star 'Baby' LeRoy (Now 32) Seeks Anonymity,** the following story appeared:

HOLLYWOOD (AP)—Somewhere on a Southern California beach, tall against the sky, stands a movie star you'd never recognize—Baby LeRoy, erstwhile bane of the bibulous existence of comedian W. C. Fields.

As a roly-poly child star of the 1930s, Ronald Leroy Overacker, then known as LeRoy Winebrenner, was a star at 8 months and a has-been at 4.

Today, tanned, lanky, ruggedly independent and 32, Baby LeRoy hankers after anonymity—so much so that he moves often, when too many people find out where he lives. Even his mother, who lives in nearby Alhambra, doesn't know the address of his present apartment in San Pedro.[3]

The story went on at some length to stress how earnestly Overacker strove to stay out of the public eye ("Ron has been a lifeguard for the past 14 years. He won't say where, because it would make it easier for people to trace him") and also rehearsed the details of his short-lived acting career. Ironically, the story also included two pictures, one of Baby LeRoy in his starring days and one of Overacker as he was now. Apparently the writer of the story saw no inconsistency in building the entire account around the theme of the man's craving for privacy, while at the same time providing all sorts of clues—the town in which he lived, his occupation, even a current picture—that would enable anyone to locate him without trouble.

This was not a major ethical lapse, to be sure. But it was representative of one kind of misuse of the gatekeeper function, either through lack of sensitivity or out of deliberate intent to build up a story.

Just What Did He Say?

In the handling of quotations, a staple of journalism, the reporter's integrity as a gatekeeper is put to more frequent and more severe tests than in almost any other aspect of the work.

Much news of necessity must be gathered through interviews of various kinds. Other news surfaces in the form of statements, speeches, press conference responses, or debates in meetings. In many of these situations the reporter has no prepared manuscript to turn to for reference; nor is it always feasible to make use of a tape recorder.

So quotes must be captured as fully and as accurately as can be managed, by careful listening and note taking, and then sorted over for use on the basis of representativeness.

These obviously are gatekeeping activities, and crucial ones. How responsibly they are carried out can significantly influence the perception that the reading or viewing public will gain of the news source.

It is axiomatic that virtually all persons who are in the news, and whose comments reach the public through the filters of the news media, are firmly convinced that the readers and viewers are getting a flawed and distorted impression. It is a rare day when a reporter gets a pat on the back from a news source for the fairness or accuracy of a quote. Usually it is something like: "You missed my whole point!" or "What were you trying to do to me with that speech story, anyway?" or "Why can't you guys ever get anything straight?"

Ben J. Wattenberg, adviser to Senator Henry M. Jackson of Washington during his bid for the Democratic presidential nomination in 1972, probably spoke for many other political managers when he observed:

Everybody that I've ever known who has worked on a political campaign— right, left, or center—comes up with the same basic viewpoint—that what you read in the media isn't what's happening. It's a fairy tale. It's distorted.[4]

The candidate wanting to make the best possible impression on the electorate, or the Rotary Club speaker who labored hard over every golden phrase and can't see why the reporter's account left out so many of them, will of course be disappointed. Sometimes they may have a legitimate gripe (though Wattenberg's was overstated) since the handling of quotes is one of the most taxing of journalistic gatekeeping chores, and no assignment for a novice.

Most of the newspaper codes or canons tend to stress literal accuracy when quoting news sources. The *Springfield* (Mass.) *Republican* once instructed its staff members:

When people are quoted, the paper is placed in the position of assuring its readers that the quoted passages were literally spoken; consequently, inaccuracy in quotation is unpardonable.[5]

Yet, as a practical matter, it is not always possible for a reporter to be so literally accurate, unless there is a prepared manuscript, a trial transcript, or a tape recording to turn to.

So some working conventions have been built into the journalist's ethic where quotations are concerned. Even if every syllable hasn't been captured as uttered, even if every article isn't exactly in place, the quote can still be considered an acceptably accurate one if it honestly reflects what the speaker said.

But note that essential qualification—if it honestly reflects what the speaker said.

No reporter has the right to manipulate the words of others so as to convey impressions that are distortions of the spirit of those words. You may misplace a comma or substitute one adjective for another and still not alter the thrust of a quote or paraphrase. But you have no license to violate the source's intent by changing the meaning of what he said, no matter what the motivation or temptation.

Consider this brief wire service dispatch:

PARIS—Liberace flew into Paris today and was practically ignored—except by a wasp which stung him on the right thumb.

The pianist insisted upon being taken at once to the airport dispensary, where the physician expressed sympathy.

"But my thumb doesn't move now," Liberace complained.

The physician said it would be all better by Sunday, when the pianist opens at the Paladium in London.

Note that last sentence: "The physician said it would be all better. . . ." It is a virtual certainty that he did *not* say that. The reporter in all probability chose the particular wording (from the familiar parental: "Mommy'll kiss it and it will be all better . . .") in order to generate in the reader a certain perception of Liberace.

Perhaps no reader of this book is likely to work up much indignation about Liberace being held up to ridicule. The flamboyant pianist has been deliberately courting publicity of all varieties; some of it is bound to be denigrative.

But there is a journalistic principle involved, even though the news item in question is inconsequential and the target of the reporter's manipulation is a person who has voluntarily put himself in the public eye. The manipulation—or fabrication—of a quote in order to condition the reader's perception of a news figure or a news situation is a breach of journalistic ethics whether the story is a major one or a filler, and whether the individual wronged is a public figure or a hitherto anonymous citizen.

Absolute, literal accuracy can rarely be achieved, as we have noted earlier, but it is a firmly-rooted journalistic convention that the central meaning, the spirit, of a speaker's words must be truly conveyed.

Side by side with this principle there also grew up the convention of laundering the poor grammar or sloppy syntax of persons quoted in the news, in order to keep them from coming through as loquacious illiterates in the news columns. This practice has somewhat fallen into disuse in the electronic age, when news sources can be heard and seen delivering themselves of their observations without benefit of filter.

This is perhaps just as well. The laundering practice had several drawbacks. For one thing, it tended to present news figures in a false light. Ward leaders were quoted in primly correct phrases, when actually they expressed themselves in cruder, though perhaps more eloquent, terms. Sports stars always came out scrubbed and even scholarly. Politicians with foot-in-mouth disease often were rescued by reporters who covered over the awkward lapses.

The practice also lent itself to manipulation by reporters with an ax to grind. If it was standard operating procedure to clean up quotes before committing them to print, then letting one person's bloopers go through without change could wreak terrible havoc on the subject so harshly handled. The tactic wasn't unknown, when a given politician or corporation spokesman earned the enmity of the reporters.

Perhaps the most persistent and troublesome problem with the handling of quotations, however, has to do with the degree to which the reporter honestly reflects the spirit of what the speaker had to say.

The quotation is almost always much briefer than the original comment. In the boiling down, the selection of the key phrase or sentence, the reporter can do considerable violence to the theme of the original statement as the speaker intended it to be perceived. Even persons without journalistic experience know how drastically the impact of a speaker's words can be altered by out-of-context use. The effect is enormously increased, of course, when the multiplier factor of the mass media comes into play.

In their book *Responsibility in Mass Communication*, William Rivers and Wilbur Schramm quote an unnamed reporter on his policy toward quotes:

I'll change a man's quotes when I write the story. How much I change them depends on the circumstances. . . .

If it moves the story, I'll rejigger the order of his statements. I often condense a number of quotes just to get the nut of the man's message.

The only thing about a man's quotes that is really sacred is his point of view. If you conserve that, almost any other change is perfectly proper.[6]

There are a couple of points worth noting about the reporter's observations—or rather, about the segment of them quoted in Rivers and Schramm, and then requoted in this text.

Note the fact that in a quotation in a text such as this one the omission of some words or phrases is indicated to the reader by an ellipsis notation, the series of dots . . . . In most news stories, this is dispensed with. Sentences widely separated in a speech or a statement can be fitted together cheek by jowl without any signal to the reader that any such rearrangement has been effected.

Also note the reporter's observation that he wouldn't hesitate to "rejigger" the order of the speaker's statements. In some circumstances this wouldn't do any real violence to the ideas being expressed. For example, in chapter 4, the order in which the account by Horst Faas of the Dacca massacre was originally presented in the *Editor & Publisher* article was shifted around in the quotation included in this book in order to clarify the chronology of the episode. No change in emphasis or context was involved.

But in some cases the order in which quoted material is used can become crucial to the impression conveyed to the reader, listener, or viewer. An example:

Several years ago a student was arrested during a protest demonstration in which a policeman was seriously injured. The front page news story reporting the episode included a picture of the student, fist cocked to strike the crouching policeman who was being held by another demonstrator.

The lead on the news story, published in the *San Francisco Examiner*, read:

A University of California student was arrested late yesterday for the Tuesday attack by anti-war demonstrators on San Francisco Policeman William Navin.

Speaking slowly and deliberately after his arrest Morgan Gilbert Doyle, 19, said at City Prison:

"You people just don't understand. Young people have to have some way of expressing themselves."

Navin suffered numerous bruises and cuts outside the Fairmont Hotel early Tuesday afternoon when demonstrators rioted against the Commonwealth Club appearance of South Vietnam Vice-President Nguyen Cao Ky.

At least five persons jumped the officer, ripped off his helmet and beat him about the head and body. Navin is now convalescing at home.

Doyle, whose shoulder-length hair had been trimmed back to well above his collar, was arrested at his parents' Marin County home, Inspector Frank McFarland and Edward Erdelatz said.[7]

Look back now at the quotation attributed to the arrested student. It is sandwiched between elements of the story describing the attack on the policeman, and thus it is almost inevitable that a reader of the story will associate the quote with the attack and thereby gain the impression that the boy was contending that young people have to be able to beat up policemen as a means of expressing themselves.

But is it certain—or even likely—that this is what the arrested person was referring to when he made the statement? Isn't it probable that he was attempting to offer a justification for the demonstration that had been taking place at the time the scuffle with the police occurred? Had the quotation been placed elsewhere in the news story, perhaps juxtaposed with passages describing the sign carrying and picketing at the hotel, would the reader have perceived it—and the arrested student—in a different light?

(Incidentally, you might want to think back to the discussion earlier in this chapter of the gatekeeper function involved in selecting what details to include in a story, and then consider the consequences of the reporter's description of the arrested person as "speaking slowly and deliberately" and as having "shoulder-length hair" recently trimmed.)

The impression created by a quotation can be as important as the literal accuracy of that quotation, and thus placement and context become elements of reality so far as the perception of the quote may be concerned. So when a reporter—or the writer of a book, for that matter—undertakes to "rejigger" someone else's ideas or observations he lies under a strong ethical obligation to be sure that he has not tampered with the essential reality of the material.

Editing copy is just as consequential an act of journalistic gatekeeping as reportorial selection of detail or choice of quote fragments.

The Fuss over "Selling"

How difficult it may sometimes be to draw the line between defensible rearranging or editing and the kind of "rejiggering" that significantly and unethically alters meaning was illustrated by a case in which two different branches of the media wound up on opposite sides of the argument.

On February 23, 1971, the CBS television network carried a documentary program entitled "The Selling of the Pentagon." The program detailed the ways in which the Defense Department undertook to generate public support for its policies and activities by making use of recruiting offices, touring speakers, and exhibits of military hardware. The tone of the program was highly critical of what the producers described as the propaganda tactics of the Pentagon; as a *Columbia Journalism Review* editor noted, the program "went about its business with a crispness and unsparing bluntness that have become all too rare in this age of the declining documentary."[8]

However, in the course of selecting, boiling down, and editing material to be used in the documentary, the CBS editors cut and spliced some film footage of an interview and a speech. In both instances, elements were fitted together in a sequence different from the one in which they had originally been delivered; in some cases, a CBS questioner would be shown asking one question and the Pentagon spokesman would be shown giving a response he had made to an earlier, or a later, question. The splicing was of course very skillfully done and, so far as the viewer was able to tell, the chronology was unaltered.

The two persons whose comments were thus "rejiggered," a Pentagon colonel and an Assistant Secretary of Defense, both protested the result. Their case was taken up by several officials, including the then Vice President of the United States, the chairman of the House Armed Services Committee, and the chairman of the House Interstate and Foreign Commerce Committee.

The complaint against CBS was that the changes made in the colonel's speech and in the interview with the assistant secretary had materially altered the meaning of their original comments.

Richard S. Salant, president of CBS News, responded that the handling of the two segments of the documentary program had been within the proper limits of journalistic editing, and that the spirit of the two men's statements had not been misrepresented.

At that point, the *Washington Post*, usually no friend of federal officialdom, entered the lists. In several editorials, the *Post* editors took issue with the CBS position. Rearranging the sequence of a man's speech so that he appears to be saying something different from what actually was said, or splicing an interview film so that a respondent is shown giving an answer different from the one he actually made to a question, is not the same thing as conventional journalistic editing, wrote the *Post* editors.

The debate resulted in an unusual exchange of letters between the CBS officials and the *Post* editors. Some excerpts from them illuminate the particular issue involved in this case and also the larger question of what constitutes editing and what distortion of the news:

From a letter sent to the *Post* by CBS News president Salant:

The question of how a news or documentary broadcast is edited is at least as important as you obviously consider it. It is precisely as important as, and possibly no more complicated than, questions pertaining to editing in the print medium (newspapers and news magazines)—the process by which any journalist rejects or accepts, selects and omits, and almost always compresses material available to him. You do not question the right, indeed the professional obligation of your reporters to do this, nor of your editors to continue the process once the reporter has done his job, nor indeed, of your senior editors to impose their professional judgment upon the same piece of work when and if it comes to them.

But you question not only our right to do the same thing, but also the methods by which we edit and even our motives. . . . You do not, in other words, grant us the right to do precisely what you do—and must do if you are journalists as distinguished from transmission belts. . . .

Then you go on to suggest, indeed recommend, that our rules should be different from your rules, that sound journalistic ethics and the First Amendment are somehow divisible between rights granted to journalists whose work comes out in ink and somewhat lesser rights for journalists whose work comes out electronically. You say we should go out of our way to "preserve intact and in sequence" the response of those we interview. We both "go out of our way" to be fair and accurate, but we both have limitations of space, and we both seek clarity. Except in verbatim transcripts, neither medium preserves intact or in sequence everything it presents. You say at the very least we should indicate that something in the interview has been dropped. If we asked you to do this, you would properly respond that readers know, without a blizzard of asterisks, that material in your paper is edited, that these are not the complete remarks. Our viewers know it, too. And so do those whom we cover. . . .

We are all after the same thing: to be fair, to inform the public fairly and honestly. We do not suggest that we—or any journalistic organization—are free from errors, but nothing in the First Amendment suggests that we must be perfect, or that we are not human. And nothing suggests that if our responsibility is larger, our job tougher or our coverage broader there should be some new set of rules for our kind of journalism, as if to say the First Amendment is fine so long as it doesn't count for much. You don't seem to mind if our end of the dinghy sinks, so long as yours stays afloat. . . .

In a public letter, the editors of the *Post* responded:

In time the U.N. may have to be called in to arbitrate the burgeoning dispute over the CBS documentary "The Selling of the Pentagon," but for now we would like, in a unilateral action, to respond to the complaint of Richard Salant of CBS News.

We think it is off the point. And we think this is so because Mr. Salant invests the term "editing" with functions and freedoms well beyond anything we regard as common or acceptable practice. Mr. Salant taxes us with unfairly recommending two sets of standards in these matters, one for the printed press and another for the electronic. But he reads us wrong. We were and are objecting to the fact that *specifically, in relation to question-and-answer sequences,* two sets of standards *already* exist—and that what he and others in television appear to regard as simple "editing" seems to us to take an excess of unacknowledged liberties with the direct quotations of the principals involved.

Before we go into these, a word might be of use about the editorial practices (and malpractices) common to us both. When a public official or anyone else issues a statement or responds to a series of questions in an interview, the printed media of course exercise an editorial judgment in deciding which part and how much of that material to quote or paraphrase or ignore. . . .

That bad or misleading judgment can be made by this newspaper in both our presentation and selection of such news goes without saying. . . . There is, for example, a distorting effect in failing to report that certain statements were not unsolicited assertions but responses to a reporter's question. . . . What we have in mind, however, when we talk of the license taken by the electronic media in the name of "editing" is something quite different, something this newspaper does not approve and would not leap to defend if it were caught doing. It is the practice of printing highly rearranged material in a Q-and-A sequence as if it were verbatim text, without indicating to the reader that changes had been made and/or without giving the subject an opportunity to approve revisions in the original exchange.

It is, for instance, presenting as a direct six-sentence quotation from a colonel, a "statement" composed of a first sentence from page 55 of his prepared text, followed by a second sentence from page 36, followed by a third and fourth from page 48, and a fifth from page 73, and a sixth from page 88. That occurred in "The Selling of the Pentagon," and we do not see why Mr. Salant should find it difficult to grant that this type of procedure is (1) not "editing" in any conventional sense and (2) likely to undermine both the broadcasts's credibility and public confidence in that credibility. . . . We agree with Mr. Salant's premise that we are all in the same dinghy. That is why we are so concerned that neither end should sink.[9]

The spokesmen for the two media never did arrive at any point of agreement in the debate, but their exchange effectively illustrated some of the difficulties involved in exercising the gatekeeping function whether in print or on the air.

A third party, observing from the sidelines, did make an effort to explain why the two distinguished news media spokesmen saw the issues so differently in their public exchanges. F. Leslie Smith, writing in *Mass News: Practices, Controversies, and Alternatives,* observed that:

When "broadcast news" began to mean "television" as well as "radio," the networks faced the task of putting pictures with their words. They used as models for their early efforts the theatrical newsreels produced by divisions of the major Hollywood studios. In fact, some of the original television newsfilm units were the newsreel organizations themselves on contract to the networks. When the networks began expanding their television news operations, they hired former newsreel employees. Naturally these men brought with them the production techniques and values of the newsreels, many of which came in turn from Hollywood. In Hollywood, the emphasis was on anything but reality. Hollywood earned its living by spinning celluloid webs of fantasy, precisely joined to present a slick, polished product. While the newsreel people left behind the fantasy in most cases, they did bring with them to the networks the concept of the slick, polished product and the film editing practices needed to create it. In this way, purely pictorial devices such as avoidance of jump cuts, use of establishing shots, and composite editing · found their way into TV newsfilm. They still exist, and TV newsmen accept them as norms of professional behavior, as means to achieving the ends of objective reporting. Finally, to further confuse the issue, the Murrow era of the 1950s established at CBS the tradition of producing documentaries which, at least in some cases, might be more accurately called "advocacy by reporting" or even "editorial."

Given these professional norms, CBS did not consider "The Selling of the Pentagon" as deceptive or unethical; it had simply done what a network was supposed to do in putting together a documentary. The president of CBS News, Richard Salant, wrote that "in accordance with customary journalistic practice, in some cases the editors rearranged material for purposes of the broadcast so that a composite answer was included. Where material from another question was added to a particular answer, it was solely to include points which CBS News felt were relevant to the discussion." To him, such editing techniques, along with "reverse shots", were perfectly acceptable so long as they did not "distort in content or in meaning the *impression* of the questions and answers conveyed to the viewer."[10]

(An ironic sequal to the *Post*-CBS exchange over what constitutes legitimate editing came a little more than four years later. A May 8, 1975, front page story in the *Post* had reported an interview with Gov. George Wallace of Alabama in which Wallace was quoted as saying that the United States should have fought on the side of Germany and Japan in World War II. Several weeks later, the *Post's* ombudsman, or monitor of staff performance, pointed out in his editorial page column that the startling quotation had been composed of one brief comment plucked from page 49 of the interview transcript and fitted together with another equally brief bit from page one of the transcript. The ombudsman, Charles B. Seib, declared that his paper had been guilty of "improper quote-juggling" in order to achieve "impact at the expense of accuracy.")[11]

A Footnote to "Selling"

The case of the CBS documentary gave rise to a different sort of problem, one which is outside the scope of this book and for that reason won't be explored here in detail. But it should at least be noted in passing.

Rep. Harley O. Staggers (Dem.-W.Va.), chairman of the House committee that investigated the charges of unfair editing in the "Selling" program, at one point in his inquiry demanded of CBS officials both the original print of the program and all of the raw materials on which the final version was based—scripts, interview texts, and outtakes (the film footage that was shot but not actually used on the program). He said that the committee needed this material so it could determine by comparison whether there truly had been distortion of reality in the way the documentary was pieced together.

CBS president Frank Stanton refused to provide most of the material sought by the committee, on the grounds that this represented an invasion of First Amendment rights. The committee persisted, and finally voted to cite Stanton and CBS for contempt of Congress. This posed a press-vs.-government issue of major proportions, and in these circumstances all of the media—including the *Washington Post*—rallied in defense of the CBS stand. It should be noted that the matter had by then moved far away from the intramural debate between the network and the newspaper over the ethics of editing; the issue now had become whether an arm of government could move in to second-guess journalists and influence the way in which they reported the news. When the issue finally came to a vote on the House floor the contempt citation was tabled, an inconclusive resolution of the press freedom issue but at least one that left the network free of that specific threat. And all the media spokesmen welcomed that, among them Harry Reasoner, ABC anchorman, who asserted on his nightly news program: "We are not second-class citizens, and when we do our job we should think only of high professional responsibilities. We should not have to think, what will Mr. Staggers say? And we won't."[12]

Notes

[1]Quoted in J. Edward Gerald, *The Social Responsibility of the Press* (Minneapolis: University of Minnesota Press, 1965), p. 146.

[2]Ignaz Rothenberg, "Newspaper Sins Against Privacy," *Nieman Reports*, XI, No. 1 (January 1957), 41–44.

[3]*Eugene* (Oreg.) *Register-Guard*, February 3, 1965, Sec. B, p. 8.

[4]Quoted in "The Press in the 1972 Campaign," a symposium, *Nieman Reports*, XXVII, No. 3 (Fall, 1973), 3–9.

[5]Nelson A. Crawford, *The Ethics of Journalism* (New York: Alfred A. Knopf, 1924), p. 217.

[6]William L. Rivers and Wilbur Schramm, *Responsibility in Mass Communication* (New York: Harper & Row, Publishers, Inc., 1969), p. 139.

[7]*San Francisco Examiner*, December 6, 1970, p. 18.

[8]"A Tradition Revived," *Columbia Journalism Review*, X, No. 1 (May/June 1971), 2.

[9]Laura Longley Babb, ed., *Of the press, by the press, for the press (And others, too)* (Washington: The Washington Post Company, 1974), pp. 57–61.

[10]F. Leslie Smith, "CBS Reports: The Selling of the Pentagon," in *Mass News: Practices, Controversies, and Alternatives*, ed. David J. LeRoy and Christopher H. Sterling (Englewood Cliffs, N.J.: Prentice-Hall, Inc., 1973), pp. 200–210.

[11]See "Inside Stories," *Newsweek*, LXXXV, No. 25 (June 23, 1975), 51.

[12]"CBS: Off the Hook," *Columbia Journalism Review*, X, No. 3 (September/October 1971), 5–6.

Reporters and Sources...

"For the edification of those who may be unaware of the etymology, the family tree, so to speak, of the wellsprings of news, it goes something like this:Walter and Ann Source (nee Rumor) had four daughters (Highly Placed, Authoritative, Unimpeachable, and Well-Informed). The first married a diplomat named Reliable Informant. (The Informant brothers are widely known and quoted here; among the best known are White House, State Department, and Congressional.) Walter Speculation's brother-in-law, Ian Rumor, married Alexandre Conjecture, from which there were two sons, It was Understood and It Was Learned. It Was Learned just went to work in the Justice Department, where he will be gainfully employed for four long years." — Editorial in the Washington Post [1]

6 In the process of gathering the news for the media of mass communication, journalists develop various kinds of relationships with news sources. Some of these relationships are adversary in nature, some symbiotic. Some of them facilitate the reporter's job, while some others compromise the central journalistic ethic of reporting the news honestly and fully.

There isn't space enough available in this book to catalog all of these numerous kinds of relationships, but in this chapter (and to some degree in later ones, too) we'll be looking at some of them and at the problems they create both for the journalist and for the consumer who is being served and informed by the mass media.

Manners and Morals

There's no need to spend much time on certain kinds of reporter-source interaction, since they are so blatantly ill-mannered and unethical that simply pointing them out is enough. Fortunately, they aren't so often encountered today as in journalism's earlier, lustier, and less principled eras when a reporter trying to pry news out of a source would stop at little. In *The Press and Its Problems*, Curtis D. MacDougall took note of this unsavory aspect of journalism:

Reporters may pose as detectives, coroner's assistants or other public or semi-public officials to gain access to places from which they otherwise would be barred, and to persuade news sources to talk. They may steal photographs, peek through windows, climb fire escapes to effect entrances into apartments, waylay servants, relatives and friends and virtually besiege the dwelling of someone reluctant to be interviewed.

Editors and publishers may deny that such practices are common, but anyone who has had reportorial experience knows that they exist, although not as much as formerly in these monopolistic days. Maybe the bosses don't know what is going on; maybe they don't want to know[2]

As MacDougall observes, such strong-arm and shady tactics are no longer so prevalent as they were in strongly competitive periods when ethical codes and professional responsibility got more lip service than genuine respect.

That is not to say, however, that bad manners and boorish behavior by the members of the press have altogether vanished from the scene. They are very much evident in herd coverage situations, in which large numbers of newsmen and newswomen are assigned to an important event. When Premier Khruschev visited the United States, one of the most memorable scenes of his tour of America was the moment in the Midwestern cornfield when an irate farmer who was the Russian leader's host that day finally resorted to throwing ears of corn at the hordes of crowding reporters and photographers pushing and jostling to catch every conversational exchange.

Most television viewers have seen situations in which a dozen bristling microphones are thrust into the face of a witness or an official, blinking in the glare of the kleig lights, while questions are shouted, sometimes several at a time and sometimes rudely personal or hostile.

Also, as William L. Rivers and Wilbur Schramm point out, some tactics today may be less blatant and more subtle than in the bad old days, but their legitimacy may nevertheless be questionable:

A reporter got a story by having a drink in a bar with a newly elected public official. The reporter hid the fact that he represented a newspaper, and the official opened up and talked quite freely about his plans for the office—a matter which he had so far refused to discuss with the press. When the reporter revealed his identity at the end, the official was restrained with difficulty from attacking the reporter physically. The reporter admitted that he might have used dubious professional ethics, but argued that any such story which the official was willing to tell a chance acquaintance in a bar should hardly be kept out of the public press.[3]

Most present-day journalists are fully aware that corner cutting and deceit are no longer acceptable, however, and when they employ such tactics they know they have overstepped the ethical line. Unfortunately, that knowledge doesn't stop some of them.

Getting to Know You...

Being beastly to a news source can cause a reporter one kind of problem; being too cozy with such a source can generate other ones.

We noted in an earlier chapter the kinds of ethical difficulties created by conflict of interest relationships, in which a reporter became beholden to a news source for gifts or favors. But problems can develop even when the consideration involved is not so overt or so commercial.

Any seasoned city editor knows that he runs a risk if he keeps a reporter for too long on a given beat, whether it is city hall, county courthouse, or the business scene. True enough, the longer the reporter is assigned to the same news sources, the more likely it is that he will be able to get at the hidden recesses of news. But it is also likely that he may begin to identify with his sources; in some respects, his interests will begin to overlap with theirs.

In time, a kind of "you scratch my back and I'll scratch yours" situation may develop, in which the reporter accepts news tips and leaks from the source and the source can count on the reporter being "friendly" if a pinch comes and some bad news break threatens.

This symbiotic relationship is unhealthy for the news consumer, the reader or viewer who believes his news report is telling him what is really happening, when actually it may be telling him only what an informal but nonetheless efficient cabal of news sources and reporters has decided he should know.

The classic flowering of this relationship has traditionally been at Washington, D.C. There the press corps is numerous, and its nerve lines run out to all the corners of the nation. The Establishment is numerously represented, too, and its interests also span the country. The two inevitably discover mutual interests and mutually advantageous relationships.

Most of the well established Washington correspondents have widespread contacts among officials in all the departments of government. It is a mark of status in the press corps to belong to the coterie of insiders who meet weekly with this cabinet officer for dinner, or with that congressional leader for an intimate lunch. At these occasions, the officials feed out informational tidbits they want to see in the mainstream of news (but not attributed to them), and the reporters pick up the handy items they can use to give substance to the stories they file the next day "from authoritative sources close to . . ." The public is impressed, and so are the correspondents' bosses back at Minneapolis or Kansas City. The officials get a chance to float trial balloons, to stick anonymous knives in the backs of rivals, or to counter some adverse report making the rounds.

Samuel J. Archibald, executive director of the Fair Campaign Practices Committee in Washington and a long-time observer of the Washington news-go-round, has compiled some definitions of the terms most often used by government "ghosts" and reporters. They include:

—Off the record: the information is not to be published in any way, with
or without attribution; no story is to be written, although a reporter is free to
inform his editorial superiors of the facts.

(Washington correspondents regularly send back a stream of confidential memos to the publisher, or to the chief editorial writer back
home, laden with hush-hush inside tips. These tips may then surface
sooner or later as profound observations on the editorial page or juicy
items dropped conversationally by the publisher at his club.)

—Lindley Rule: stories may be written but there must be absolutely no
attribution; the story must appear to come from the reporter himself.

(This convention, named for Ernest K. Lindley, a former *Newsweek*
writer, provides the basis for many of the insights and informed guesses
that stud the columns and background stories filed by Washington correspondents.)

—Not for attribution: the remarks of the government spokesman can be
quoted, but not as coming from the individual himself; a cloaked source
such as "high government officials" or "Navy experts" or "the Department
of Defense" is agreed upon between the spokesman and the reporters.[4]

Mr. Archibald observes that the "anonymous spokesman technique
can be a useful tool to make more information available to the public
or it can become a self-serving device to convey distorted information."
And he also points out that "no code of ethics for the handling of
anonymous government news has ever been developed."
There are solid reasons why such a code hasn't been developed, and
isn't likely to be developed. The convention of the backgrounder, the
symbiotic relationship, the game of government ghost—whatever you
choose to call it—has too many practical advantages for both parties; they
won't be quick to jettison it.
Benjamin C. Bradlee, executive editor of the *Washington Post*, has
noted the advantages that accrue to the newsmen:

It is a cardinal if regrettable rule of journalism that a story dropped in the lap of a reporter is "better" than a story that must be dug from a dozen different mines. It is easier to write, easier to edit, easier to read and often easier to understand, even if it may be incomplete, misleading or even false. Normally querulous editors are easily mollified by the knowledge (which they often dine out on) that the high government official quoted in the story is in fact the President of the United States. The lazy reporter can file his backgrounder and be out on the golf course after lunch. The confused reporter can convince himself he has the truth by the tail at long last. And even the conscientious reporter knows that if he doesn't file the story fast, he will get scooped.[5]

From the standpoint of the government, Bradlee points out, there are equally important advantages to the practice:

By its control of the briefing, it can withhold whatever information it wants to withhold, and by forbidding identification of the briefer, it prevents accountability.[6]

But where, in all this, are the advantages for the public?

In some instances, perhaps, information gets into the open that might otherwise remain hidden. But in other cases the end result may be just the opposite: information that properly *ought* to be relayed to the public is quietly suppressed. Washington correspondents talk freely among themselves about the drinking habits of notable government figures, joking about senators or congressmen reeling into the legislative chambers so far gone that they cannot find their seats. But none of this gets into the correspondents' reports to the home-town papers of these same congressmen.

Admittedly, whether a congressman has two martinis or six before dinner at home is not really the public's business. But when his drinking becomes so chronic and disabling that it interferes with his ability to meet his responsibilities as an elected official, shouldn't his constituents be informed? Usually they never find out from the correspondents unless, as sometimes happens, there is an auto accident or some other police blotter episode that forces the situation on to the public stage and obliges the reporters to record the extra-curricular antics of their cooperative and valued news sources in high places.

Drawing the line between what is legitimately the private business of a person in public life and what ought to be part of the public record is never an easy matter. It becomes an even more ticklish situation when there is a special bond—personal or professional—between the reporters and the errant steward of the public interest.

There are many other disquieting developments that grow out of the marriage of convenience between reporter and source that are not in the public interest. They differ in nature and in the degree to which they result in compromise of the journalistic ethic. They will be better understood if we can look at them one by one.

The Official Sources Syndrome

One tendency that is encouraged by the close reporter-source relationship is that of journalists to become too dependent on the official spokesmen as sources of news. It is so easy, so convenient, as Bradlee points out, to turn to the official at this or that executive department, or to the office of the majority whip, to get the Word on the latest news break. These are spigots, handy and reliable. Turn the handle and the tips flow. So why take the hard, digging route of tracking down details for yourself? One of the most aggressive and old-fashioned of the Washington correspondents' corps, Clark Mollenhoff of the Cowles publications, once asserted that there were really only half a dozen true reporters in Washington; the rest lived on handouts from the public relations offices of government, on tips from their privately cultivated sources, and on gossip exchanged at the Press Club bar. (Mollenhoff himself rarely had friends or contacts in government; he was too prickly, too persistent, and too successful in his digging. And for those efforts he won the Pulitzer Prize and just about every other award given for journalistic enterprise. For one brief period at the start of the first Nixon administration, he uncharacteristically forsook his role of offstage gadfly and got into the political act himself. He became an aide to President Nixon with the assignment of keeping corruption out of the White House. He soon quit and went back to his typewriter and his digging, becoming one of the most strident of administration critics in the later Nixon years.)

Another Washington reporter, Tom Wicker of the *New York Times*, also complained about the "official sources" syndrome, the tendency to turn to the easy access to news provided by the friendly bureaucrats and the public relations officers. He sees it, however, as more widespread than at Washington:

I think that we have had, historically, an orientation toward nationalism in politics and toward establishmentarianism in other areas of society, such as the economy or the academic world. Particularly in politics and diplomacy the orientation toward nationalism has been very pronounced in recent years. The obvious example, I think, is the failure of the American press, exemplified by the Washington bureau of the New York *Times*, of which I was in charge at the time, adequately to question the assumptions, the intelligence, the whole idea of America in the world–indeed the whole idea of the world—which led this country into the Vietnam War in the 1960s. It is commonplace now, when the horse has already been stolen, to examine those assumptions. But where were we at the time we might have brought an enlightened public view to bear on that question? We were not, I think, very forward in challenging the rationale for that unhappy episode in American history.[7]

Wicker also cites the failure of the press to recognize the news area represented by consumerism—until Ralph Nader, a nonjournalist, showed what deep concerns and hitherto uncovered news existed there.

The journalists' preoccupation with official sources and institutional spokesmen makes it likely that they will miss much important news—the kind of news that isn't going to be given out by the spokesmen for organizations or bureaucracies because it might be awkward or embarrassing or inconvenient:

To the extent that you are reliant upon institutional sources for news you are reliant upon a self-serving source which in every case will attempt to put the best face on the news, to interpret information for you in the light of its own interests. That is obviously not something to be criticized; only the degree to which an institution would distort the news to serve its own interests is really to be criticized. You always attempt to put the best face on your behavior. It is only when you tell an outright, flat, provable, damaging lie that you really transgress moral bounds. So this is a truism—a fact of life— that reporters have to understand if they are relying on institutions: they are relying upon a self-serving interest.[8]

Wicker points out, too, that reliance upon the official sources syndrome causes the reporter to miss some kinds of news for which there just aren't any formal spokesmen. The swelling of unrest among the young, exemplified by the disturbances on college campuses in the late 1960s and early 1970s, came upon the country unperceived and at first widely misunderstood—largely because the press couldn't get a handle on the phenomenon. There were no "official sources," no spokesmen able to reflect the organized, institutional viewpoint of the movement; so journalists fell back on the police beat approach of covering the riots and the building seizures without ever coming to grips with the root causes of the surface outbreaks. So, too, Wicker contends, with the mishandling by the press of the diffuse, half-seen forces behind the dissatisfaction among blacks and among women. Major news of our era was only partially reported, only half-understood, because journalists couldn't find any handy spigots to turn for prepackaged news releases that would sum it all up neatly and without further effort.

Nor is the official sources syndrome a peculiarly American journalistic trait. In a *Nieman Reports* article, Louis Lyons quotes a Canadian newspaperman, Robert Fulford of the *Toronto Star*, who describes what he calls a built-in bias of the press in his country and elsewhere:

He [Fulfold] says it takes its cues from established Authority. Authority is whatever is organized, that has a name and gives speeches—industry, trade unions, government, chambers of commerce, cultural institutions. The newspaper is dominated by articulate opinion, he says. It is easier to accept conventional wisdom than to challenge it.[9]

The Users and the Used

This reluctance to challenge the version offered by the official source allows such sources to manipulate newsmen and news institutions for their own ends.

When, in the middle 1960s, American armed forces were deployed in the Dominican Republic, reporters accompanied the U.S. mission but, because of fighting in the streets, they were not permitted to cover the scene directly. Instead, they got briefings from the U.S. ambassador. He told them of a "Communist takeover," of atrocities being committed in the streets, of 1,000 to 1,500 persons summarily taken "to the wall" and executed. The rebel leader, the correspondents were told, had personally machine-gunned to death a Colonel Juan Calderon, a high government aide.

The correspondents dutifully passed all this on to their offices at home, and it appeared in such publications as *Time* and *U.S. News & World Report,* as well as in newspapers and on newscasts. Later it developed that the atrocity stories were all untrue—there had been no heads on spikes, not 1,500 persons but only six or ten had died in the fighting, and the machine-gunned Colonel Calderon was discovered in a hospital suffering from a slight neck injury.[10]

89

Edward Jay Epstein, author of *News From Nowhere* and a close observer of journalistic practice, records another instance in which officials exploited the reporter-source relationship in order to manipulate the media to serve Machiavellian aims:

Consider, for example, the disclosures by the columnist Jack Anderson of the minutes of a secret National Security Council meeting on the 1971 Indo-Pakistani war for which he was awarded the Pulitzer Prize for national reporting. Anderson claimed that the blunt orders by Dr. Henry Kissinger in these private meetings to "tilt" toward Pakistan contradicted Kissinger's public professions of neutrality. This claim received wide circulation, and sharply undermined Kissinger's credibility. . . .

At the time it was generally presumed that the leak came from a dissident within the Administration who favored India, or at least, opposed the Administration's policy in the subcontinent. Only two years afterward, as a by-product of the Watergate investigation, was some light cast on the source of the leak.

A White House investigation identified Charles E. Radford, a Navy yeoman who was working at the time as a stenographer, as the proximate source of the National Security Council minutes supplied to Anderson. But the investigation further revealed that Yeoman Radford was also copying and transmitting to members of the Joint Chiefs of Staff highly classified documents in a "surreptitious operation" apparently designed to keep them aware of Kissinger's (and the President's) negotiations.

And Yeoman Radford has testified that he acted only on the express orders of the Joint Chiefs of Staff, and not on his own initiative, in passing documents. If this is indeed the case, it would appear that members of the Joint Chiefs of Staff authored the Anderson leak in order to undermine the authority of Henry Kissinger (who was involved in developing the détente with China and Russia at that time.)

In this case, Anderson was used as an instrument in a power struggle he probably was unaware of—and which might have had nothing to do with the Indo-Pakistani War he was reporting.[11]

Ironically, that same Henry Kissinger himself made adroit use of the press on more than one occasion to further his diplomatic objectives. One such occasion was during the period when he was in the process of negotiating a settlement of the Arab-Israeli war in 1974. The following is from *Time:*

Background Music. As part of his "atmospheric," Kissinger at times unabashedly uses the American press corps that travels with him aboard Air

Force Two. During the shuttle flights between Jerusalem and Aswan in January, which eventually led to disengagement along the Suez Canal, the press was an integral part of Kissinger's diplomatic gap closing. Whenever he was asked how far along the negotiations had come, Kissinger would answer, "Oh, 60% completed." The next time it was 75% and the next 90%. As the two sides kept reading these daily stories, they could not help being nudged into believing that a settlement was nearly at hand. "He played the press like a cello," recalls one reporter. "We created all the background music he needed."[12]

Even in cases where there is no complex intrigue involved, or even orchestrated background music for a Kissinger diplomatic ballet, the tendency for the press to accept the version of events as it is given out by official sources can lead to misinforming the public.

When a disturbance broke out at New York's Attica prison, and inmates seized an entire cell block and numerous guards as hostages, newsmen from throughout the country converged on the scene. Some of them (including Tom Wicker of the *New York Times*) even took part in some negotiating sessions as officials tried to work out a means of freeing the hostages and restoring order. News interest mounted and readers and viewers all over the United States were following the day-by-day developments.

Then the decision was finally reached that troops would have to storm the prison; no other way to resolve the situation had worked. The attack took place, and of course in the circumstances the reporters were kept outside the walls and had to rely on the information relayed to them by state officials, the prison wardens, and leaders of the troops sent in to retake the cell block. In the chaotic hours that followed, bulletins and fuller stories went out on all services and networks, describing how hostage guards had been slaughtered by the inmates as the troops closed in. Some guards, the reports recounted in gory detail, had been thrown from the walls to die on the pavement below; others died when convicts slashed their throats with knives·in full view of the oncoming troops (a *New York Daily News* headline: **I Saw Seven Throats Cut**); at least one guard had been castrated before he was murdered. Such reports were carried as fact, without attribution, by seven major news organizations represented on the scene (the Associated Press was the lone exception to include adequate attribution). By the time the shooting was finally over, more than 40 persons—guards and inmates—were dead. Reporters were not allowed inside the smoking ruins for many hours, until order had been restored throughout the prison.

When they did get in and began to investigate more fully, and when the autopsy reports began to come out, it developed that the hostages had died from bullets fired by the charging troops, that no throats had been slashed, no one castrated. By then, two days had passed; the original stories had gotten bulletin treatment on the networks and bold banner headlines in the newspapers. Editorials had been written condemning the bestiality of the prisoners and demanding a crackdown in penal policies, not only at Attica but at prisons everywhere.

The corrections and explanations poured forth, but it is probably fair to say that they never caught up with the lurid initial stories. Mention Attica, and many Americans will still retell for you the castration and throat-slitting stories. Because the reporters on the scene accepted the versions put out by prison spokesmen who had a strong stake in having the story viewed as one of inmate savagery rather than official bungling, a major news story of the era went into the public consciousness erroneously.

Attribution—the assignment of a source or authority for some statement or purported fact presented in a news story—in some cases isn't essential. A story reporting that the city council will meet tomorrow night doesn't need to spell out the fact that this information came from the office of the city manager. But there are some kinds of news situations—and Attica was one—in which the reporter fails to meet a basic obligation if attribution is not complete and clear. The identification of the source of information itself becomes a vital element of the information; without it the story may be both incomplete and potentially misleading.

In the sober aftermath of the Attica affair, editors and reporters swore once again to be more careful about the attribution problem, more careful about qualifying the authenticity of inflammatory accounts before they were put out as fact, more careful about specifically identifying "official spokesmen" when no other, independent source could be reached to verify a story.

Yet it was not long after Attica that the same kind of situation was played out once more.

This time the locale was Munich, Germany, and the time the summer of 1972. The Olympic Games were under way, and a large international press corps was on hand, including the top-ranking TV sportscasters. Then a brutal interruption halted the athletic competition that the whole world, literally, had been watching on TV screens. A band of Arab terrorists crept over the walls of the Olympic Village in the night and shot their way into the building where the Israeli team was quartered. A coach was killed in the break-in, some team members escaped, but a group of hostages was taken.

Then followed a melodramatic scene of mounting tension—much of

92

it depicted on television—as German officials attempted to negotiate with the terrorists, and various others also tried to intervene. Finally the nighttime climax, the Arabs and hostages swiftly driven to an airport where a getaway plane was supposed to be awaiting them, then a burst of firing from hidden snipers, and the terrorists' retaliation.

Once more, the press corps was held at a distance, getting word from the police and Olympics spokesmen. They accepted the assurances of Munich authorities that the hostages had been rescued; the bulletins flashed out, precipitating tearful thanksgiving in Israel. Then, again as TV viewers saw bits and fragments, hours passed while slowly the terrible truth seeped out around the edges—the initial police reports had been falsely optimistic. The hostages, all of them, had died, partly because a nervous sniper fired too soon. The dismayed authorities held back the dreadful news, and the press accepted the official version.

But what, it is proper to ask, were the reporters and TV sportscasters to do? They couldn't flock to the airport, follow the action. They had to rely on the reports that came to them.

True enough. But, as Attica had earlier taught another set of reporters, in such circumstances the public is entitled to have the report presented as it is—a version, unverified, supplied by sources with self-interest to protect. Instead, the reporters passed on the version as fact—as their colleagues had done at Attica—and put their own credibility on the line as warrant for its accuracy. The official sources syndrome, combined with the pressure to get the news out quickly, had led to misinformation on a global—if short-lived—scale.

The Nameless Ones

Let's turn now to examine another kind of reporter-source relationship that can sometimes be an invaluable avenue to important news, and at other times can be a vehicle for serious abuse of the journalistic ethic. This is the concept of reporter privilege—the thesis that there are certain circumstances in which a journalist ought to be allowed to keep the sources of his news secret from all others, including even the courts.

Proponents of reporter privilege argue that some kinds of news cannot be obtained through conventional channels. These kinds of news can be had only from secret informants, who insist on their anonymity being protected for one reason or another.

For example, a patrolman providing details of a linkup between high police officials and local Mafia families has obvious reasons of personal safety for wanting to keep his name out of the situation. Reporters relying on such secret sources have broken stories of major national impact, disclosing graft, corruption, and malfeasance.

Perhaps the most celebrated instance of reliance on secret sources to crack a far-reaching story occurred in the complex chain of events that will be known to history as Watergate.

The reportage of Watergate and its momentous consequences spanned several years. It included some of American journalism's greatest moments, and some others that weren't so admirable. We'll be looking at some of the latter in subsequent chapters.

But in the initial stages of the coverage of this national scandal, there stood out a classic example of investigative journalism by two previously unsung reporters, Robert Woodward and Carl Bernstein of the *Washington Post*.

They weren't among the elite of capital journalism, the correspondents' corps. They were local beat reporters for the *Post*, which is the hometown paper for the District of Columbia. They were initially assigned to the break-in at Democratic headquarters in mid-June of 1972 because it at first seemed to be a relatively minor police blotter story. Then, as it took on wider and wider dimensions, Woodward and Bernstein's energetic and effective pursuit of the story's ramifications led their editors to keep them on the story, rather than putting some of the paper's luminaries to work on it.

It was a shrewd, inspired decision by managing editor Howard Simons, backed up by his superiors, executive editor Benjamin C. Bradlee and *Post* owner Katherine Graham. For it was the *Post*, more than any other journalistic enterprise in the country, that unraveled the incredible skein of Watergate—and the job was done largely by two young reporters using old-fashioned fact-gathering methods and relying almost entirely on secret sources whose identity they promised to keep secret.

In Bernstein's own words:

There is one central point about Watergate that might be helpful to anyone who's interested in journalism, especially Washington Journalism. And that is we used very basic, tested reportorial techniques—empirical police reporting techniques.[13]

The two reporters' sources during the long months they worked on the story were secretaries in government offices, disgruntled FBI men, and other dissidents in the Nixon administration, including one code-named Deep Throat who yielded up the most useful leads of all. But in virtually every case, the Woodward-Bernstein stories that traced out the sorry tale of Watergate were based on anonymous, faceless sources so far as the reading public was concerned.

The two young *Post* reporters weren't bemused by the "official sources syndrome," partly because as lowly members of the journalistic hierarchy they didn't have access to these sources. As Bernstein notes:

In Washington the press corps is largely accustomed to learning things over lunch and perhaps not doing the kind of digging that younger reporters have always been asked to do or are accustomed to doing.[14]

During the election-year stretch of 1972 when the *Post* pair was doggedly working away at the story, most of the Washington press corps accepted at face value the statements from Administration and Nixon campaign spokesmen that it was nothing more than a "third-rate burglary" by underlings—a stupid bungle, but nothing consequential. Even when some others began to catch on to the fact that the *Post* had a tiger by the tail (or perhaps, more appropriately, an elephant), they couldn't seem to match the Woodward-Bernstein pace of dogged, tireless digging at the odd, obscure corners where the leads could be turned up.

During the last six months of 1972, before the *Times* and the other media had begun to lock onto the Watergate story, Bernstein, Woodward, and the *Post* were out on a lonely limb. Ben H. Bagdikian, a Washington press critic, has calculated that during the initial stages of the story only about 15 media persons in Washington were assigned to cover it, out of 433 who might have been sent to join the two *Post* men.

Bradlee, the executive editor, admits to having many a nervous moment during the time when his staff members were producing one incriminating story after another—all of them based on material that could not be attributed. He and managing editor Simons insisted that Woodward and Bernstein check out every lead with exacting thoroughness, getting at least one or two cross-checks, before going into print with it. As matters turned out, virtually all of the stories held up; one did contain an inaccuracy, but the overall score constituted a pretty solid average considering the stakes.

It should perhaps be noted that not everyone had praise for the performance of the two young reporters; some revisionist evaluations of their efforts came along later, notably from Edward Jay Epstein, who wrote:

Even in the case of Watergate, which has become synonymous with "investigative reporting," it was the investigative agencies of the Government and not the members of the press who assembled the evidence, which was then deliberately leaked to receptive reporters at the Washington *Post*, the Los Angeles *Times, Time,* and other journals.[15]

It was the FBI which turned up most of the leads, Epstein contends, and it was John Dean and James McCord who revealed the rest under pressure from judges and investigators. The reporters, including Woodward and Bernstein, served as "conduits for the interested parties who wanted to release information about Watergate and other White House abuses of power."

But, on balance, not much can be taken away from the achievement of the two *Post* men. They dug when others settled for handouts; they persisted when others went off to what seemed to be more exciting stories; and they made highly effective use of the secret leads that came to them.

A Claim to Privilege

In the case of the Watergate reporting by Bernstein and Woodward, reliance on anonymous sources did not result in complications or difficulties for the newsmen—except perhaps for the anxious time editor Bradlee went through.

But in many other cases where reporters have similarly based their accounts on leads fed to them by persons who insisted on anonymity, some very real problems have arisen.

Such reporters have been hauled into court or before legislative committees and ordered to divulge the identity of the persons who gave them the material for their exposé stories. And then the reporters faced a painful dilemma, both professional and personal.

If they gave up the names, as requested, they would be violating a pledge made to the news sources; moreover, as a practical matter, they would forever cut themselves off from future access to those sources and perhaps to a good many others who would learn of the betrayal. But the alternative was hardly palatable: a jail cell, on charges of contempt of court, or of Congress, or of the legislature.

The journalistic codes examined earlier in this book rarely make specific mention of the notion of reporter privilege, other than to emphasize that journalists ought to respect an off-the-record pledge. But there is a strong craft convention, embedded in the lore of the business and in the textbooks, that when the cause is important a journalist ought to protect the confidentiality of his sources whatever the consequences— up to and including a jail term.

The rationale runs thus: there are some kinds of news it is important for the public to know about (for example, the Watergate horrors) that cannot be obtained by conventional means. To get at such news, reporters must sometimes promise anonymity to the sources who constitute the only avenue to the news. When such a promise is made, it is in the public interest; the public's right to know is being served, and that right-to-know concept derives from the First Amendment.

The other side of the argument is a legal one. Judges and others associated with the administration of the law contend that it is every citizen's obligation to give evidence in court when he is in possession of such evidence and when he is requested to provide it. Unless citizens accept this obligation, the system of justice at once breaks down. The Sixth Amendment right of an accused person to a fair trial by an unbiased jury of his peers will be abridged, because some of the relevant testimony will not be forthcoming in court. Exceptions to the obligation to testify are recognized in certain circumstances, and to a limited degree. Lawyers may not be forced to reveal information given to them in confidence by their clients, nor may doctors be obliged to give out information about their patients obtained in the course of doctor-patient relationships.

In approximately half of the states, a similar but still more limited privilege to withhold testimony has been extended to newsmen by statute. But these "shield laws" are typically equipped with various loopholes that make them less than totally protective. Even where they exist, journalists have in some cases had to resort to the First Amendment line of reasoning to justify their claim to reporter privilege, since the state statute has proved to be a porous buckler.

For a good many years the issue of reporter privilege was not a lively one. Few cases came up in which it was necessary for a reporter to invoke the concept; judges and district attorneys tended to veer away from head-on confrontation with newspapers and broadcasters, and usually found other ways to get the needed evidence.

But beginning with the mid-1960s the instances involving reporter privilege began to increase, both numerically and in terms of the seriousness of the consequences visited on the untalkative journalists.

The increase in the incidence of cases stemmed partially from more aggressive investigative reporting, partly from a toughening attitude on the part of the courts and others associated with the administration of justice.

The list of cases that have popped up one after another since about 1965 is a lengthy one, but a few representative examples will serve to indicate the kinds of situations that gave rise to the confrontations:

—TV news reporter Stewart Dan and cameraman Roland Barnes of WGR-TV, Buffalo, refused to tell a grand jury what they witnessed inside the Attica prison during the riot.

—Earl Caldwell, a black reporter for the *New York Times*, refused to tell a grand jury about the sources on which he relied for published stories on the Black Panther organization. Caldwell contended that his access to those sources would be destroyed if he so much as entered the grand jury room.

—Annette Buchanan, managing editor of a student newspaper at the University of Oregon, refused to reveal to a judge or grand jury the names of persons who had provided her with information about drug use on the campus.

—Radio station WBAI declined to submit to a trial subpoena for original tape recordings of interviews with prisoners involved in a riot in the Tombs Prison in New York City, claiming that the originals could be used to identify prisoners who wanted to remain anonymous.

—Reporter Joseph Weiler of the *Memphis Commercial-Appeal* was threatened with contempt for refusing to disclose to a state legislative investigating committee the confidential source of information about abuses at a home for retarded children.

—Reporters Jack Nelson and Ronald J. Ostrow and Washington bureau chief John F. Lawrence of the *Los Angeles Times* were subpoenaed to produce confidential tape-recorded information obtained from a key witness in the Watergate bugging trial.

—Reporter William Farr of the *Los Angeles Herald-Examiner* refused to disclose to a county court judge the confidential sources who supplied him with a confession obtained by the prosecution in the celebrated Manson-Tate murder case.

—Paul Pappas of a New Bedford, Mass., TV station refused to disclose to a county grand jury confidential information he obtained during several hours' stay inside a black militant group's headquarters.

—Paul Branzburg of the *Louisville Courier-Journal* refused to disclose to a county grand jury his confidential source of information about local drug abuse.[16]

Of the journalists involved in the above cases, some were fined (including student editor Buchanan) and many went to jail for varying terms (among them Farr, Lawrence, and WBAI station manager Edwin A. Goodman).

In all instances, the contempt citations or threats (some never went beyond the threat stage) were resisted by the journalists and their employers. Cases mounted through the various court levels, with most of the decisions going against the privilege claim.

The Watershed Case

The climactic case—and one that promises to be a landmark or watershed decision—was decided by the United States Supreme Court in June 1972. In it, the court ruled simultaneously on three separate incidents joined in the single case—those involving Caldwell, Branzburg, and Pappas. And once again, at the highest level of all, the newsmen lost.

As Norman E. Isaacs wrote in *Columbia Journalism Review:*

The date was June 29, 1972—and while the countdown to 1984 stood at eleven years and six months, one had to reflect that George Orwell was, after all, author, not infallible seer. The Supreme Court of the United States, by 5 to 4 vote, ruled that the power of a grand jury took precedence over the heretofore presumed protections of the First Amendment.[17]

The majority decision was joined in by those justices regarded as the conservative bloc on the Court at that time. The decision held, in part:

The great weight of authority is that newsmen are not exempt from the normal duty of appearing before a grand jury and answering questions relevant to a criminal investigation. . . .

These courts have . . . concluded that the First Amendment interest asserted by the newsman was outweighed by the general obligation of a citizen to appear before a grand jury or at trial, pursuant to a subpoena, and give what information he possesses. . . . We are asked . . . to grant a testimonial privilege that other citizens do not enjoy. This we decline to do.[18]

There were two dissents to the historic decision. One of them, written by the Court's most consistent champion of press freedom, Justice William O. Douglas, asserted that:

The function of the press is to explore and investigate events, inform the people what is going on, and to expose the harmful as well as the good influences at work. There is no higher function performed under our constitutional regime. . . . A reporter is no better than his source of information. Unless he has a privilege to withhold the identity of his source, he will be the victim of governmental intrigue or aggression. If he can be summoned to testify in secret before a grand jury, his sources will dry up and the attempted exposure, the attempt to enlighten the public, will be ended.[19]

The other dissent, authored by Justice Potter Stewart and supported by Justices William Brennan, Jr., and Thurgood Marshall, underlined the significance of the flurry of government and court subpoenas in recent years as efforts to force journalists to do the courts' investigative work for them:

The error in the Court's absolute rejection of First Amendment interests in these cases seems to me to be most profound. For in the name of advancing the administration of justice, the Court's decision, I think, will only impair the achievement of that goal. . . . The Court's crabbed view of the First Amendment reflects a disturbing insensitivity to the critical role of an independent press in our society [and] invites state and federal authorities to undermine the historic independence of the press by attempting to annex the journalistic profession as an investigative arm of government.[20]

It is possible, of course, that *Caldwell* will be modified, or even reversed, by the Court in some future decision. Even more dramatic about-faces have occurred in the Court's history.

But until that happens, journalists are left with the unhappy knowledge that the amorphous but comforting contention that reporter privilege had roots in the First Amendment has now been rejected by our highest judicial authority. And the other elements of protection for that privilege—the various shield laws—have been shown to be flimsy barriers indeed. (Most of the cases in recent years, including those joined in the Caldwell decision, arose in jurisdictions where a state shield law was on the books.)

Virtually all of the state shield laws have some loopholes (for example, the provision that a judge may determine that "overriding public interest" requires that the privilege be set aside in certain kinds of cases). The existence of these loopholes, emphasized by the various court tests that have centered on them, leaves news sources uneasy about a newsman's promise that is dependent on such variable statutes.

Attempts have been made to draft a national shield law, but they have faltered on several points. How do you define in a law which journalists should be able to invoke a confidentiality privilege? Is it only for reporters for the *New York Times* or CBS News? Does it cover reporters for college and high school papers, or for underground journals? Does it apply to someone who prints up a single-issue broadside to call attention to a problem in the community? (The First Amendment covers all persons, of course, and embodies a free-press protection that is a public right, not one vested in any special class.) If you use a definition in any form, aren't you coming perilously close to the basis for government licensing of journalists, a First Amendment no-no?

Also, if you do try to frame a shield law, how inclusive should it be? That is, should it be so expansively drawn that it would allow a reporter to use the claim to justify withholding the identity, say, of a murderer or a rapist? But if you begin with exceptions, where do you stop?

And, finally, there is the fact that what the Congress may give, the Congress may also take away. Do journalists really want to be dependent upon a statute that could at any time be repealed by a Congress irritated by the "irresponsibility" of the press?

So, deserted at least temporarily by the courts, and with little realistic prospect of help in statutory form, where is the journalist left? Under what professional obligation does he lie when he faces the proposition from a news source: "I'll tell you this, but only if you can promise that my name will never get out"?

If the journalist accepts the validity of the central ethic of journalism—to report the news the public needs to know, as honestly and as fully as possible—he or she will also have to shoulder the concomitant obligations and risks. Those risks may include—as they did for Bill Farr, John Lawrence, Edwin Goodman, and a good many others—going to jail, sometimes more than once. That's not a cheerful prospect.

Nor is there much comfort to be had by assuming that the situation, after all, really isn't likely to come up in *my* case, that it isn't an everyday thing, the invoking of reporter privilege.

A survey of daily newspaper editors cited by David Gordon in *Columbia Journalism Review* indicated that the issue is no longer so rare an occurrence as it once may have been. The editors were asked for a rough estimate of the number of stories published annually in their papers which were based on information from confidential sources. Their answers ranged from "one or two" to "350 to 1,000." Erwin Canham of the *Christian Science Monitor* estimated that from a third to a half of the major stories in that paper raised the problem of protecting confidential sources in some way.[21]

If the editors' estimates are representative, and if courts and prosecutors feel emboldened by *Caldwell* to challenge the reporter privilege concept more regularly, the potentialities clearly exist for frequent tests in years to come of journalists' willingness to hold to a basic tenet of journalistic ethics in the face of tangible risks.

As in virtually all areas of journalistic ethics, a hard-and-fast rule is difficult to devise. Journalists may agree in a general way that the concept of reporter privilege must be lived up to in certain cases. But what cases?

Where the news cannot be obtained in any other way, and where the news involved is truly vital to the public interest, journalists of future years may have to take the hard decision that Bill Farr and Ed Goodman took. Newsmen and newswomen run various kinds of occupational risks; the war correspondent's beat, or that of the reporter covering a beleaguered inner-city ghetto, may be physically hazardous. Not all journalists are willing to accept those risks, but many are. And many will face in the same spirit the threat posed by the reporter privilege issue. Whenever they do, they ought to have the unreserved support of their publications or broadcast stations, and the united backing of their fellows in the field.

Playing Catch-up

One further aspect of the anonymous source question remains to be examined before we turn to other kinds of ethical problems.

As was noted earlier, the Watergate revelations developed through the months by *Post* reporters Woodward and Bernstein would have been impossible to get at without the use of the secret source. And the two, supervised by conscientious veterans of the *Post* editors' group, did try to make sure that they had multiple substantiation for the reports they put into print. James McCartney observed in a *Columbia Journalism Review* report on the Woodward-Bernstein feat that "In reading over the voluminous *Post* file of clippings on Watergate of last year, there is no story in which the facts appear to have been handled carelessly. No conclusions were drawn that have not been more than proven by disclosures now."[22]

Mr. McCartney may have been a bit too sweeping in his endorsement; as Woodward and Bernstein point out in their own account, *All the President's Men*,[23] a few errors did slip into their stories because they trusted their secret informants just once or twice too often. Nonetheless, for the most part, the use of the anonymous source by the two *Post* men was in a sound tradition of journalism. But the gambit isn't always so responsibly employed.

For example, when the Watergate story entered the second stage—that is, when reporters other than those from the *Post* began to scent what was up and joined the hunt—there were some newsmen who tried to emulate the tactics used by Bernstein and Woodward but without the same care and professionalism.

In an effort to grab at the Pulitzer coattails of the *Post*, writers for other media picked up and disseminated any snatch of rumor that came along, always "from a source close to. . . ."

In many instances, unlike the Woodward-Bernstein team, these writers did not check out the secret leads carefully, did not adequately determine the reliability of their sources, and most emphatically did not respect the ethical standards of the news-gathering business.

The results were often shoddy, indefensible journalism.

As *Wall Street Journal* columnist Vermont Royster wrote:

The pressure for scoops has led to reports of what congressional witnesses might testify on the morrow—sometimes correctly, sometimes not. Grand jury testimony, taken in secret, has been reported second-hand, relying on anonymous sources. And all too often it seems that many reporters have cast themselves in the role of prosecutors.[24]

Some instances of what Royster was writing about:

1. ABC network newscasters broadcast on Oct. 22, 1973, a story to the effect that Charles G. Rebozo, a friend of President Nixon, was administering an investment fund of more than $1,000,000 on behalf of the President, using money from unreported political contributions. The White House branded the story as false, yet for three months the "million-dollar slush fund" story was repeated over and over again on national news media—newspapers, television, and news magazines. Finally, on January 27, 1974, the Associated Press moved on its main wires a report that the story had turned out to be a complete fabrication.

There was no million-dollar fund being administered for the President, made up of political contributions or anything else. Yet by then the story was embedded ineradicably in the public consciousness, one of the bill of particulars in the indictment of the President.

2. On September 26, 1973, the *Wall Street Journal* published a remarkable editorial, a *mea culpa*, in which the paper acknowledged that a long-circulated set of stories about vast sums having been spent by the General Services Administration to provide private improvements to the presidential homes at San Clemente and Key Biscayne had been, in effect, nonstories. The expenditures, as the *Journal* editorial pointed out, and as was documented in detail in an accompanying news account, had been legitimate and defensible in virtually all respects (for example, landscaping charges were necessary to restore grounds that had been torn up for installation of conduits for power lines, alarm systems, and TV cables required by the Secret Service; trees had in some instances to be relocated to prevent line-of-sight visibility of windows to distant sharpshooters). The *Journal* editorial, commenting on the failure of the press to heed the explanations that had been offered in justification of the "boondoggle" and "scandalous" spending, observed that: "lately it has been popular to take every explanation not as a settlement of the charges it addresses but a backhanded confirmation of the charges it does not address. . . . we suspect it is one of the best ways for non-stories to catch on."

3. During the last part of January 1974, wire services and individual newspapers carried repeated reports "from sources close to . . ." that when one of the convicted Watergate conspirators, Egil Krogh, was finally sentenced he would then "spill his guts" and link President Nixon to various of the Watergate offenses. Krogh had just been waiting, according to the faceless informants, until he had been sentenced, refusing all offers to plea-bargain, so that when he finally did talk no one would be able to discount his revelations as having been bought for a lesser penalty. Then on January 27 Krogh was sentenced, and he did, indeed, issue a statement—but it insisted flatly and repeatedly that President Nixon had not given Krogh directions in the Watergate capers, neither directly nor indirectly. In short, the long-awaited gut-spilling was exactly the opposite of what the faceless sources had been quoted as forecasting.

4. Edward Jay Epstein reports another instance, this one involving a news magazine:

For instance, in what purported to be an interview with John W. Dean III, the President's former counsel, *Newsweek* reported that Dean would reveal in his public testimony that some White House officials had planned to assassinate Panama's head of government but that the plan was aborted at the last minute. This *Newsweek* "exclusive" was circulated to thousands of newspapers in an advance press release, and widely published. When it turned out that the story was untrue—Dean did not testify about any such assassination plot, and denied under oath that he had discussed any substantial aspects of his testimony with *Newsweek* reporters—*Newsweek* did not correct or explain the discrepancy. Presumably, Dean was not the source for the putative "Dean interview," and the unidentified source had misled *Newsweek* on what Dean was planning to say in his public testimony. Since the error was that of an unidentified source, *Newsweek* did not feel obligated to correct it in future editions.[25]

It would be possible to document numerous other instances of gross misuse of the secret source device by newsmen who failed the ethical test that Woodward and Bernstein met in their Watergate reportage.

Such abuse of the convention of the anonymous source could well lead to further erosion of the concept of reporter privilege. At the very least, it had the immediate effect of significantly besmirching the credibility of the press, just at a moment when the Watergate exposés had seemed to be providing a triumphant justification for the role of the Fourth Estate in our society.

Notes

[1]Laura Longely Babb, ed., *Of the press, by the press, for the press (And others, too)* (Washington: The Washington Post Company, 1974), p. 129. The editorial first appeared in the *Post* on February 12, 1969.

[2]Curtis D. MacDougall, *The Press and Its Problems* (Dubuque: William C. Brown Company, Publishers, 1964), p. 338.

[3]William L. Rivers and Wilbur Schramm, *Responsibility in Mass Communication* (New York: Harper & Row, Publishers, Inc., 1969), p. 166.

[4]Samuel J. Archibald, "Rules for the Game of Ghost," *Columbia Journalism Review*, VI, No. 4 (Winter, 1967/68), 17–23.

[5]Benjamin C. Bradlee, "A Conspiracy in Restraint of Truth," in *Of the press, by the press, for the press (And others, too)*, pp. 124–27.

[6]*Ibid.*, p. 126.

[7]Tom Wicker, "The Greening of the Press," reprinted from the *Columbia Journalism review*, X, No. 1 (May/June 1971), © 7–12. (Edited from an extemporaneous speech.)

[8]*Ibid.*, p. 10.

[9]Louis M. Lyons, "The Pressures of News," *Nieman Reports*, XX, No. 3 (September 1966), 2, 18–24.

[10]Gene Graham, "History in the (Deliberate) Making: A Challenge to Modern Journalism," *Nieman Reports*, XX, No. 3 (September 1966), 3–7.

11Edward Jay Epstein, *Between Fact and Fiction: The Problem of Journalism* (New York: Vintage Book Division of Random House, Inc., 1975) . © by Random House, Inc., and quoted by permission. This excerpt first appeared in an article in *Commentary*.

12*Time*, CIII, No. 13 (April 1, 1974), 31.

13Carl Bernstein, "Watergate: Tracking It Down," *Quill*, LXI, No. 6 (June, 1973), 45–48. (*Quill* is published by The Society of Professional Journalists, Sigma Delta Chi.)

14*Ibid.*, 45.

15Epstein, *Between Fact and Fiction*, p. 10.

16Compiled from cases reported in various issues of *Press Censorship Newsletter/Media Law Reporter*, published by The Reporters Committee for Freedom of the Press, Washington, D.C.

17Norman E. Isaacs, " 'There May Be Worse to Come from This Court' ", reprinted from the *Columbia Journalism Review*, XI No. 3 (September/October 1972), © 18–24.

18*Ibid.*, p. 19.

19*Ibid.*

20*Ibid.*

21David Gordon. "The Confidences Newsmen Must Keep," *Columbia Journalism Re-* X, No. 4 (November/December 1971), 15–20.

22James McCartney, "The Washington 'Post' and Watergate: How Two Davids Slew Goliath," *Columbia Journalism Review*, XII, No. 2 (July/August 1973), 8–22.

23Carl Bernstein and Bob Woodward, *All the President's Men* (New York: Simon & Schuster, Inc., 1974).

24From his column on the editorial page of the *Wall Street Journal*, April 3, 1974.

25Epstein, *Between Fact and Fiction*, pp. 8-9.

Problems Built In... "Often it seems that our society is a tremendous cave of sound, in which voices bounce back and forth, calling to one another, responding to one another, stimulating one another. The journalist stands in the middle of this huge roaring chamber, trying to catch the most significant voices, the rising new voices, the receding old voices. As he listens, he must think—think for himself, forming his own judgments out of all the pieces of his knowledge of the past and the present; and think for the public, for the millions who rush from the confusion of their private lives to the perplexities of trying to be citizens of the world."—Frank K. Kelly [1]

7 It isn't an easy place to keep one's footing, where the journalist stands immersed in the flow of the news, trying to make sense of it somehow. He is beset by the pressures of time, conscious of obligations, aware that reputations, lives, even the future of nations may depend on how well he does his filtering task for the benefit of those who read, listen, and view.

Often, as anyone in the business knows, that job isn't done as well as it should be. When that happens, it may be the fault of the journalist, in ways that we have to some extent explored in earlier chapters. But it may also be at least in part because of the kind of business it is.

The gathering, processing, and disseminating of the news goes on in an atmosphere of deadlines. Many other pressures also impinge, some of them built into the craft. It is often difficult to know with any certainty whether a given lapse—minor or consequential—can be laid to a reporter's or editor's lack of professional skill or ethical standards, or to the nature of the work itself.

Consider the ever-present bugbear, the error.

Every issue of every newspaper or magazine, every live broadcast, almost certainly contains some errors. If it is an early edition of the newspaper, one that hasn't yet been gone over carefully by proofreaders, or if it is a rip-and-read news broadcast that the announcer hasn't had time to skim through before going on the air, the mistakes may be many.

Some of them will be unintentional typographical errors, or verbal fluffs by the newscaster. Others will have been caused by some of the pressures that infuse the news business.

The typos or fluffs may be harmless enough. When you read that an offer has been made "with no stings attached" you know what was meant. The same with: "There is a majestic strength and a sense of immorality to be gained from looking at the Capitol."

But some simple, accidental errors can be the cause of embarrassment and even tragedy. A picture and caption were transposed in one paper, and under the photograph of a respected clubwoman of the community appeared the cutlines: "Former call girl writes memoirs." A libel suit resulted from that one.

And the accidental omission of "not" from a crime story in which a defendant entered a plea of "not guilty" has more than once caused nightmares for a courthouse reporter.

These are essentially mechanical errors that slip through the elaborate, multistage system that most publications and broadcast outlets try to maintain to keep them from occurring.

Some other kinds of errors get into the mainstream of the news for different reasons, but ones that are nevertheless associated with the nature of the news business. Consider one instance that involved some of the best-regarded news outlets in the nation.

Those Controversial Birds

In February of 1969, Fred L. Hartley, president of the Union Oil Company, was in Washington to testify before the Senate Subcommittee on Air and Water Pollution. He was making some comments on problems caused by a leaking oil well owned by his company and located off the coast of Santa Barbara, California. Oil from the leaking well had spread to nearby beaches, and birds and other wildlife had been coated with the black, sticky mess.

The hearing was being covered for the *New York Times* by one of its ablest reporters, Warren Weaver. But Mr. Weaver was obliged to be absent from the hearing room for a few minutes while Mr. Hartley was on the stand and he asked another reporter, a *Christian Science Monitor* staff member, to fill him in when he returned.

During Weaver's absence, the witness was asked about the effect of the oil spill on beach wildlife. The oil company president responded, as the transcript of the hearings shows: "Mr. Chairman, I would like to comment further here. I think we have to look at these problems relatively. I am always tremendously impressed at the publicity that death of birds receives versus the loss of people in our country in this day and age."[2]

When reporter Weaver returned to the room, the *Monitor* staffer gave him a rundown of the testimony he had missed. But in the condensing, summing-up, and transfer, the testimony by Mr. Hartley came out: "I'm amazed at the publicity for the loss of a few birds." That was how the account appeared under Weaver's byline in the next day's *New York Times*. The day following, the *Wall Street Journal* picked up the quote from the *Times,* and added to it a comment obtained by one of its correspondents from an unnamed Union Oil official at San Diego: "Lord, I wish he (Hartley) hadn't said that."

David Brinkley appropriated the quote for his nightly TV news program, and soon after it appeared in *Time* with a few embellishments typical of that publication ("the blunt, short-tempered executive" was "amazed at the publicity for the loss of a few birds"). Finally, the quote showed up on the editorial page of the *Washington Post*, paraphrased as the title of an editorial comment: "The Loss of a Few Birds."

By then the aggrieved Mr. Hartley was making protests to everyone concerned about the pejorative spin that had been put on his words. Whether or not all of the other publications did him the courtesy of correcting the error, the *Post* generously did so in an editorial which traced the whole sequence of events.

But of course by that time the comment had gone into the conventional wisdom, and the impression had been implanted firmly in the public mind that oil company executives are coldly indifferent to the fate of wildlife besmeared by leaking crude.

Another unfortunate lapse caused by slippage in communication, and by an additional factor as well, occurred during the dramatic days of the summer of 1972 when Senator Thomas Eagleton of Missouri was named by the Democratic National Convention as the party's vice-presidential candidate. A few days later came the revelation that Senator Eagleton had at one time been under psychiatric treatment. That story, although it was actually released by the senator at a press conference, had first been uncovered and put together by the Knight Newspapers. Reporters for the Knight organization carefully checked out all the leads, and before breaking the story decided to let the McGovern people know about it and get whatever comment might be forthcoming. It was then that Eagleton and McGovern decided to take the initiative and release the story before it could come out elsewhere. The handling of the matter by the Knight reporters was thoroughly responsible. But an episode that immediately followed was not.

Columnist Jack Anderson got a tip from an informant that Senator Eagleton, in addition to the psychiatric treatment background, had a record of drunk-driving arrests. Without checking out the tip, Anderson went on radio with it at once. It turned out to be false, and Anderson later attempted to correct the error, but by then the senator had been dropped as the nominee—chiefly, of course, because party strategists felt that the record of hospitalization for mental illness would handicap the ticket; the drunk-driving charge was not a major factor. Nonetheless, as *Columbia Journalism Review* observed editorially:

The dramatic Eagleton case provided two textbook examples of how to handle accusations against public figures. One was a model of the kind of careful work for which the media seldom get credit; the other, the kind of cheap shot that makes the public forget all the good work. . . . Anderson's report on drunken driving—too flimsy to put in his column—was broadcast on radio in terms that suggested he had seen documents. Anderson talks like a crusader. In this instance he showed that his game was self-aggrandizement.[3]

110

He also showed that in his haste to get a scoop on a fast-breaking story he was willing to take unethical shortcuts with the accuracy of his reporting and too readily accept from an unchecked source what appeared to be a hot lead on an important news situation. That sort of expedient compromise of ethical standards results in an erosion of public confidence in all of the media of communication.

The Murdered Panthers

Another instance in which a significant error was not only allowed to get into the stream of the news but was also then magnified by careless journalistic handling involved the charge that police in various parts of the country had "murdered" 28 members of the Black Panther organization.

The episode began with the assertion by Charles R. Garry, legal counsel for the Panthers, that two members of the party who had died in a Chicago police raid were the "twenty-seventh and twenth-eighth Panthers" to have been "murdered by the police."

At first, newspapers and broadcasters reporting the charge attributed it to Garry, and indicated his relationship to the Panthers. But then, as the item was repeated in various stories and newscasts, the attribution shifted to others, or faded away altogether. Witness this sequence of references in the *Washington Post:*

December 7, 1969, news story: "Twenty-eight Panthers have died in police shootings since January, 1968, according to Charles Garry, San Francisco attorney and general counsel for the Panthers."

December 9, 1969, news story: "Jay Miller, Illinois director of the American Civil Liberties Union, asked for an inquiry into a whole range of reported Panther slayings. A total of 28 Panthers have died in clashes with police since Jan. 1, 1968."[4]

Soon the qualifications and attributions disappeared entirely from broadcasts and news accounts, and it became accepted fact that 28 members of the Panther party had been "murdered" or "killed" or "shot down" by police, depending on what story you read or heard.

This went on for more than a year until press critic Edward Jay Epstein took the trouble to trace down all of the facts in the matter. In an article in the *New Yorker* he demonstrated that these facts did not support the charge that the police had "murdered" 28 Black Panthers. Some had died in shootouts in crime situations; some had been victims of internal fighting within the organization; what number had actually died in one way or another was not even clear. Certainly the non-attributed use of the "28 murders" item as established truth was unjustified by any of the facts that Epstein tracked down.[5]

In the episode was reflected the tendency of reporters to accept an item of news provided by an "official spokesman" (Garry, in this case) and then to pass it along, trade it around among the media, allowing it in the process to take on the aspect of proven fact rather than a possibly self-interested claim.

As *Columbia Journalism Review's* editors observed. Epstein's painstaking detective work on this long-circulated story "provides a therapeutic corrective for all journalists who not only used the dubious statistic (concocted by the party's lawyer) but elevated it into acceptability by eliminating the attribution."[6]

In a quite different and less consequential instance the element of attribution was preserved, at least technically, but the net effect of the story was the same: facts were distorted significantly out of shape, and unwary reportorial use of attribution only made the matter worse.

In this case, a casual comment made during an interview by the author of a small book on how to buy food inexpensively was later quoted in the report of a Senate subcommittee. From there it was elevated to national attention by reporters and columnists who accepted it on its face and made no effort to check out its validity. The burden of the report, as it finally made the wire services and the headlines: As much as one-third of the dog and cat foods sold in city ghetto areas is being eaten by humans, according to a panel of nutrition experts.

Actually, as a later digging expedition revealed, there was no documentation for the assertion, even at the point where it first had been made in offhand fashion during the interview with the book author. The official aura of the later sources—in this case the staff authors of a Senate subcommittee report—was apparently enough to satisfy the reporters and columnists who passed on the startling claim and even magnified it. (Jack Anderson wrote a column, accepting the accuracy of the item and enlivening it with some additional vivid color: "My associate Les Whitten tried some of the pet foods. . . . He found the canned pet foods, though edible, had a rank taste which made him queasy. . . . The dry foods, sold in bulk quantities, were coarse tasting and hard to swallow. . . . Peanut butter or cheese spread made dog food easier to get down, he found. But the poor can seldom afford these tasty spreads.")

As the free-lance writer who finally tracked the story down to its source concluded, "The media had transformed casual conversation and mere guesswork into hard fact."[7] In the process, the reporters, desk men, and columnists had violated the principle that the journalist's obligation is to sketch as honest a picture of reality as possible.

The Pittsburgh Riot

Ralph Z. Hallow, an editorial writer for the *Pittsburgh Post-Gazette*, had an excellent vantage point from which to analyze another case in which some of the built-in pressures and conventions of journalism combined with reportorial lapses to magnify a news story into something that was larger than life and several times more lurid.

On October 17, 1971, the Pittsburgh Pirates won the baseball World Series, and Pirate fans streamed into the streets to celebrate. What followed became the subject of angry debate among newspapermen, wire service officials, and Pittsburgh civic leaders.

The Associated Press report that went out that night began thus:

A massive World Series celebration exploded last night into a rampage of destruction, looting, and sex-in-the-street.

Newsmen reported two apparent assaults, some of them in full view of hundreds who cheered the assailants, displays of public lovemaking, nudity, and drinking. . . .

"This isn't a riot, it's an orgy," a motorcycle policeman said. . . .[8]

Around the nation the report was published in various newspapers, topped by such headlines as:

100,000 Pirate Fans Stage Orgiastic Riot

Fort Lauderdale (Florida) *News*

Thousands Run Riot in Pittsburgh

Detroit Free Press

113

Pittsburghers Ugly on Victory Binge

Wilmington (Del.) *Evening Journal*

Looting, Sex-in-Street Follows Pittsburgh Victory

Wilmington Evening Journal

Some correspondents for foreign newspapers, or writers on the home desks, embroidered the story further. The *London Daily Mail,* for example, told its readers that the victory "sparked off the most incredible riot in American history." The *Mail* report said there had been two shooting deaths, 13 rapes, stores set on fire and "crowds cheering as gangs of youths dragged girls to the roadway and raped them."

Pittsburgh Post-Gazette writer Hallow notes in his *Columbia Journalism* Review account:

If an "orgiastic riot" or "extraordinary orgy of destruction, looting, and sexual excess" of this magnitude did occur, evidence of it could scarcely be concealed. Yet investigators who have sought evidence of such an occurrence have found themselves in part in pursuit of a will-o'-the-wisp. In fact, neither the Pittsburgh *Post-Gazette* nor the city Police Bureau has detected a single rape complaint or a building set ablaze. Police Superintendent Robert E. Colville has said that the events of that Sunday afternoon and evening constituted neither a riot nor an orgy.

Separate, peripatetic observations for six hours throughout the downtown area by this reporter and another *Post-Gazette* newsman revealed nothing which approximated a riot or an orgy.[9]

Then how did the reports get into the news stream, there to be magnified and embellished and built out of proportion? Hallow traces down the details of one of the sensational elements, the assertion that there had been several rapes:

Where did this report originate? Pat Minarcin, the AP bureau chief in Pittsburgh, said that he witnessed an incident which he first described as "rape." But since then he has had second thoughts about it. Between 8 p.m. and 9 p.m. on traffic-jammed Fifth Avenue, downtown, in the midst of the celebration, Minarcin, from his automobile, saw "one pretty damned drunk" young woman, who had been waving a beer can, pulled from an automobile. Apparently frightened, she seemed to resist as her hot pants, sweater, and underwear were pulled off, but according to Minarcin she then appeared to cooperate enthusiastically as four men pressed her against a car fender and had intercourse with her.

The report of this incident, minus the observation that the woman "seemed to be enjoying it," went out in an AP wire story. Reading it in the *Post-Gazette* city room a short time later, a *P-G* reporter incorporated the "assault" report into his own story. Still later, the AP read about the "assault" in the *P-G* and, believing it was a second incident, added it to its "overnight" wire story. Thus, the same incident viewed by one AP reporter inadvertently became two "assaults" in a later AP story.

The third AP paragraph said that at "the height of the melee a police desk sergeant said he had calls reporting about a dozen rapes. But officials denied they had such reports." The AP, in this instance, did properly check with police, therefore, for confirmation of rape reports and found none. . . .

The AP reported that "more than a dozen cars were overturned and in same cases burned" and that seven taxis were destroyed. But the only vehicle damaged which police knew of was one taxicab on Liberty Avenue. . . .

Had there been "sex in the streets"? Apparently, yes—to the following extent. There was a report of a bare-breasted girl dancing atop a car, of an elderly intoxicated woman lifting up her skirts as she danced at Liberty and Sixth, and of the young woman who was made love to on an auto fender on Fifth Avenue. . . .

Were these, in the context of a huge, jubilant celebration, indecent public displays? Perhaps. But with an estimated 100,000 or more persons jammed into less than a square mile of the city, these incidents hardly justify calling the victory celebration an orgy.[10]

Any of us now—distant in time and association from the episode—can read the accounts and Mr. Hallow's analysis of how they came to be and recognize that here was no simple black-and-white situation. The Associated Press did somewhat later acknowledge that such terms as "riot" and "orgy," considering their vivid and sensational connotations, should not have been so freely used in the wire service reports that night. But the AP editors also pointed out that their reporters *had* personally witnessed instances of gross public misbehavior, and that the difficulty of covering the whole of a sprawling, crowded demonstration scene made it easy for eyewitnesses to extend and generalize those individual observations.

Those who, later on in the news pipeline, added touches to the story and placed it under glaring headlines, contributed to the magnifying

115

process. Were the reporters, the editors, the head-writers guilty of un-ethical acts? Were they responding automatically to craft conventions characteristic of the news business? Or a little of both?

Mr. Hallow concludes that there were various lessons to be read from the analysis he made of the coverage of the Pittsburgh episode.

The first lesson, it would seem, is that sensationalized reports of events still attract greater prominence than restrained accounts—and, unfortunately, more prominence than denials and postmortems which attempt to unbend a warped record. . . .

There remains . . . a wire-service tendency to "hype" things up, to strive for the punchy lead. There is also the old problem of haste. Wire services operate on continuous deadlines, having to satisfy the multiple schedules of print and electronic customers in differing time zones around the world. Then there is the news service-newsmagazine tradition of having someone in a New York bureau rewrite someone else's report for added zing, perhaps without checking the nuances of a situation, even though the rewriteman wasn't on the scene. . . .

In the Pittsburgh case, finally, there were too few local reporters covering the story and, because it was a Sunday (traditionally a ho-hum-no-news-day) no experienced editors to check a reporter's tendency to assume that what he saw was typical of the whole event. . . . The hidden heart of that problem is money and city room budgets. For in the wire services as elsewhere in the media, it is still principally economics, not the lofty professional principles of the Fourth Estate, which set the parameters of journalistic achievement—an observation which should shock few, if any, working journalists.[11]

Mr. Hallow's conclusion is valid up to a point; ameliorating ex-planations can be developed for some kinds of ethical lapses by jour-nalists, whether on the basis of newsroom economics or of long-standing craft conventions. But these are only explanations, not excuses. The principle of accuracy is demanding, but it is also inescapable. The ethical journalist knows that and does not seek refuge in rationalizations.

'The Attributes of Fiction'

The built-in circumstances that tend to nudge the journalist toward ethical shortcuts exist in the electronic media as well as in the wire services and the newspapers, of course.

When a television news director is putting together a program, for example, he is conscious of the need to keep the screen alive as much of the time as possible. The "talking head"—a newscaster reading the news report to the camera—is to be avoided, since impatient viewers may be tempted to turn to another channel where there is more action.

So as a consequence, when choices must be made between stories that have some accompanying film footage and others for which there are no pictures, the nod will usually go to the visualized news item—even if conventional news standards would ordinarily dictate otherwise.

Moreover, since the overall context of television is that of an entertainment medium, it is inevitable that TV newscasts, at least in some cases, will be put together as though they were dramatic presentations rather than recitals of news as it happened. (Recall the description of the influence of Hollywood newsreel makers on TV newsfilm set out in chapter 5.)

Reuven Frank, at that time the president of NBC News, observed that:

Every news story should, without any sacrifice of probity or responsibility, display the attributes of fiction, of drama. It should have structure and conflict, problem and denouement, rising action and falling action, a beginning, a middle and an end.[12]

There is, in this directive to staff members, the saving clause: ". . . without any sacrifice of probity or responsibility . . . ." But it may be difficult to reconcile that with the other implications of the policy position Frank lays down. Sometimes, it would seem, the reconciliation doesn't come off.

Edward Jay Epstein describes an instance:

In filming delayed stories, newsmen are expected to eliminate any elements of the unexpected, so as not to destroy the illusion of immediacy. This becomes especially important when it is likely that the unusual developments will be reported in other media and thus date the story. A case in point is an N.B.C. News story about the inauguration of a high-speed train service between Montreal and Toronto. While the N.B.C. crew was filming the turbotrain during its inaugural run to Toronto, it collided with—and "sliced in half," as one newspaper put it—a meat trailer-truck, and then suffered a complete mechanical breakdown on the return trip. Persistent "performance flaws" and subsequent breakdowns eventually led to a temporary suspension of the service. None of these accidents and aberrations were included in the filmed story broadcast two weeks later on the N.B.C. evening news. David Brinkley, keeping to the original story, written before the event, introduced the film by saying, "The only high-speed train now running in North America has just begun in Canada." Four and a half minutes of shots of the streamlined train followed, and the narration suggested that this foreshadowed the future of transportation, since Canada's "new turbo just might shake [American] lethargy" in developing such trains. (The announcement of the suspension of the service, almost two weeks later, was not carried on the program.)[13]

Some of the interviews that are one of the most reliable staples of TV news are very much in the tradition of show business. The subjects are rehearsed before the cameras turn; the general topic is gone over so that the interviewer can determine which questions are going to elicit the liveliest responses; sometimes the subject of the interview is permitted to put together a list of questions he wants to be asked.

Then when the interview is actually being filmed, the same question may be asked several times, in slightly different ways, so that the best and sharpest answer can later be selected for showing. I was thus interviewed once for the Huntley-Brinkley Nightly News, and out of about six minutes of questions and answers on camera, 15 seconds of footage appeared on the air. Those 15 seconds included a single question and answer, but the answer was one I had provided to an earlier question, not to the one shown on the televised exchange.

These built-in characteristics of the television news field lead, certainly, to some distortions. They also, in some cases, introduce errors into the news as it is presented to the viewing audience, just as the pressures of the craft insinuate errors into the news report offered by the print media.

Are these errors to be chalked up as ethical lapses—or as the inevitable price to be paid for getting the news swiftly and excitingly packaged?

As was noted earlier, some allowance can fairly be made for the built-in pressures. But it is equally fair to say that a better job—in many cases a *far* better job—could be done than the journalists of the print and electronic media are doing today.

As Nat Hentoff, the press critic of the *Village Voice* in New York once commented:

I wonder how many of you are aware of how little checking goes on anywhere in journalism. I've written for a wide variety of magazines and newspapers and only two of them fully check out the facts in a writer's piece.[14]

118

Back in the Classifieds?

When errors are made in reporting the news—for whatever reason—they ought to be corrected, to the most effective degree possible. The qualifying clause is necessary, of course, because it is a provable fact that corrections never do catch up with the first, erroneous version, no matter how well intentioned they may be.

Most journalists will agree in principle that the correction of errors is in the best tradition of journalistic ethics. (Recall the canons of the American Society of Newspaper Editors: "VI . . . 2. It is the privilege, as it is the duty, of a newspaper to make prompt and complete correction of its own serious mistakes of fact or opinion, whatever their origin.")

But principle is one thing, practice often quite another.

Just as it is rare to find anyone who has been satisfied with the accuracy with which his words have been quoted in the press, so is it equally unusual to find someone who has been the victim of a journalistic error and feels that the mistake was adequately corrected. The more typical complaint: "Sure, they said on page one that I was arrested for drunk driving, and then ran the correction back on page 46, with the classifieds, two weeks later."

An Associated Press study discovered that of 50 newspapers that ran the Jack Anderson story about Senator Eagleton's drunk-driving record on page one, 15 printed the correction on the same page. Yet if the true version doesn't get the same prominence as the incorrect one, how can the matter possibly be rectified, how can a reputation possibly be made whole?

Another survey, this one by the Associated Press Managing Editors Association of some 300 APME editors, reported that the "vast majority" of those responding felt an obligation to correct mistakes and do it wholeheartedly.

Some of them quite clearly were attempting to do just that.

For example, the *St. Paul Pioneer Press* and *Dispatch* sends out form letters to persons mentioned in news stories, along with a clipping of the story. The form letter asks such questions as: Are the facts in this story correct? Was the story complete? Is the headline accurate and fair? The responses from the persons thus solicited are published, if corrections are called for.[15]

Other papers take this approach, too, while still others run a regular department to handle corrections and acknowledgments of omission, among them the *Decatur* (Ill.) *Herald* and *Review*, and the *Chicago Sun-Times* and *Daily News*. The *St. Louis Post-Dispatch* in 1974 began running corrections under a standing headline, and always on the same page—3 A. The *Wall Street Journal* also developed a standing head—"Corrections & Amplifications"—but did not always anchor it to the same page daily; it usually was positioned within the first four or five pages, however, and was hard to miss.

If corrections are run separately, some papers make sure they will be noticed as such. Managing editor Ed Donohue of the *Scranton* (Pa.) *Times* said that "The correction must be clearly understood as such. No pussy-footing. If we were wrong, we say so."

It is evident, however, from a close reading of the APME study findings that many publications do not print corrections and retractions on as prominent a page, and in as large a display space, as was the case with the original, erroneous report.

Some of the comments printed in the APME publication that reported on the findings of the accuracy study were revealing:

If the error will create trouble for the person we correct it. If it is something like a wrong age in an obit or other minor problem, we try to skip corrections—*Enid* (Okla.) *News* and *Eagle*.

Generally speaking, we try to avoid having the pages pockmarked with "correction" because that helps increase any reader credibility gap. But we don't hedge on correcting a real error that can be harmful.—*Greenfield* (Mass.) *Recorder*.

Errors which have no libel potential generally are corrected by republishing the original story, if practical, with errors corrected.—*Atlanta* (Ga.) *Journal*.

No policy on corrections except that we try not to call attention to them (except, of course, for retractions on possibly libelous material).

We try to disguise the headline over a correction, rather than just writing "correction." . . .

In other words, we want to be able to say to the person offended: "Yes, we ran a correction on that report." But we don't want to advertise it unnecessarily to the other readers.—*Hutchinson* (Kans.) *News*

There are some disturbing strains running through that last set of responses. Why should corrections be attended to with care only if a libel threat is pending? Isn't a reader who is less gravely injured also entitled to have the error put straight?

Is republishing the original story, with errors corrected, a genuine effort at correction—or a finessing of the matter?

Who decides what is a "real error" that will be corrected *(Greenfield Recorder)*? If there is an error of any kind, it is real to the reader and he ought to be entitled to have the record adjusted.

And read through the comment from the Hutchinson paper again. If there is an ethical spirit reflected therein, it is no more than ethics of expediency, and not much of that.

It would be reassuring to readers—and gratifying to anyone concerned about the ethics of the press—if all editors had the philosophy of managing editor George N. Gill of the *Louisville* (Ky.) *Courier-Journal:*

We decided to publish all corrections in the same place any day that it was necessary. And it seems to be necessary almost daily.

We settled on the front page of our second section, and on a standing headline that reads: "Beg Your Pardon." . . . Some days we carry two or three (corrections) under the same head.

Of course, we shouldn't make mistakes at all. I've offered $100 of the publisher's money for a staff party any time we go seven days without a "Beg Your Pardon."

I'm afraid the publisher's money is safe, sorry to say, as long as mortals publish 100,000 words each day.

The publisher's money may be safe, but so are the interests of the readers of the *Courier-Journal.* The same can't be said for the subscribers to a good many journals in other communities.

One conservative critic of the press, Irving Kristol, has painted the situation in grim colors, charging that it is a "fact that all of our major newspapers will normally refuse to publish letters from public officials or experts challenging the accuracy of their news reporting."

In a footnote to his contention, he observes:

To those who know only about newspapers what they read in the newspapers, this will sound incredible. But it is so. To be sure, a very superior newspaper like the New York *Times* will occasionally publish a very short letter that takes issue with one of its stories. But behind every such letter there stands [sic] a dozen unpublished ones—to say nothing of the dozens that do not even get written, since it is known that their chances of being published are negligible.[16]

Mr. Kristol's charge is sweeping, so much so that it oversimplifies and even misrepresents the true situation. My own experience of several decades, either working on newspaper staffs (a large part of the time with editorial pages, on which letters to the editor typically appear) or in journalism education as a consistent observer of the press, would lead me to dispute the blanket nature of Mr. Kristol's charge.

I would say that most of "our major newspapers" *do* publish letters challenging the accuracy of their reporting or the cogency of their editorial arguments. It is true enough that most papers are not able to publish *all* of the letters that they receive, but the reason for this is limitation of space rather than defensive censorship. The *New York Times* receives about 40,000 letters from readers in a typical year and can find space to publish only about 6 percent of them.

However, the *Times* and other reputable journals—a majority of the American papers, I would argue, not just the "very superior" few—do make a consistent effort to be sure that the letters that they do publish present a faithful reflection of the pro-con views of the unpublished others for which space was not available. In other words, they try to publish a *representative sample* of the overall volume of mail received. And conscientious editors actually give priority to those letters that are critical of the newspaper's performance or policies.

But if Mr. Kristol had not been so all-inclusive in his complaint, he would have been able to justify and document it to some degree. Some papers, at least, and other media as well *are* vulnerable to criticism for their handling of complaints about inaccuracy, imbalance, or other kinds of lapses.

A case in point: Syndicated columnist William F. Buckley included in one of his columns an attack on the Most Reverend Leo C. Byrne, a Catholic archbishop coadjutor, taking the clergyman to task for a policy statement he had made. Archbishop Byrne wrote a rejoinder to the Buckley column and asked Buckley's syndicate to send the rebuttal out to all of its subscribers, together with a note from Byrne requesting that they publish his response "in the name of fairness."

The National Conference of Editorial Writers later checked the pages of all of the newspapers that had printed the Buckley column and had also been sent the Byrne response to see how many had given the archbishop a chance to reply. The NCEW survey showed that 72 percent of the editors had run the rebuttal column and 28 percent had not used it. Gilbert Cranberg, chairman of the professional standards committee of the NCEW observed: "It's cause for concern that nearly 30 percent of the editors did not print even excerpts from Archbishop Byrne's response to Buckley's attack."[17]

Those editors who made up the 28 percent of the NCEW survey

group might be legitimate targets for Mr. Kristol's complaint cited earlier. And he could find additional targets, as well.

There are, for example, some few editors who deliberately stack the decks in the letters column. That is, they distort the reader's perception of the real situation by printing more letters in favor of the paper's pet causes than against them, even though the actual flow of mail is running the other way. The editor of a prominent Midwest metropolitan daily once told me quite candidly that he did this regularly, in order to "reinforce" the paper's editorial positions by suggesting public support of them through manipulation of the letters column. And I know of a small-town daily editor who sorts through the incoming letters each morning, tossing into the wastebasket those he disagrees with and okaying for publication the ones that accord with his own prejudices.

Other editors take advantage of their ability to get in the last word; they append snide editor's notes to letters, putting down the letter writer with sarcasm or ridicule. That's a cheap tactic, and clearly unethical. The editor has plenty of space in which to offer his own comment in the editorial columns across the page; he has no business poaching on the territory theoretically allocated as a public forum, except to correct a clear misstatement of fact.

As with other aspects of journalism, there are ethical practitioners and there are less admirable corner-cutters. It is important to acknowledge and deplore the latter without censuring the whole establishment with the sort of blanket condemnation issued by Mr. Kristol.

In the broadcasting media, the situation is somewhat different. Because of the evanescent nature of broadcasting and the difficulty therefore of documenting the commission of errors, demand for corrections of mistakes are likely to be rarer than in the case of newspapers and magazines, where there is a permanent record of the offending lapse.

But both radio and television operate under the fairness and equal-time rules of the Federal Communications Commission, which require that broadcasters who express a point of view or who attack someone on the air must provide the aggrieved party an opportunity to respond. Such an opportunity is most often sought with respect to editorial observations made by the broadcaster, but it sometimes can be used also to obtain correction of a factual error made in a newscast.

In a move more directly comparable to the newspapers' handling of corrections, NBC's "Nightly News" in 1974 added a new segment to its program. Under the title "Editor's Notebook," the program's anchormen attempt to catch up "on stories we never finished, correcting those on which we made mistakes, and generally dropping the other shoe," in the words of John Chancellor.[18] If others follow the NBC example one ethical weak spot will have been at least partially shored up.

Errant Heads

Another journalistic sector where special craft conditions sometimes provide severe tests of ethical integrity is on the copy desk.

Here editors go through copy destined for broadcast or print publication and refine and polish it. They may change a word here, strike out a phrase there, move a paragraph up to the top from a place near the end, or insert new material that in their judgment will improve the story. And, so far as the print media are concerned, they also devise headlines to go above the story.

There is obviously gatekeeper power being exercised at this point, and it can be awesomely effective. A slight change in a phrase can make a vast difference in the way a story is perceived by the viewer, listener, or reader.

Consider for a moment a story reporting the testimony of a defendant in a trial or a hearing. Whether the story reports that he "stubbornly insisted on his innocence" or that he "firmly maintained his innocence" can subtly but significantly affect the way in which the reader of that story will feel toward the person described.

Whether the account reads that the governor "hurried solicitously" to the bedside of a wounded civil rights leader, or that he "fleet-footedly turned up" at the hospital, can portray him in the one instance as humanely concerned and in the other as trying to make political capital of the situation, behaving like an ambulance chaser.

The process of distilling the essence of a half-column story into a six-word headline inevitably brings some distortion. Only a facet, a fleeting glimpse, of the complex substance of the account can be squeezed into the tiny format of a headline. Even with the best of intentions, it is difficult for the copy editor to fashion a head that will fairly reflect the content of the story that follows; if the editor is careless, or if he abuses his gatekeeper power, he can twist the impact of the story around 90 or even 180 degrees.

Sometimes, when the head-writer's effort is well meant but ambiguous, the result is unintentionally amusing, but harmlessly so. For example:

124

Ex-Sen. Hill Cited for Mental Health Progress

Tuna Recalled After Death

Women in Political Campaigns to Be Explored at Workshop

In other circumstances, a headline may involve some person whose name is well known locally, but might have another meaning to an outsider reading the same head:

Lord Finds Paradise in Hawaiian Lifestyle

Pope to Be Admitted to Vt. Bar

No harm is inflicted by either category of mangled headline. But some others are not so innocent.

At the time when the My Lai massacre of Vietnam civilians by American troops was almost daily in the news, the following headline appeared:

General Faces My Lai Charge

The casual reader—and there are very many such—would take the headline to mean that a general officer was to be charged with complicity in the murder of the Vietnam civilians. But the story below indicated that a sergeant charged in the affair had signed a complaint saying that the U.S. Chief of Staff, General Westmoreland, ought to be held accountable for not controlling the troops at My Lai since at that time he had been in command of the entire Vietnam theater.

On another occasion, a headline read:

White House Aide
Arrested as Drunk

Consider the connotations of the words used in that headline. "White House Aide" certainly suggests to most persons some high staff member, an assistant to the President. "Arrested as Drunk" conjures up the picture of a disheveled, unshaven derelict picked up as he staggered down the street. But what was the story below the headline actually about?

Those persons who read it discovered that the person involved had been arrested for "investigation of drunken driving," and if the reader was persistent enough to get down to the fourth paragraph he found that the "White House Aide" was a "Navy enlisted man attached to the White House Communications Agency. A specialist in walkie-talkie and other mobile communication, he was assigned to check radio contacts in the Lancaster area when apprehended."

This story and headline combination appeared at the time the Watergate investigations were very much in the news. Did the headline writer choose his words only because in his judgment they fairly reflected the thrust of the story? Or was he reinforcing a viewpoint—perhaps his own—that was prevalent among media people at the time?

Some years earlier, when the Vietnam fighting was still underway, some newspapers took strongly antiwar positions. A large number of staff members of other newspapers also were opposed to the war, even though the papers had not taken an editorial stand. Sometimes those staff members who were on copy desks took advantage of their gatekeeper leverage to "hype" wire service stories that were susceptible to such treatment. One headline of the time:

Giant Bombers Pound Antiaircraft Positions

And the lead on the story read:

SAIGON—Waves of Air Force B52 bombers swept in to smash Communist antiaircraft positions and supply bunkers just seven miles south of the main headquarters for the Demilitarized Zone (DMZ) defense line at Quang Tri city today . . .

By now what impression does the reader have of the situation? Consider the frame of reference that has been established for him by such phrasing as "Giant Bombers Pound . . ." and "Waves of Air Force B52 bombers. . . ." He can visualize the sky darkened as great fleets of the giant aircraft "pound" the Communist positions.

If the reader goes on through the rest of the story—and bear in mind that a great many newspaper readers do not get beyond the headline and lead, just as many listeners to radio and TV news take in only the first elements—he will find that the "waves" of bombers were two in number, and that in each "wave" there were three aircraft. Six bombers in all.

How much violence, in this instance, was done to the reality by the one-two punch of the reporter and the headline writer involved in producing the final version that was put before the reader? What were the motivations behind the reshaping of the news?

"Framed" News

In several of the instances involving headlines the accompanying discussion raised questions about motivation, and about the assumptions with

127

which the journalist approached the task of distilling the essence of the news into a tiny snippet of headline space, or into the few seconds of news highlights on the air. This is a point that deserves some further exploration, since it relates to an area in which craft attitudes and ethical considerations are closely intertwined.

Ben H. Bagdikian, one of the most perceptive of contemporary press critics, observed in *The Information Machines* that:

No reader and no local editor could possible review the total available news; the editing down at each step will always occur simply to produce a manageable body of information. But the more limited the capacity of the system, the greater the dependence of the reader on the decisions of unknown men who exercise their crucial function. The decisions on selecting news are made on the basis of mixed motivations—the intense time pressure for fast decisions which makes the quantity of decisons more important than the quality; the social values of the individual and his superiors; the perceived social values of the local editor who buys the service; the perceived social values of the reader to whom the local editor presumably will be sensitive; and, finally, professional judgment of what is important regardless of all the above.

The more restricted the capacity of each link in the process, the greater the chance that the surviving items will be compatible with conventional wisdom, since each gatekeeper in the system is scored on how successfully he guesses the acceptances of his selections by the next decision point. The more severely the incoming items have to be cut to fit the capacity of the next link in the system, the more the system will reject those items that seem to be contrary to prevailing ideas.[19]

What constitutes "conventional wisdom" or "prevailing ideas" within the news-processing organization may be ideological in nature, as seemed to be the situation with some of the headline cases cited. Or it may be something altogether different. It may, for example, be a frame of reference that has been built up by past associations with the personalities or organizations in the news; the reporter or editor then reacts to some new development in terms of earlier developments that have conditioned his thinking, providing the frame through which he sees the latest occurrence.

For example, in 1973 the Long Island, New York, newspaper *Newsday* noted the fact that the death of a coed at Hofstra University had been erroneously reported in two major New York papers as resulting from drug abuse.

The headlines on the death story read:

Hofstra Coed Dies of Drug Overdose
(*New York Times*)

Hofstra Coed, A Diabetic, Found Dead, Apparently of Overdose
(*New York Daily News*)

But the facts were that the girl had not died of a drug overdose, illegal or prescriptive. She had died of heart disease. Why had the reporters for the two New York papers, able newsgatherers, gotten the story wrong?

As *Newsday* writers pieced the situation together, it had developed because just the day before the death of the girl, police had arrested 28 Hofstra students on drug charges. The arrests had nothing to do with the girl's death. But the reporters who were assigned to cover the death story came with a preconceived mental set because of the previous day's events. Then when they questioned university and medical sources at the scene and got somewhat ambiguous responses, they jumped to conclusions that turned out to be unwarranted.[20]

A similar "frame of reference" explanation was among those advanced for the mishandling of the Attica death reports, discussed earlier in this book. The reporters covering that story were aware of an attempted prison break earlier that year in which hostage guards had been slain by inmates, some by throat cutting. So when the first rumors spread in the confusion of the Attica storming, the reporters were mentally ready to credit the reports and forward them on as unattributed fact.

Terry Ann Knopf, a research associate at the Lemberg Center for the Study of Violence at Brandeis University, made a detailed study of the ways in which mental sets and frames of reference can result in a wrenching of the reality of the news.

One case she explored was set in York, Pennsylvania, where in the summer of 1968 there were instances of racial unrest; bottle throwing and other disturbances had been reported. Then a wire service stringer was asked by his head office to get a picture to illustrate some of the copy being filed from York. A photographer got a photo of a motor-cyclist with an ammunition belt around his waist and a rifle strapped across his back. A small object dangled from the rifle. When the picture appeared in the *Washington Post* it was above this caption:

ARMED RIDER—Unidentified motorcyclist drives through heart of York, Pa., Negro district, which was quiet for the first time in six days of sporadic disorders.

The same picture also was used by the *Baltimore Sun*, with a somewhat different caption:

QUIET, BUT . . . An unidentified motorcycle rider, armed with a rifle and carrying a belt of ammunition, was among those in the heart of York, Pa., Negro district last night. The area was quiet for the first time in six days.

Now let Terry Knopf pick up the situation:

The implication of this photograph was clear: The "armed rider" was a sniper. But since when do snipers travel openly in daylight completely armed? Also, isn't there something incongruous about photographing a sniper, presumably "on his way to work," when according to the caption the city "was quiet?" Actually, the "armed rider" was a sixteen-year-old boy who happened to be fond of hunting groundhogs—a skill he had learned as a small boy from his father. On July 16, as was his custom, the young man had put on his ammo belt and strapped a rifle across his back, letting a hunting license dangle so that all would know he was hunting animals, not people. Off he went on his motorcycle headed for the woods, the fields, the groundhogs—and the place reserved for him in the nation's press.[21]

Miss Knopf notes also another case, at a time when student disturbances on university campuses around the country were almost weekly occurrences. An AP man in Dallas filed a story on a student takeover at Southern Methodist University. The *Fort Worth Star-Telegram* put the story on the front page and gave it a banner headline:

130

Blacks Seize Office of S.M.U.'s President
Police Are Called to Stand By

And the story itself read:

DALLAS (AP)—Black students with some support from whites took over the office of the president of Southern Methodist University today and swore to remain until their demands are met. . . .

Reports from the scene said from thirty to thirty-five students were in control of [President] Tate's office.

The takeover occurred during a meeting of Tate and a campus organization, the Black League of Afro-American and African College Students. . . .

Miss Knopf comments:

The story had one major flaw—it wasn't true. While about thirty-five students had met with the university president, they were not "in control" of his office; nor had they "swore (sic) to remain" until their demands were met. No such "takeover" had occurred. . . . Apparently the wire service reporter had accepted the many rumors of a student takeover. . . .

Even when the reporters did not use the scare terms in their copy during that period, copy desk headline writers sometimes added them automatically, conditioned to regard any development on a university campus as one involving disorder. A story appeared in the *Boston Globe* about then, reporting a rally by a small group of students at a theological seminary, a "peaceful and orderly" gathering, according to the story. But the headline above the story read:

Newton Campus Erupts

Characteristic of journalists' knee-jerk reaction to kinds of news for which they had already-fashioned frames of reference was the tendency to use stereotypical terminology. Miss Knopf's studies indicated that "Value-laden words receive unusual emphasis. The participants are 'marauders,' not men; they 'rove' instead of run; they move in 'gangs,' not groups; they engage in 'vandalism,' not simply violence."

Journalists are far from alone, of course, in reliance on stereotypes. All of us make use of the device in much of our everyday existence, to help fit new acquaintances and new ideas into convenient pigeonholes and sort out the bewildering complexity of life.

But there is a particular pressure on journalists to foster and make use of stereotypical images, not just in political cartoons (where they are an essential stock-in-trade), but in written or oral journalism as well. They constitute a journalistic shorthand, a means whereby to bridge the difficult communication gap between news disseminators and their audiences. They are thus tempting. They are also insidious, destructive of individuality, and sometimes gross distorters of reality.

Richard Harwood of the *Washington Post* reports that when novelist James Michener went to Kent, Ohio, to investigate the shooting deaths of four students by National Guardsmen in the spring of 1970, he encountered some consequences of such distortion:

Some townspeople in Kent, carrying around in their heads certain pictures of "hippies" and how they live, insisted to Michener that the two girls killed on the campus by National Guardsmen were "covered with lice," "on drugs," "pregnant," ridden with syphilis," "tattooed from head to toe." None of these things were literally true, according to the coroner's report, but they were absolutely "true" in the minds of some townspeople because they seemed to fit a stereotype.[22]

Harwood observes that:

. . . the mass media are still full of stereotypes, labels, clichés and code words that confuse or mislead more than they inform. We still write about "hippies"

132

and "hard hats" as if they were scientifically delineated species of mankind. We still talk about "suburbia" and "ghettos" as if these geographical concepts had assembly-line characteristics. We still discourse on the "middle class," the "military-industrial complex," "the poor," and the "Eastern establishment" as if, like bottles of milk, they are homogenous entities. We still hang on our politicians empty labels such as "liberal," "conservative," "hawk" and "dove" as if we—and the audience out there— had some clear idea of what information these labels are intended to convey. . . .

Newspapers can do better than that. They can use language with more precision. They can develop better definitions of "news." They can recognize diversity. . . . Above all, they can ignore the labels and stereotypes that are hung on people and things and seek out the reality of the human condition.[23]

Harwood is of course correct. The newspapers, and all the other media of mass communication, can do better than they have been doing with respect to reliance upon the shorthand of stereotypical communication. But if they do, it will be an upstream struggle. All the pressures, all the conventions built into the business of gathering, packaging, and swiftly passing on to the consuming public a reasonably recognizable picture of reality, tend to nudge the journalist toward reliance on the shortcut description, the pigeonhole term, the dehumanizing stereotype. Walter Lippmann wrote about the problem in the 1920s, in *Public Opinion*, and so did Plato when he talked of the flickering shadows on the cave wall as man's chief basis for judging what was going on in the world outside.

"Happy" News

Let's shift to another area of journalism to consider one more form of built-in problem that bears upon the effectiveness with which journalists are able to do their job in a responsible and ethical fashion.

This is a condition particularly notable in the electronic media, and it stems from the origins of these media as entertainment-oriented agencies of communication.

News was very early a part of the program mix, first on radio and then carried over to television. But initially it was typically a subordinate element. Announcers picked up stories from the local newspaper and read them or condensed them for use on the air. Later, as the electronic news programs developed their own character, newsmen from the

133

print media were brought on board to gather local news for broadcast, and the wire services developed specially tailored reports of national and international happenings.

Many of the concepts of objective reporting which were dominant in the print media during the formative years of radio were brought over to the new medium, and later were reflected in early television news as well.

But in recent years, with growing recognition that broadcast news was gaining in audience favor and becoming as marketable an item in the programming mix as soap operas or sports, some changes have been introduced. And these changes have their roots in the entertainment function that has always been the primary concern of the broadcast media.

Richard Townley, news director of KWTV in Oklahoma City, describes the trend:

They call him Billy Blue Collar. He never went to college, has never been on an airplane, has never seen a copy of The New York *Times*. He rarely reads anything, in fact. And for the most part he ignores television news. Yet, in an official policy memo at KPMB-TV in San Diego, and in a growing number of other TV newsrooms across the nation, he is the accepted stereotype of the average television news viewer. And his tastes and preferences are having a profound influence on the kinds of news programs you are watching on television.

In cities from Philadelphia to Oakland broadcasters are designing news programs to attract Billy Blue Collar and other audience prototypes discovered through motivational research and sophisticated surveys. And what the viewer often ends up with is a slick, breezy news show, dispensing glib headlines, sock action films and orchestrated "spontaneity"—newscasts, as one critic says, "for people who can't stand television news."

Their creators operate on the premise that news programs—like everything else on TV—can be merchandised, packaged to appeal to the "massest" mass audiences. After all, they reason, broadcasters are licensed to give the public what it wants. But a good many TV newsmen see the rapid spread of action-oriented "happy-talk" formats as a menace—a danger to TV news' integrity, a hindrance to public understanding of complex issues and a threat to many newsmen's jobs.[24]

The spread of the new approach of action and happy talk is fostered by consultant firms that specialize in pepping-up the programming of a station low in the audience ratings that are life and death in broadcasting.

One of the leading consultant firms is Frank N. Magid Associates, with a staff of 85 "action-oriented, commercially aware" researchers and advisers. A team from such a consulting firm will come into a community, analyze the appeal of the anchormen and news program format being used by the faltering station, and then suggest changes. The changes are usually very similar to ones already found to have been successful elsewhere—more news stories per program block, shorter stories, lots of visual action, and of course the breezy "happy talk."

The consultants' recommendations *do* produce results; the stations that follow the pattern see their ratings rise, and those that stick with the traditional approach of a comprehensive, balanced report suffer. As one consultant told a meeting of broadcast educators: "The country is filled with stations that have . . . gone down in absolute flames to a station that comes on with a contemporary style of presentation."[25]

That contemporary style is distinguished to the casual observer chiefly by the informality and the emphasis on personalities. Two *Columbia Journalism Review* writers, Byron Shafer and Richard Larson, catch the spirit well:

The Eyewitness News ("just folks") approach is the clearest example. Local anchormen may now show their displeasure at the day's report, or kid it into insignificance. ("Well, John, 150 women and children were found dead at Ban Dahn Hee today." "Was that Bin Din Haa, Barry?" "Come on, John; give me a break." "Ha. Ha.") . . . Anchormen camp across news ads in Wyatt Earp garb (e.g., Channel 7, San Francisco) or pose as "Newshounds" in large, Muppet-like dogs' heads (Channel 4, San Francisco.)[26]

Weather and sports segments of the news report get the ham-it-up treatment with a vengeance. Weathermen with far-out accents, or weather girls in skimpy costumes, vie for honors in devising new gimmicks to serve as vehicles for purveying the day's statistics and the morrow's forecast.

But the happy talk aspect of the new programming pattern, distinctive as it is, may not be the most disturbing dimension of the trend.

The consultants almost invariably recommend that more and briefer stories be crammed into the newscast time block. They insist that no story should run longer than 90 seconds, and that the goal ought to be to handle from 18 to 20 stories in a typical 27-to-30-minute newscast period.

As news director Townley observes:

. . . If a program crams in 20 stories instead of the usual 10, something's got to give. Especially since more time now is taken with chatty interplay and feature material. A California news director worries that his consultant's influence has "subtly caused us to change the coverage of some important stories." Where he once sent a reporter to spend the morning covering the city council, that's no longer done because of the demands of a high story count. Besides, official meetings are mostly talking heads. The restrictions, he confesses, "make it difficult to cover stories about ideas which just do not have visual possibilities."[27]

Underlying the rationale for the new format is the assumption that the broadcaster ought to be giving the viewer what he or she *wants* to know about, not what *ought* to be reported in order to give the public the information it needs in order to make effective decisions in a democratic system. This is clearly in harmony with the philosophy of programming elsewhere in broadcasting; the audience ratings, theoretically signaling what the public wants, are the final arbiter for entertainment segments. So why not, reason the consultants, use what works elsewhere in the broadcast mix as a guide to making the news programs into hits?

It is a line that a good many stations in the mid-1970s were buying —and finding profitable. But at what cost to the central journalistic ethic of reporting the news fully and fairly—all kinds of news, not just "happy talk" and weather?

One old-line newsman, Walter Cronkite, one of the most respected figures in the history of broadcast journalism, thinks the cost is too great:

We newsmen are not jugglers, dancers, ventriloquists, singers or actors seeking applause. We are not in the business of winning popularity contests. It is not our job to entertain, nor, indeed to please anyone except Diogenes.

Unfortunately, we have seen lately the growth of "happy news time" on some stations, promoted by managements willing to sell their journalistic responsibility for a few fickle Nielson points. . . .

To seek the public's favor by presenting the news it wants to hear, is to fail to understand the function of broadcast news in a democracy.

Radio and television journalists and enlightened executives have spent 35 years convincing the public that broadcast news is not part of the entertainment industry. It is a shame that some would endanger that reputation now.[28]

One Los Angeles newscaster put it less eloquently but more succinctly: "The question is, are we in show biz or the news biz? Today it looks more and more like we're in show biz."[29]

136

Stolen News

Let's turn now to look into a somewhat different sort of built-in problem involving ethical considerations.

This has to do with what the posture of a journalist ought to be toward stolen goods—specifically news or information taken from private files or government archives without authorization and then fed to the news media.

It should be noted that this is a different question from that posed by other kinds of thievery of news cited in an earlier chapter in this book. In those earlier instances, characteristic of the days of anything-goes competition, reporters stole pictures from the homes of persons who had just died, bribed or dissembled their way into situations where they could overhear private conversations, and in other ways acquired various kinds of stolen news. Such tactics are now generally discredited and understood to be beyond the ethical pale.

It is not so simple, however, to make a quick ruling on cases involving reporters who have come into possession of facts or documents taken from confidential government files, and which constitute news of major significance. This can happen at various levels, but perhaps the classic case to use as a vehicle for exploring the problem is the publication of the Pentagon Papers in the *New York Times* and several other national publications.

The famed papers were a set of analyses prepared by Pentagon officials at the direction of then Defense Secretary Robert McNamara. He wanted to get down a comprehensive account of the ways in which this country first became embroiled in the Southeast Asia fighting and then later escalated that involvement more and more disastrously. Once compiled, the analyses remained in Top Secret files in the Pentagon.

But one of the analysts who had prepared the studies, Daniel Ellsberg, had made and kept an unauthorized copy of the papers, and in early 1971 he decided to turn them over to the *New York Times* so that they would be published and the entire American public would have the benefit of the analysis of "How we got there."

As the matter later developed, the federal government sought to prevent the publication of the papers through court injunction, precipitating one of the most momentous press-government confrontations in American history. That, however, is a First Amendment question, and has nothing to do with ethics. So let's put that aspect of the Pentagon Papers case aside and focus only on the much narrower issue of the ethical questions that may have been involved in the decision to accept the stolen documents for publication. (An excellent exploration of the press freedom aspects of the case may be found in the September/ October 1971 issue of *Columbia Journalism Review*, which is devoted entirely to the Pentagon Papers episode.)

It has already been suggested in this volume (by reference to disapproving mention of the stealing of photographs and the like) that it is less than ethical to traffic in stolen goods, whether journalistic or not. A reporter who appropriated a competitor's notes and used them to write his own story would get more condemnation than plaudits for his enterprise.

What, then, is there to be said about the fact that the *New York Times*, the *Washington Post*, the *Boston Globe*, and the *St. Louis Post-Dispatch* served, in effect, as fences for Dr. Ellsberg's stolen property? Is there a difference between this celebrated case and simpler, less consequential ones?

As the various editors who made the decision to accept and publish the Pentagon Papers saw it, there was indeed a difference. Many of them agonized over the decision, yet came to it in the end on the ground that the matters dealt with in the papers involved historic developments of enormous consequences to a whole generation of Americans.

The public, these editors felt, had a legitimate right to know how and why our nation had become so fatally enmeshed in the long, ugly struggle in what had been Indochina. More than 55,000 Americans had died in the fighting, tens of billions of dollars had been expended, and the nation had been riven by dissension stemming from the war. As A. M. Rosenthal, managing editor of the *New York Times*, later put it:

We are dealing with decisions made in government that affect the people. Can you steal a decision that was made three years ago and that has caused consequences that a country now pays for, good or bad? How can you steal a decision like that? How can you steal the mental processes of elected officials or appointed officials? . . .

It just seemed to us that this information was essential to understanding the course of the war and decision-making in the U.S. Government, and we had no right not to print it. How could we say to ourselves that we have this information, which we do not consider classified, not bearing on military security; it is a treasure house of, not secrets, but insights into the process of government; and then say, sorry, we'll keep it to ourselves. That is not what the American press is all about.[30]

But the issue was not seen so simply by others, including the Chief Justice of the United States, Warren Burger, who observed in his opinion on the case:

To me it is hardly believable that a newspaper long regarded as a great institution in American life would fail to perform one of the basic and simple duties of every citizen with respect to the discovery or possession of stolen property or secret government documents. That duty, I had thought—perhaps naively—was to report forthwith, to responsible public officers.
This duty rests on taxi drivers, Justices, and the New York *Times*.[31]

Was the decision to accept the stolen goods and publish them, taken first by the *Times* and then by the other newspapers, one by one, an ethically defensible one?

Certainly the matters at stake were momentous. That was the basic defense mounted by editors and spokesmen for the press: that the importance of the material involved was sufficient justification for a course of action that might otherwise not have been followed.

Some critics were quick to point out that the *Times* and other papers had taken a wholly different position on an instance that had taken place some years earlier. The then Senator Joseph R. McCarthy (R–Wisconsin) had been probing into alleged communist infiltration in the federal government. In the course of his investigations, he had obtained and made public some material stolen from the files of a government agency. The *Times* and other papers condemned the senator in harsh terms for using such stolen material and applauded efforts by the executive branch of government to prevent further thefts.

The *Times* editors would seem to have applied a double standard of sorts in the cases. Presumably they would argue that McCarthy had been pursuing a personal, headline-grabbing vendetta, and using the stolen papers to destroy others' reputations, while in the Pentagon Papers case the editors were acting in the public interest. But if you shake all that down to its essentials it strongly resembles an "end justifies the means" argument. Philosophers, moralists, logicians, and theologians have never had much regard for that line of reasoning, although it has always had at least some supporters in their ranks.

Moreover, there is one disquieting footnote to the *Times*'s handling of the Pentagon Papers case which must be considered since the context of our discussion is an ethical one. Edward Jay Epstein has pointed out that:

139

But even in the rare cases in which newspapers allot time and manpower to study a leak, as the New York *Times* did in the case of the Pentagon Papers, the information still must be revised into a form and format which will maintain the interest of the readers (as well as the editors). Since the *Times* decided not to print the entire study of the Vietnam war—which ran to more than 7,000 pages and covered a 25-year period—or even substantial parts of the narrative, which was complex and academic, sections of the material had to be reorganized and rewritten along a theme that would be comprehensible to its audience.

The theme chosen was duplicity; the difference between what the leaders of America said about the Vietnam War in private and in public. The Pentagon study, however, was not written in line with this theme. It was an official Department of Defense analysis of decision-making and, more precisely, of how policy preferences crystallized within the department.

To convert this bureaucratic study into a journalistic exposé of duplicity required taking certain liberties with the original history. Outside material had to be added, and assertions from the actual study had to be omitted.

For example, to show that the Tonkin Gulf resolution (by which in effect Congress authorized the escalation of the war, and which was editorially endorsed at the time by most major newspapers, including the New York *Times* and the Washington *Post*) resulted from duplicity, the *Times* had to omit the conclusion of the Pentagon Papers that the Johnson Administration had tried to avoid the fatal clash in the Tonkin Gulf, and had to add evidence of possible American provocations in Laos, which were not actually referred to in the Pentagon Papers themselves.[32]

This analysis by press critic Epstein, admittedly written some years after the fact, may be compared with a comment made by *Times* managing editor Rosenthal shortly after the publication of the documents:

The decisions were not taken lightly. We had long discussions among editors and reporters about how we would present the material. A key decision was that we were going to tell the Pentagon story of the study. Our story was the Pentagon study—and the supporting documents—not the New York *Times* story of the war as pieced together from these sources plus others.[33]

So the decision to use the stolen Pentagon Papers, with its momentous implications and far-reaching consequences, was another of the difficult, ambiguous, unclear challenges that confront journalists at all levels, all of the time. In this case, great matters of history and national policy were involved; most of the time the stakes are less significant. But the ethical calls are nonetheless agonizing ones to make, and not always can the journalist be sure that the decision taken can be fully supported.

Nor can he be sure where the decision may be taking him in the long run, as was suggested by an episode that occurred several years after the Pentagon Papers case.

This was an ironic sidelight to the long months of press coverage of the Watergate scandals, which turned so very importantly on the surreptitious wiretaps that President Nixon had made of his Oval Office conversations. The press generally had been righteously indignant about the wiretaps, the secret surveillance, the "dirty tricks," and other trappings of the spy trade which were characteristic of the Watergate exposures.

Yet in mid-1974, while the Watergate skein was still unraveling, two reporters from the respected *Louisville Courier-Journal* were arrested while eavesdropping on a closed meeting of the Louisville Fraternal Order of Police (as a final ironic twist, the eavesdropping took place in a motel—not a Howard Johnson's, however). The two reporters were caught in a room adjoining the meeting room, lying on the floor with a tape recorder.

The publisher of the *Courier-Journal* said that, while he considered eavesdropping "morally wrong," he defended the two reporters because they were "exhibiting the vigorous enterprise and competitive spirit that is not only an unalterable policy of these newspapers but also a standard of excellence in journalism."[34]

Well . . . um . . . (unintelligible). . . .

Notes

[1]"Ethics of Journalism in a Century of Change," *Nieman Reports*, XXII, No. 2 (June 1968), 12–15.

[2]This and following references to the Hartley testimony are from *Of the press, by the press, for the press (And others, too)*, ed. Laura Longley Babb, (Washington: The Washington Post Company, 1974), pp. 16–17.

[3]"Two Faces of Journalism," *Columbia Journalism Review*, XI, No. 3 (September/October 1972), 3–4.

[4]Babb, *Of the press, by the press, for the press*, p. 9.

[5]Edward Jay Epstein, "The Panthers and the Police: A Pattern of Genocide?" *New Yorker*, XLVI, No. 52 (February 13, 1971), 45–77.

[6]"Ending an Acceptable Myth," *Columbia Journalism Review*, X, No. 1 (May/June 1971), 3–4.

[7]Robert J. Samuelson, "Let Them Eat Dog Food?" *Columbia Journalism Review*, XIII, No. 3 (September/October 1974), 4–8.

8Ralph Z. Hallow, "Pittsburgh's Ephemeral 'riot'," reprinted from the *Columbia Journalism Review*, X, No. 5 (January/February 1972), © 34–40.

9*Ibid.*, p. 35.

10*Ibid.*, pp.35–38.

11*Ibid.*, p. 40.

12Quoted in Edward Jay Epstein, *News from Nowhere* (New York: Random House, Inc., 1973), pp. 4–5. Copyright © Random House, Inc. Excerpted by permission of Random House.

13Epstein, *ibid.*, pp. 32–33.

14Quoted in Richard Harwood, "Can Newsmen Do Better on the Facts?" in *Of the press, by the press, for the press*, pp. 11–13.

15The several references here to the APME study are from Associated Press Managing Editors Association, *1970 Supplement—APME Guidelines* (New York, 1970), pp. 14A–15A.

16Irving Kristol, "Crisis for Journalism: The Missing Elite," in *Press, Politics and Popular Government*, ed. George F. Will (Washington: American Enterprise Institute for Public Policy Research, 1972), p. 47.

17Gilbert Cranberg, "Testing Fairness," *Columbia Journalism Review* XIII, No. 4 (November/December 1974), 56.

18Quoted in "Record" section of the *Quill*, LXII, No. 8 (August 1974), 7.

19Ben H. Bagdikian, *The Information Machines: Their Impact on Men and the Media* (New York: Harper & Row, Publishers, Inc., 1971), pp. 265–66.

20"Credulity," editorial, *Columbia Journalism Review*, XXI, No. 1 (May/June, 1973), 3.

21Terry Ann Knopf, "Media Myths on Violence," reprinted from the *Columbia Journalism Review* IX, No. 1 (Spring, 1970), © 17–23.

22Richard Harwood, "Putting People into Pigeonholes," in *Of the press, by the press, for the press*, pp. 21–23.

23*Ibid.*, pp. 22–23.

24Richard Townley, "The News Merchants," *TV Guide*, XXII, No. 10 (March 9, 1974), 6–11. Excerpted with permission from *TV Guide®* Magazine. Copyright © 1974 by Triangle Publications, Inc., Radnor, Pennsylvania.

25*Ibid.*, p. 10.

26Byron Shafer and Richard Larson, "Did TV Create the 'Social Issue'?", *Columbia Journalism Review*, XI, No. 3 (September/October 1972), 10–17.

27Townley, "The News Merchants," p. 11.

28Walter Cronkite, "The State of the Press," The *Quill*, LXI, No. 6 (June 1973), 37–40. (The *Quill* is published by the Society for Professional Journalists, Sigma Delta Chi.)

29Quoted in "The News Doctors," *Newsweek*, LXXXIV, No. 22 (November 25, 1974), 87.

30A. M. Rosenthal "Why We Published," *Columbia Journalism Review*, X, No. 3 (September/October 1971), 16–21.

31Quoted in Ben H. Bagdikian, "What Did We Learn?", reprinted from the *Columbia Journalism Review*, X, No. 3 (September/October 1971), © 45–50. Copyright 1971 by Ben H. Bagdikian. Quoted by permission of the Sterling Lord Agency.

32Edward Jay Epstein, *Between Fact and Fiction: The Problem of Journalism* (New York: Vintage Book Division of Random House, Inc., 1975) 15-16. © by Random House, Inc., and quoted by permission. This excerpt first appeared in an article in *Commentary*.

33Rosenthal, "Why We Published," p. 16.

34Peter Chew, "Press 'Enterprise' Brings a Wire-Tap Charge," *National Observer*, week ending May 25, 1974, p. 14.

Through the Side Door...

"The American press is afflicted with the country club mind. It doesn't make much difference how much of a crusading Galahad a young publisher may be when he starts; by the time he begins to put his paper across he is taken up by the country club crowd, and when that happens he is lost. He joins the country club, for that is our American badge of success. And before he knows it, he sees his community from the perspective of the country club porch, and he edits his paper to please the men who gather with him in the country club locker room." — William Allen White[1]

8 Not all of the situations that put journalists to the ethical test crop up in the reporter-source relationship, or arise out of conditions peculiar to the craft. Some may be the result of pressures that are applied subtly and indirectly from outside, or from within the news-gathering organization itself—usually from the direction of the offices of the publisher or the advertising director.

When William Allen White of the *Emporia* (Kans.) *Gazette,* wrote his pessimistic prediction about the country club syndrome, some segments of the newspaper industry were in the big business category. Today *most* daily newspapers, television stations, mass circulation magazines, the broadcasting networks—both radio and television—and some individual radio properties are very definitely classifiable as big business.

Many of the major media properties are owned by industrial conglomerates with a wide range of other interests from banking to chemicals. And, increasingly, the ownership of the channels of communication is being concentrated into fewer and fewer hands as chains and groups grow and merge with each other.

These trends have a tendency to accentuate the kind of attitudinal alteration that White was talking about. Ownership may not only begin to reflect the values of the "country club crowd" but also those of true Big Business—the vast, interlocking corporate structures that sprawl across the nation, or the world.

Now it should be made very clear at this point that the concentration of ownership, or even conglomerate takeover, doesn't *invariably* or *inevitably* convert the media managers into "profits-first" types. Many present-day publishers and owners are thoroughly conscious of the social responsibility they must shoulder. Moreover, the growing professionalism of the men and women who staff the mass media constitutes a force that is resistant to the compromise of standards in accommodation to the interests of conglomerate or corporate ownership.

Yet, when these qualifications have been entered on the record, it is necessary to add that there does exist an array of evidence of various kinds to suggest that the basic ethic of the news media is being perverted in numerous ways—sometimes in obvious ways, sometimes in only half-visible ones—because of pressures that are generated by ownership or by the friends and associates of ownership.

When such pressures prevent the journalist from adhering to the professional standards he believes are binding, he can protest, resist, even resign—and many have done all three. But personal and family obligations, the difficulty of locating another job, or a weary conviction that it wouldn't do any good in any event prevent others from putting their careers on the line in defense of journalistic ethics.

Without attempting to inventory all of the kinds of side-door pressures that can pose ethical challenges for journalists, let's look at a representative sampling of cases and comments in order to get a clear understanding of the nature and dimensions of the problem.

Where the Money Comes From

It is commonplace today to assert that large newspapers are relatively immune from direct advertiser pressure, and that this sort of thing now rarely occurs; this is a thesis expressed in most introductory mass media texts, and it is based on sound reasoning. After all, as was noted in an earlier chapter, virtually all daily newspapers are in a semimonopoly situation; in very few communities does any true, head-to-head print competition between different ownerships survive. An advertiser theoretically shouldn't be able to bring off a squeeze play, since he needs the advertising medium represented by the daily newspaper more than the paper needs any single advertiser. Or so the thesis goes. And cases can be cited in which advertiser power plays were successfully resisted by individual papers. But there are other cases to be cited as well.

The *Wall Street Journal*, whose reporters periodically present some of the most penetrating analyses of newspaper practices to be found anywhere, documented an embarrassing instance involving the respected *Denver Post.*

A reporter for another paper somehow came into possession of an internal memo from one *Post* executive to another detailing an arrangement whereby the newspaper had agreed to run 1,820 column inches of free publicity about a new shopping center because the shopping center had bought and paid for 30 pages of advertising. Nor was this the only instance of such cozy *quid pro quo* arrangements; the *Post* had also promised a block of free space to another advertiser, and the news staff was complaining that there was no more to say about them "short of repetition," even though the promised quota of puffery was far from filled.[2]

More often, of course, the pressure is not applied so openly or so brutally, and the puffery is at least partially veiled. According to the *Journal* writers, the *Dallas Times Herald* used to print each Monday from 2½ to 3 pages of what was described as commercial, business, and industrial news of Dallas. Actually, the news space assigned to a given company was carefully calculated to reflect the amount of advertising space the company had been buying in the paper.

And, as Carl E. Lindstrom, a former editor of the *Hartford* (Conn.) *Times* once wrote:

Would there be travel pages if travel agencies and airlines didn't advertise? Would there be recipes in the paper if food advertisers didn't come in with a bang on Thursday afternoon and Friday morning? Would there be a stamp column or a dog column if there were no related revenue?[3]

In the broadcast media the influence of advertisers on the content of entertainment programs has been pervasive and traditional. News departments on radio and television, by contrast, have attempted to shield themselves from similar pressures. They have not, however, in all cases been successful. Fred W. Friendly recounted in his book *Due to Circumstances Beyond Our Control*[4] how pressures generated by advertisers affected the nature and content of news and documentary shows under his direction at CBS. The experience of newsmen at other networks has been similar.

As John C. Merrill and Ralph L. Lowenstein point out in an overview book of the media, the influence of advertisers on the content of broadcasting is not necessarily overt and direct:

Sponsors do not often act in a positive manner to deliberately censor programming material, as is commonly thought. Rather their influence on the total programming picture is *negative*. Their reluctance to sponsor a program that is either controversial or likely to attract a small audience assures that such programs will not be shown frequently.[5]

Still, there are cases in which television advertisers have been known to bring a more direct pressure to bear to prevent, say, mention of a competitor on a sponsored news show.

And others have been successful in efforts to prevent a negative reference to their company or their product from getting attention on broadcast news programs. Robert Cirino recounts how representatives of Coca-Cola were given an opportunity to preview a documentary depicting the plight of migrant workers; Coca-Cola was one of the companies depicted as profiting from the work of migrants in Florida. When the company representatives had viewed the film, they asked the president

146

of NBC to meet with them before the film was shown, in order to consider some cuts in the film that would have the effect of softening the impact on Coca-Cola. The meeting was held and some, at least, of the requested cuts were made before the documentary went on the air.[6]

How Many Hats?

Another form of awkward internal pressure peculiar to the broadcasting news field is the prevalent practice of requiring announcers on news programs to serve also as voices for commercials.

Some of the top network anchormen refuse to switch hats, and because of their stature they can get away with it. But as we noted in the last chapter in another connection, less prominent newsmen can find themselves in cowboy costumes (or dog's heads) to push a product or a program when they are not busy intoning the latest bulletins.

In a speech to radio news executives in 1970, Walter Cronkite spoke with feeling for his fellow newsmen:

Reliability is a handmaiden to integrity and I fear that many of us are not as careful as we might be to keep our escutcheons unbesmirched. It is beyond me to understand how anyone can believe in, foster, support, or force a newsman to read commericals. This is blasphemy of the worst form. A newsman is nothing if not believable. And how can he be believed when he delivers a news item if in the next breath he lends his face, his voice and his name to extolling in words the public knows he never wrote a product or service that the public knows he probably never has tested? When a newsman delivers a commercial he puts his reputation for honesty in the hands of an advertising copy writer and a client whose veracity is sorely tried by the need to make a buck. It is difficult if not impossible for the individual newsman who wants to protect his family to stand up to a management that demands that he indulge in this infamously degrading and destructive practice.[7]

On the small-market radio or TV station, Cronkite's depiction of the vulnerability of the newscaster who is asked to double as huckster certainly does apply. The trend to the "happy talk" format, with the chummy interchanges sliding almost imperceptibly from the news to the commercial messages, poses the problem in an even more insistent form for the newscaster.

Yet the growing importance of news on the electronic media, and the discovery through surveys that increasing numbers of Americans are dependent upon these media for most of the news that they receive in a given day, ought eventually to strengthen the hand of the newscaster and give him better leverage with which to insist that his role as reporter not be confused with the different job (certainly respectable enough in itself) of the salesman.

Some broadcast newsmen have adhered to Cronkite's philosophy and have refused to do the double-hat routine even though their stand has cost them lucrative opportunities.

When Frank McGee, co-host and news anchorman for NBC's morning "Today" show, died in April 1974, there followed a search for the right man to fill the prized post with its $350,000-a-year salary. The network finally narrowed down the list to eight, but then discovered that several of the best prospects balked at the requirement that they would have to read commercials as well as serve as host and newscaster. One of them, Garrick Utley, said: "I question whether a reporter does not lose his journalistic virginity by doing commercials. And can you recover that virginity later?"

Another, who had appeared to be the most promising of the finalists in the tryout sessions on the show, was Tom Brokaw, NBC's White House correspondent at the time. He said flatly: "I find doing commercials repulsive. If that is a job requirement, it would not be negotiable with me."

Both stuck to their principles and did not take over the McGee role, but the network did find someone who would. The stakes were high, since the "Today" show was drawing about five million viewers each morning and reportedly made $10,000,000 a year for the network. For Utley and Brokaw, however, and for many others who have had to face similar decisions with less momentous financial consequences, the ethical value involved was more important than the network's profit margin—*or* the impressive salary.[8]

By the Bushel

Not all of the pressures that impinge on the journalist from advertiser or outside corporate institutions come in the form of direct power plays or through the side door of management influence. Many of them arrive courtesy of Uncle Sam.

Every newspaper city desk, every electronic newsroom, is daily deluged with vast quantities of public relations releases of various kinds. Every corporation of any size, most government agencies, trade associations, even civic groups and educational institutions, employ skilled staffs to prepare "news" stories to be sent to the various media outlets—all of them designed to result, if possible, in the publication or broadcast of an item that will depict the sending agency in a favorable light before the public.

Much of this expensively prepared material goes directly into the wastebasket, but a very large amount of it gets into print or on to the air in some form. Press critic Ben H. Bagdikian has estimated that if one were to trace down the origins of all the news items in the columns of a daily newspaper of substantial size, it could be demonstrated that up to 60 percent of the material started out as some kind of release from the news source itself.

It is obvious, of course, that most of the material put out by a public relations officer on behalf of his company or organization is going to include an element of self-interest, sometimes blatant, sometimes subtle. But it is also true that much of that volume of paper that flows over the transom each day also contains kernels of news that the newspaper or broadcasting station might not otherwise come upon.

So the welter must be gone through, and the solid substance of news sifted out and fed into the media. If the job is done conscientiously, the self-serving spin put on the releases by the public relations authors will be removed, and the genuine news will remain. The careless, hurried, or cynical desk man will "railroad" the copy through without bothering to work it over—and as a result the reader, listener, or viewer is exposed to adulterated news.

The ethical editor suffers a particularly nasty twinge when the public relations copy coming over his desk has an invisible "must run" stamp on its because it in some fashion involves an organization or a cause in which the publisher is known to be intensely interested.

On one small-city daily, for example, all staff members knew that anything involving the Boy Scouts must get special handling, for this was one of the most sacred cows in the publisher's stable and *always* must have tender, loving care—and plenty of news space.

Perhaps no great harm is done if an organization such as the Boy Scouts gets the benefit of some extra puffery. But there are more insidious critters in the sacred cow corral.

Melvin Mencher, a Columbia University professor writing in *Nieman Reports,* notes:

I know now why so many newspapers use acres of newsprint on year-end bank statements; their publishers serve on the boards of directors of the local banks. Perhaps these stories are newsworthy. After all, depositors do want to know the state of health of their banks. But I wonder how many newspapers whose publishers are bank directors will want to examine the mortgage loan policies of banks, which in many urban communities can accelerate the decline of a neighborhood by refusing to grant home improvement loans. This practice, called redlining, is well-known to real estate editors, but it's rarely made the subject of hard-digging journalism.[9]

Let me note again that in at least part of the reams of news releases turned out by public relations offices there is legitimate, significant news to be found. Persons who work in the public relations field are typically highly skilled, often former journalists. They frequently make the point that their efforts save reporters and editors valuable time, both because they dig out hard-to-locate facts and because they do at least part of the job of packaging the information for processing by the news media. These are defensible arguments.

Yet the fact remains that what the public relations man or woman is paid for is to see to it that the best possible version of the news about his or her organization or company gets through the media pipelines. The job of the journalist, if he subscribes to the ethical guidelines of his business, is to report the news without bias, without favor to any organization or cause, exposing the face of reality fully rather than focusing only on the best profile.

There may be times when these two functions coincide. Much of the time they do not. And the flood of public relations material through which desk editors must regularly wade is a wearing test of their principles and their stamina.

Sometimes it would appear that their defenses have indeed been worn down, and the gates left open wide for the public relations people to pour through. One example was chronicled by *Columbia Journalism Review* after its editors had noted a sudden spate of stories and broadcasts by the New York media about the 75th anniversary of the birth of composer George Gershwin—hardly a day of national observance under ordinary circumstances. Among those that voiced tributes, almost in chorus: the *New York Times, Saturday Review/World, Newsweek, Vogue, New York,* NBC's "Today," and public television.

When the *CJR* editors looked into the matter they discovered that the outpouring had been orchestrated by the efforts of Alice Regensburg, staff member of a New York public relations agency, as a device for promoting the sale of a new $25 book about the composer. As Ms. Regensburg put it, "People are hungry for material and if you offer them good, well-planned ideas, they welcome them."[10]

Journalists with a sense of respect for the integrity of their business will welcome legitimate news, yes. But they will firmly shut the gates on blatantly promotional copy, no matter how "good" and "well-planned."

Living-Color P.R.

In recent years public relations experts have discovered new dimensions to their field in the form of the radio or television news release.

Most public relations copy still goes out in the form of paper, handouts printed or mimeographed in handy triple-spaced format so that they can be sent to the composing room or the newscaster with a minimum of editing. But much of that handout material, as was observed earlier, goes into the round file unused. Public relations messages for broadcast, while much more expensive to produce, stand a far better chance of getting through to the ultimate target—the consuming public.

Radio and TV stations at the local level—TV stations in particular —need material to fill out their local news shows. It is expensive to send reporting and camera crews out to get local footage, and many kinds of local stories are unproductive in any case; they result only in "talking-head" interviews with inarticulate city managers or school board members.

Then along comes a lively, colorful, beautifully produced short film about an interesting, topical subject. It's all free, and it can be used anytime. There's even a script with it so that the local announcer can "read over" the film footage to give the impression that the item was produced locally. Somewhere in the film there will be a message subtly promoting the interests of the organization supplying the film; but it usually won't be intrusive. It doesn't have to be. Just a fleeting glimpse of a recognizable product or a brand name in a favorable setting will be enough to justify the very considerable expense that has gone into producing the film.

And the beauty of it, from the standpoint of the public relations people, is that the film is very difficult—by design—for the local station to edit. Whereas the mimeographed handout can be edited so that the commercial overtones are removed, this is all but impossible with the public relations film.

As the features appear, with the local announcer's familiar tones reading the words-over, they all seem to be just parts of the regular news report—during which they typically are run, particularly by the small-market stations hard up for genuine local footage to keep the screen alive.[11]

This living-color credibility has quite understandably caught the attention of a group that classifies as just about the most indefatigable public relations practitioners in any field—the politicians. And the results pose a new set of ethical headaches for the journalists.

Greening the Grassroots

For many years officeholders have been well aware of the advantages of the conventional press release. The oftener a senator or congressman can show up in the pages of the home-district newspapers, or on the newscasts of stations in the area, the better name familiarity there will be among the electorate next time polling day rolls around. Virtually all of the members of the Senate or the House have at least one former journalist on their staffs, and some have several. These aides crank out the press releases with a sure knowledge of style, deadlines, news values, and the names of the right news editors to target.

One Western senator was famous during his incumbency for an expensive but highly effective gambit—not a single working day went by in the offices of the major newspapers of his state that some editor in each of these offices didn't get either a personal letter, a telephone call, or a telegram from the senator. He could be pretty certain that when his press releases came around to these carefully cultivated editors they usually got special treatment.

In recent years, with the growing importance of the electronic media in campaigning, the politicians have turned to radio and television press releases, emulating corporate P. R. That is not to say, of course, that the old-fashioned printed press release has been abandoned. Literally tons of them still go out of legislators' offices in a steady stream. But the same factors that make the TV press release so useful to the corporate public relations men make it attractive to the congressmen.

One of the impressive sights of Washington—and one hardly ever seen by any but insiders—are the television studios maintained for members of the Senate and the House to use in filming "news" footage to be shipped home to key TV stations nestled in the vital grassroots.

These studios have all the most up-to-date equipment—color cameras, tape facilities, and duplicating devices for producing multiple copies of video film or tape. And, according to Ben H. Bagdikian, Washington correspondent for *Columbia Journalism Review*, the cost to a congressman or senator for producing a five-minute color video tape in 25 copies for home-district stations is about one-twentieth to one-tenth of the amount that would be charged by a commercial production unit.

From these studios the films or tapes are shipped off weekly or monthly to the home front, there to be presented in some cases as "reports from our senator (or our congressman)," but in many other instances to be fitted into the regular news shows as though they were the genuine article.

To give these televised press releases as authentic a touch as possible, the legislators are able to select from several official looking "sets." As Bagdikian describes it:

There is a choice of backgrounds for the representative. He can choose a scholarly-looking "library" background with legal-bound books. He can also appear in front of a blue curtain or a carefully contrived photograph of the Capitol as though seen through his office window. Unfortunately, this view of the Capitol is not seen from the office of any senator or representative, either in size or perspective, but it has appeared in thousands of TV shots, implying that the local politician occupies a high-status office overlooking the great dome.

Another background is a special screen on which a slide or movie (provided by the member, not the studio) can be projected, either for a stable background or for action footage that dramatizes the subject the member wishes to discuss.

The other basic set is the "office," with a big congressional desk, the standard black-leather high-backed chair behind it, a desk pen, perhaps the blue and red books, and the choice of backgrounds. . . .

There is one other scene, not exactly a full set. It is a paneled wall with two hooks on it from which may be hung the standard gold-plated nameplate of every standing committee of the House—Agriculture, Appropriations, Armed Services, so on; thus, the member may be photographed as though standing outside a committee room from which he has just emerged to share with his voters the inner secrets and wisdom. . . .

Last year 352 of the 435 members of the House repaired to their studio, most of them every week.[12]

It seems obvious that the home stations that integrate such living-color press releases into their regular news programs without flagging them for what they really are, have failed the ethical litmus test. They also may be helping to magnify the advantages of incumbency to almost unbeatable proportions.

Any incumbent officeholder has an advantage over a challenger, whether the race is for the presidency or the state legislature. He is likely to be better known, more often legitimately in the news, and able to use the platform of his office to generate pseudo-news in the form of releases of various kinds that command at least some attention simply because they come from a current public official.

But the advantages accruing to a member of Congress who has learned how to make the most of his cut-rate private studios for the production of TV news releases far outclass anything previously known in politics, particularly as television assumes more and more significance in campaigning.

As one congressman told a committee on ethics of the New York Bar Association, "A challenger needs $25,000 just to get even with me."

The end result, as Bagdikian points out in his *Columbia Journalism Review* analysis, is that there tends to be less and less turnover in Congress as the firmly entrenched incumbents deluge the home folks with see-it-now evidence of their impressive labors at the Capitol. The struggling challengers have to be extremely well heeled, or extremely well known, before they start, in order to overcome the incumbents' built-in advantages. And so, as Bagdikian writes:

Congressional Quarterly tells us that in the 1870s more than half the members of each session of the House were newly elected, but that by 1900 only a third were first termers and that by 1970 the figure had dropped to 12 per cent. Of 330 incumbents running for re-election in 1972 (the other 135 having retired, died or given up in primaries), only ten incumbents—3 per cent— were defeated.

Obviously, as these figures show, the renewal of the House on the basis of performance and changes in public desires is not working. One important reason is that the news media simply don't tell the folks back home what their member of Congress really does. Worse than that, most of the media are willing conduits for the highly selective information the member of Congress decides to feed the electorate.[13]

As Bagdikian points out, the turnover rate for congressmen has been strikingly higher in districts where voters have access to newspapers or broadcasting stations with their own Washington bureaus. Reporters in such bureaus can keep tabs on what the State's representatives at Washington are really up to, and relay that information to the reader or viewer back home to weigh along with the press-release picture painted by the legislators and reproduced by complaisant local media. But few newspapers and even fewer broadcasting stations can afford full-time Washington bureaus, and the wire service, network, and news magazine bureaus cannot provide individual coverage of senators or congressmen except in very special circumstances; the big bureaus quite naturally concern themselves with the flow of the major news at Washington. The answer, according to Bagdikian, is more pooling of Washington coverage by papers or stations unable to afford their own bureaus, and above all more honesty in the handling of the various forms of press release material—print and broadcast—that come their way.

One Small, Sad Footnote

Before turning from the topic of side-door pressures and the ethical tests these ubiquitous forces impose on journalists in all media, let's note one final item that bears on the subjects that we have been discussing. It pretty much points its own moral, without any exposition or embellishment.

It is taken from the introductory comment to a searching analysis of the press of New England, undertaken in 1973 by newsmen and press observers in the area with financial support from a foundation.

The editor of the survey report, Loren Ghiglione, himself an editor, observed in the prefatory comments:

If the editorial page is the newspaper's soul, then a large number of New England dailies are in danger of going to hell.

At least one-third of the region's dailies occasionally—or almost daily—publish editorials purchased from one of a half-dozen services located outside the region.[14]

These canned editorials are presented in the papers as though they were the home-written opinions of the local editors. And, as Ghiglione points out:

The services produce editorials for hundreds of papers throughout the country. The pieces discuss nonlocal topics and rarely take a stand on anything more controversial than motherhood (pro) and heart disease (con).[15]

And Melvin Mencher, a Columbia University professor who served as one of the evaluators in the New England newspaper survey, adds this:

The Survey gives us a picture of newspapers that will not endorse candidates, will not take a position on controversial local issues, will not permit staffers to write columns. Our inheritors of the tradition of Elijah Lovejoy, William Allen White, and Joseph Pulitzer willingly preside over their own emasculation. But the loss of virility can be profitable. It does keep the newspaper from offending the partisans among its readers. The non-combative editorial page tells readers the newspaper has no axes to grind at a time of public suspicion of the press. . . . Publishers buy up syndicated columnists by the score to make a sufficient din to conceal their quavering voices.

But is this journalism? Is the journalist, to use a phrase of Harvey Swados, "a publicly useful man" when he refuses to put himself on the line?[16]

These comments on editorial page lapses were made with respect to the small-city newspapers of New England, but the practice is by no means characteristic only of that region.

Papers short of manpower—and editors short of ethics—plug up their editorial columns with mislabeled factory-produced editorials or with "safe" columnists in many areas of the country. They represent exceptions rather than the rule, but even so they are too numerous for comfort.

Notes

[1]Quoted in Paul Hutchinson, "What Makes Public Opinion," *Survey Graphic*, XXVIII, (June 1939), 376.

[2]"Conflict of Interest, Pressures Still Distort Some Papers' Coverage," *Wall Street Journal*, July 25, 1967, pp. 1, 10.

[3]Carl E. Lindstrom, *The Fading American Newspaper* (Garden City, N.Y.: Doubleday & Company, Inc., 1960), p. 264.

[4]Fred W. Friendly, *Due to Circumstances Beyond Our Control* (New York: Random House, Inc., 1967).

5John C. Merrill and Ralph L. Lowenstein, *Media, Messages, and Men* (New York: David McKay Co., Inc., 1971), p. 86.

6Robert Cirino, *Power to Persuade: Mass Media and the News* (New York: Bantam Books, Inc., 1974). p. 133.

7Quoted in Irving Dilliard, "Random Thoughts on Press Performance," *Grassroots Editor*, XIII, No. 5 (September/October 1972), 3–7.

8Quoted in "The Great Host Hunt," *Time*, CIV, No. 3 (July 15, 1974), 96.

9Melvin Mencher, "A View from the Inside," *Nieman Reports*, XXVII, No. 4 (Winter, 1973), 6–11.

10"Filling the Gaping Void," *Columbia Journalism Review*, XII, No. 5 (January/ February 1974), 2.

11For a detailed description of how such TV news releases are utilized, see William McAllister, "More Business Firms Provide TV Stations With 'News' on Film," *Wall Street Journal*, February 10, 1972, pp. 1, 10.

12Ben H. Bagdikian, "Congress and the Media: Partners in Propaganda," reprinted from the *Columbia Journalism Review*, XII, No. 5 (January/February 1974), © 3–10. Copyright 1974 by Ben H. Bagdikian. Used by permission of the Sterling Lord Agency.

13*Ibid.*, p. 4.

14Loren Ghiglione, ed., *Evaluating the Press: The New England Daily Newspaper Survey* (Southbridge, Mass., published by the editor, 1973), p. 10.

15*Ibid.*, p. 8.

16Melvin Mencher, "A View from the Inside," pp. 6–11.

Saying It with Pictures...

"The news camera . . . is responsible for more public dismay and resentment than any other newspaper tool or technique."
—Carl E. Lindstrom[1]

9 The ratio may not be precisely 1 to 10,000, but there is no denying that pictures have more immediate impact than do words in a great many circumstances. And because they do, their use in the mass media—whether as still shots in the newspapers and magazines or as film or video tape on television—gives rise to a variety of perplexing and painful dilemmas for journalists.

Pictures engage the emotions of the viewer, draw him into the news situation being depicted, and let him share in a vicarious but vivid sense the excitement, the tragedy, or the exultation being experienced by the persons caught up in the news.

Pictures thus are newsworthy, by any definition you choose to apply. They are also capable of causing agony and embarrassment for the subjects or those who are the close associates of the subjects.

The journalist knows well that pictures attract readers or viewers, that by all the yardsticks they are heavily infused with human interest appeal, the most sure-fire ingredient of newsworthiness. But the journalist knows also that pictures can inflict lasting pain in various ways; and the ethical standards of the field impose an obligation to consider the sensitivities of individuals as well as the larger need of society to be informed.

The photographers, cameramen, and editors are caught uncomfortably in the middle. Decisions with ethical overtones are forced on them constantly.

Consider, for example, one of the commonest photographic topics in the flow of the news—scenes of tragedy and grief. They are on every day's picture agenda of the wire services or the television cameramen: auto accident scenes, fires, murder sites—often with the sheeted victim in the foreground. Readership surveys indicate again and again that readers linger over such pictures while ignoring many other aspects of the newspaper; these dramatic glimpses arrest the passing eye.

But the journalist always has to weigh—or, rather, he *ought* to weigh—whether the obvious newsworthiness in such pictures justifies their use when other implications are also considered. Does the picture represent a gross, unseemly intrusion on a private moment of wrenching grief—and is that why it so catches the viewer's attention? Will the lasting memories of the pictured scene trouble the thoughts and dreams of the victim's survivors as long as they live—and is that worth the transitory exploitation of newsworthiness?

Curtis D. MacDougall, professor emeritus of Northwestern University's distinguished school of journalism, published a book full of such borderline pictures, *News Pictures Fit to Print . . . Or Are They?*,[2] gathered through many years of observing the press. It is a disturbing collection.

And in his thoughtful exploration of *Pressures on the Press*,[3] Hillier Krieghbaum of New York University devoted a chapter to a similar consideration of the kinds of tough decisions news photographers and editors are called upon to make about such pictures as those of the burning monk and the shooting of the Viet Cong suspect which we have considered in another context in chapter 4.

Many of the photographs that Professors MacDougall and Krieghbaum cite are dramatic, classic cases, such as the memorable picture of a young girl kneeling, with outstretched arms and anguished face, over the body of one of the four students shot by National Guardsmen at Kent State University in 1970, or the equally famed picture of Lee Harvey Oswald clutching at his stomach a split second after Jack Ruby had fatally shot him while in the basement of the Dallas Police Headquarters.

In such cases, however, the news significance of the photograph involved may be so overriding that other considerations can be set aside without much debate. Other, less momentous instances may involve more difficult decisions.

One such decision confronted the editors of the two Honolulu, Hawaii, newspapers one February day in 1975. The decision did not have to do with a major news break of momentous dimensions. But it did embrace all of the facets involved in a sensitive decision between news values on the one hand and human values on the other. In that respect it was a classic illustrative case.

A 15-year-old girl had been appearing in juvenile court in Honolulu for a hearing. During a recess in the proceedings, she crawled out of an open window and edged out onto a narrow ledge above the street, distraught and seemingly about to leap to death or injury below.

The judge, still in his flowing black robes, came to an adjoining window and talked soothingly to the girl for nearly 20 minutes, finally persuading her to take his hand and come back into the courtroom. Meanwhile, firemen had been holding nets below, a crowd had collected, and both newspaper and TV cameramen had arrived on the scene. They got some highly dramatic shots. The set taken by the photographer for the afternoon paper, the *Star-Bulletin*, included two particularly striking ones. The first was of the girl, mouth open as though screaming, and of the judge leaning partially out of the window about 15 feet away. The second shot showed the girl, her tear-stained face now with a trusting look, holding the judge's outstretched hand and about to step back in through the courtroom window. (See page 162.)

The two pictures told a compelling, arresting story. In all likelihood they were destined to be prize winners. The photographers for the *Advertiser*, the morning paper, and those from the local TV stations, had comparable film and photos. By all measurements of newsworthiness, this was great material. But consider how many factors other than newsworthiness the editors felt obliged to weigh as they tried to decide whether or not to use the photos and the film.

The sensitivities of the girl could not be ignored, nor those of her family. What impact would the publicity have on her? Might it exacerbate the problems that had brought her into juvenile court in the first place? Moreover, the standard practice with most news media (enforced by law in some jurisdictions) is to shield juveniles from publicity when they are involved in Family Court proceedings; publication of the pictures in unretouched form would violate that privacy convention.

Some among those debating the decision urged that the girl's features be masked so that her identity would be concealed from all those readers who did not have personal knowledge of the case (as has been done with the reproductions of these same pictures in this book). Others pointed out that this would detract from the dramatic impact of the two photographs; and for the TV editors, masking would be an almost impossible technical problem.

So the decisions came, and in a kind of domino fashion. First, a local TV station showed the film of the episode on that evening's news-

161

Photographs by Ron Edmonds, Honolulu *Star-Bulletin*, reproduced with permission of the *Star-Bulletin*.

cast, just as the *Advertiser* editors were conferring about how they would handle the photos for their next morning's paper. Seeing the film on office monitors, the *Advertiser* editors decided that since the girl's identity was known to the crowd on the scene, and now to the TV audience as well, there would be little additional harm in running a picture in the next morning's paper. So it ran, top of page one, three-column size, with no masking of the girl's face.

The *Star-Bulletin* editors then had to make their decision for the afternoon paper. Although the issue of exposure of the girl's identity was by this time increasingly academic, they still debated whether they should follow the competition's lead or hold back out of deference to the sensibilities of the girl and her family. But the decision finally was to run the two shots, again without masking.

What is most interesting about the case is that even after the papers had been published and the TV news programs had long ago flickered out, the various journalists involved were still torn by the ethical issues involved. An editor of the *Star-Bulletin* acknowledged a week later that the consensus in his newsroom was that if the decision had to be faced all over again, the pictures would have been masked, or not run at all, no matter what the competition had done.

And the morning paper, the *Advertiser*, ran an editorial page column by Managing Editor Mike Middlesworth which acknowledged two weeks after the fact that:

In retrospect it was probably a wrong decision. It was made in haste, and we let our admiration for a fine photograph outrun thoughtfulness.

Newspapers have the capacity to do great good. . . . They also have the capacity to do harm.

In this case we may have done some harm. The only good to come out of it is that we have now thought long and hard about what we did and why— and having thought about it, perhaps we'll be wiser the next time an equally sensitive decision has to be made.[4]

Let's explore some other cases in which newsworthiness had to be weighed against other values in making the decision whether or not to publish.

A West Coast metropolitan daily published in large format (2 columns $\times$ 8 inches) a closeup shot of a grieving man. His eyes were puffed and downcast, his jaw slack with shock. Beneath the picture were the following cutlines:

GRIEF—Robert Jones, 41, bows head in grief on learning his six children had perished in fire which swept his home early Thursday.

What were the values involved here? Certainly our sympathies for the subject of the photograph are aroused; certainly few readers will fail to see the picture and read the cutlines to find out what brought about this devastation of a man's spirit. So in these respects, the picture has newsworthiness. But are the reasons for the viewer's interest in the picture ones that the newspaper ought to be exploiting? Is there a kind of uncomfortable voyeurism here, and should that be made the basis for attracting or holding readers?

Consider another tragedy shot. This one pictured a young woman lying on a street, dressed in a housecoat. Her face was turned toward the camera, and her eyes were open. Sprawled on top of the woman was her mother, gray hair in a bun, her mouth wide and her face twisted with anguish. The cutlines:

DEATH PLUNGE—Ella Goldberg, 70, throws herself across her dying daughter, Gloria Lanzet, 38, after her aged fingers proved too weak to hold back death Tuesday. Mrs. Lanzet fell from outside the window of her sixth floor apartment in Brooklyn as her mother clung to the tip of her daughter's housecoat for a few despairing moments.

Again, the ingredients of newsworthiness unquestionably are present. We can share the tearing remorse of the mother as she clutches her dying daughter. We can see the daughter's eyes, still open but glazing with death. The cutlines tell us of the poignant circumstances that preceded the pictured scene, heightening our feeling of sympathy and involvement.

But what business have we as witnesses to this scene in the first place? How seemly is it of the newspaper to take advantage of our (morbid?) fascination with a moment of tragic death? Should someone somewhere in the news pipeline have decided that in this instance the scales should not dip on the side of publication?

Such pictures as these are not rarities, as anyone who regularly reads a newspaper or watches television newscasts well knows. Many of them are prize-winners in annual news photography competitions, simply because they have such powerful impact.

The *AP Log*, a weekly publication distributed to newspapers that are members of the Associated Press, regularly notes the "best" pictures of the week, and usually most have to do with violence or tragedy of one kind or another. A sample, from the *Log* for May 10 to 16, 1971:

FOR THE SHEER DRAMA of spot tragedy, the outstanding picture of the week showed a shocked 8-year-old looking down at the body of his father, killed in a shootout with police. It was taken by *Jerry Wolter* of the *Cincinnati Enquirer*.

Other dramatic photos of the week: Police firing into a house as officers drag a wounded policeman to an ambulance, by *Fred Griffith, Memphis Commercial Appeal*; Elderly woman caught in scuffling demonstrators at a flower show, by *Lloyd Pearson, Baltimore Sun*; Three-picture sequence as police captured teen-ager who threatened to jump from a building, by *Joe DeMaria, Long Island Press*; Dazed and injured motorist sitting on highway between two wrecked cars, by *Mrs. Hazel Thiel, for the Appleton*, Wis., *Post-Crescent*.

There are some tragedy shots that are so regular and predictable that they have almost become photographic clichés—the spread-eagled figure plunging to his or her death from a high-rise apartment fire; the would-be suicide, poised to jump from the ironwork of a bridge, or the ledge of an office building; and of course the auto wreck scene, usually with at least a glimpse of a mangled body.

So far as car accident pictures go, editors offer a specific argument in support of printing at least some of them. Such pictures, the reasoning goes, serve as a reminder and warning to other drivers to be more careful lest they wind up in a similar scene.

Traffic safety officials don't entirely agree, however. They say that the wholesome-warning notion really isn't very effective. The drivers who are inclined to be reckless, or to drink too much, aren't likely to be straightened out by a photograph of a grisly accident scene. Yet there is at least some plausibility to the warning-bell notion, at least so far as auto accident and even home mishap pictures are concerned.

But for the grief and voyeurism pictures, no very persuasive case can be made. John Hohenberg, in *The News Media: A Journalist Looks at His Profession*, quotes one newsman:

Michael J. Ogden, the executive editor of the *Providence Journal-Bulletin*, argued for a policy against printing the pictures that can serve no conceivable use except to capitalize on someone's grief. "I can understand the printing of an auto accident picture as an object lesson," he said, "What I can't understand is the printing of sobbing wives, mothers, children. . . . What is the value of showing a mother who has just lost her child in a fire? Is this supposed to have a restraining effect on arsonists? I am sure that those who don't hesitate to print such prictures will use the pious pretense of quoting Charles A. Dana's famous dictum that he always felt that 'whatever the Divine Providence permitted to occur I was not too proud to print.' Which is as peachy a shibboleth to permit pandering as I can imagine."[5]

And another editor, Oxie Reichler of the *Yonkers* (N.Y.) *Herald Statesman*, took a similar position:

Are we misguided do-gooders because we rebel at printing pictures of dead bodies and gory scenes that tear at the sensibilities of many readers? . . .
I don't think so—and I want to suggest that it is a direct and important form of public service to edit our papers so that they are clean and refreshing, informing and morale-building, with no do-it-yourself columns for committing crimes, defeating justice or circumventing the orderly processes of our society and our economy.[6]

But there are obviously a good many other editors who hold differing views, as anyone with an eye to see can testify. It is a rare day when the morning newspaper doesn't include at least one or two photographs that trade on grief, tragedy, or violence; and few installments of the nightly television newscast are free of film footage of a similar character.

For the persons who suffer as a result of this kind of pictorial news, there often is little recourse. Curtis D. MacDougall cites a 1949 case in which a federal court judge refused to find against the *Minneapolis Tribune* on an invasion of privacy count when it had published a picture of parents in a divorce action who were comforting their child. And:

In 1951 the parents of a child killed in an automobile accident were unsuccessful in an action against the Boston *Post*, which used a picture of the mangled body. Similarly, in 1956 the Iowa Supreme Court upheld the Sioux City *Journal-Tribune* which used a picture of the mutilated and decomposed body of an eight-year-old boy who had been dead for a month.[7]

The concept of the right of privacy, which is still taking shape as court decisions build up into a body of precedent, typically is considered not to be applicable in situations in which the subject is legitimately a part of the news.

Accident victims are in the news, as are the shocked onlookers. But as we observed in an earlier passage in this book, this does not mean that they have thereby been stripped of their humanity, their sensibilities.

It is relevant—and very much a matter of journalistic ethics—that the figures in the news be treated not as grist for the journalistic mills but as individuals entitled to respect and consideration despite the fact that events, often not of their own doing, have thrust them into the stream of the news.

As Paul G. Kauper, a Michigan law professor has argued, "A greater sensitivity to the right of privacy needs to be emphasized as against any competing claim of the press that it is free of any responsibility to consider this right in publishing what it thinks is a matter of public interest."[8]

The courts have extended to the press great latitude so that the public's right to know may be served. Libel laws that once severely restricted the press from publishing unfavorable information about persons in the news have been watered down repeatedly by Supreme Court decisions. The end result has been much more energetic investigative reporting, particularly of politicians and officeholders; instances of misuse of the public trust have been uncovered, and malefactors driven from their posts and sometimes into prison. Such results have clearly been in the public interest.

But as a by-product of the relaxation of libel and right-of-privacy limitations on the press, many innocent individuals have been pained, embarrassed, or even more consequentially injured by photographers and editors conscious of their new freedom and less careful than they once might have been about the rights of those in the news.

As Anthony Harrigan of the *Charleston* (S.C.) *News* and *Courier*, wrote in *Nieman Reports:*

Readers of news magazines have thrown up before their eyes each week picture stories which show theologians in undershirts heavy with sweat, a bride changing her clothes after the wedding service, the reaction of a pregnant woman to the result of a saliva test used in determining the sex of her unborn child, an exhausted athlete vomiting under the stands after a grueling race. The moments in life which ought to be private, the property of the individual experiencing whatever is happening to him, are recorded on film and transferred to the pages of several millions of copies of magazines.[9]

The same kinds of critical comments could be aimed at the newspapers and the television newscasts. The new freedom that has been opened to journalists by the courts' interpretation of libel and right-of-privacy doctrines could someday be curtailed if ethical concepts continue to be brushed aside in the pursuit of newsworthiness, no matter what the ingredients.

In fact, one 1974 Supreme Court decision (Gertz *v.* Robert Welch, Inc.) suggested that the Court might be considering backing away from some of the earlier, liberalizing decisions in the area of libel and privacy. It was a very small backward step, however, and it did not materially reverse the trend. Columnist James Kilpatrick, commenting on the decision, observed that:

What all this means is that those of us in the news business are pretty well relieved of the awful anxieties we used to live with. In the absence of willful or malicious or reckless publication—something that happens very seldom—we are home free.

This is good, but something more remains to be said. The old anxieties were worrisome, but they also were useful: They tended to make careless editors careful. Freed of the old risks of a disastrous judgment, it becomes all the more imperative that in writing of individuals, whether in public or in private life, we must be fair. We must open our columns voluntarily to replies. We must actively seek "the other side" of stories. And when we fall into error, we must correct our errors promptly.

The American press today is not especially loved and it is not widely respected, partly because important elements of the press have failed to couple freedom with responsibility. With the court's opinion, we have about all the freedom we reasonably could ask. I pray we use it wisely.[10]

As the cases we have been exploring suggest, using freedom wisely is not a simple, clear-cut matter. We have seen how compelling are the news values involved in the agony-and-anguish photographs, or the peeks into intensely personal moments. The journalist intent on reporting the news inevitably becomes at least somewhat calloused and indifferent to the subjects about whom stories must be written, and of whom photographs must be taken. There is no simple, one-size-fits-all rule that can be applied. Perhaps Carl E. Lindstrom, a former editor, came as close as anyone could with his injunction that "The picture which creates in the beholder the feeling of intrusion upon grief or private anguish, the feeling of 'here I should not be,' ought never to be taken."[11]

The foregoing exploration of problem pictures has, of necessity, concentrated on the lapses and the insensitivities of the journalist. There are, however, occasional grace notes, such as the observations of editors Reichler and Ogden quoted several pages earlier, or the following incident recorded in the *AP Log:*

168

TO THE PRESS in *Copenhagen* and to Danes throughout the land it had been evident for days that King Frederik was dying. The watch was set at Municipal Hospital and at Amalienborg Palace.

It was then that Queen Ingrid had a request to photographers and newsmen—not to congregate under the window of the king's sick room. And in return she promised that the autos carrying the royal family would drive slowly so that cameramen might have an opportunity to make pictures.

The request was met, the promise kept. When the time came the queen stopped her limousine, rolled down the window, personally thanked the press.[12]

What Role to Play?

One of the least enviable situations in the debate over what is ethical and what is not in the handling of news photos is that of the photographer or cameraman.

He or she is assigned to gather the pictorial dimension of the news, just as the reporter is supposed to collect the facts. The decision as to whether the photograph or film footage will be disseminated later through the media is not the photographer's. So does that relieve the cameraman from responsibility for respecting ethical values on assignment? Not really.

For one thing, just the fact of taking the picture can be an indefensible intrusion, or worse. Curtis D. MacDougall recalls that one of the chief reasons why the Charles Lindbergh family decided to leave the United States for England was the fright that had come to them when a photographer for the *New York Mirror*, intent on getting a picture of little Jon Lindbergh, had forced an automobile containing the child and his nursemaid to the curb in order to make the picture possible. (The photographer won praise and a bonus from his paper, incidentally, although he was roundly condemned by many in the field.)[13]

Another problem for the photographer on the scene, particularly if the scene is one of an accident or disaster of some sort, is how to decide which of his responsibilities is paramount—that of news photographer, or that of human being?

A hit movie of the early 1970s included a sequence in which a TV camera crew, en route to a story, happens on an automobile accident. Apparently the accident had taken place only seconds before. The car was partially overturned and bodies were lying half-in, half-out of the front seat. The two-man crew rushed to the scene and proceeded to get film of the wreck and the bodies. Then, as they returned to their own car, one observed to the other that "maybe we ought to call an ambulance; one of them seemed to be alive."

The movie scene might well have been inspired by an article that had appeared in the *Bulletin of the American Society of Newspaper Editors* nearly ten years earlier. The article was titled: "Get the Picture or Act the Samaritan?" and it included an auto wreck photograph that had been published in an East Coast newspaper, showing the body of a woman on the pavement, that of a man lying half-out of the wrecked driver's seat. A third person appeared to be giving aid to the woman on the pavement.

Readers of the newspaper in which the picture had been published had protested that the photographer had no business standing about taking pictures; he should have been trying to help the victims, since prompt aid might have saved their lives.

So the *Bulletin* editors asked three experienced photographers to comment on the basic question—which role should the photographer play, and why?

One of the responses came from Joseph Costa, chairman of the board of the National Press Photographers Association. He pointed out that rarely is the situation so clear cut as the instance cited; usually there are numerous other persons on hand to provide help to the injured. Moreover, amateur first aid efforts may do more harm than good in any case. And, finally, Mr. Costa observed:

One more factor that should be taken into consideration here, and my friends of the NPPA will probably never forgive me for this, but the question as we have posed it further presupposes that the photographer is an average human being.

He is not.

From the first day on the job, he is trained as a pictorial reporter, a visual historian, or maybe we should simply say, as a press photographer. In situations involving great emotional strain, the taking of a picture is really not a premeditated act. It is an automatic reflex—and I doubt very much that the instant, the minute fraction of a second it takes him to snap the picture, would make a vital difference in most situations.   14

Another of the trio of respondents, Lloyd B. Walton of the *Indianapolis Times*, asserted that "I doubt that there is a photographer alive who would fail to drop his camera without taking a shot if he believed quick action on his own part would save a life." But he went on to say:

A photographer arriving on an accident scene when other people are running in to give aid is honorbound to his paper and to the public to record the drama as best he can. That's what he's there for. He's not a freelance first aid man.[15]

And the third to react to the *Bulletin* editors' question, Bruce Roberts, director of photography for the *Wilmington* (Del.) *Morning News* and *Journal*, wrote:

There is no question in my mind that a photographer is first a human being with compassion for other human beings. If he arrives at the scene of an accident first before any aid has been summoned that is his first duty and a Pulitzer prize winning picture possibility should make no difference. . . .

Movies and television have done the news photographers a serious injustice. The great majority of my friends in this profession bear no resemblance to the coarse and callous portrayals of news photographers which I see on the screen.[16]

Yet it may not be only on television or in the movies that news photographers acquire the reputation of being indifferent to the human suffering they frame in their viewfinders.

For example, *Editor & Publisher*, the trade magazine of the newspaper business, published an article by a photographer whose behavior at the scene of a tragedy, as he himself recounted it, might have led others there to wonder about his motives.

The photographer introduced the story thus:

What should a news photographer at the scene of a tragedy do when told that relatives of the victims don't want pictures taken? . . .

My decision was to go ahead with the photographing.

I was attacked and slugged by fire officials. My gadget bag torn from me. My camera was thrown to the ground and some of my film deliberately ruined. State police declined to protect me.

Still, I'm sure my decision was the proper one.

The tragedy was the drowning of four small boys, three of them from a single family. They had walked into deep water in a river, and by the time the photographer reached the scene three of the bodies had been recovered and the fourth was still being sought. A policeman at the

171

scene told the photographer to leave, since the members of the family had asked that no pictures be taken of the bodies.

Let's pick up the photographer's account:

Ignoring the fire policeman, I walked down a hill to the beach where three bodies lay in a row on the bank. . . .

I spotted the parents of three of the boys. They appeared in deep shock and it was my impression that they were too numb to care whether photos were taken or not.

I quickly took a shot of the parents as they talked with a state policeman. As I did, the trooper waved his arm at me. "Get the Hell out of here with that camera!" he shouted. The parents didn't appear to even know that I was there. . . .

A second fire policeman—this one wearing a white hat—took the cue from the state policeman and ordered me not to shoot any more photos. . . .

After trying to explain to him that it was my job to get photos, I took two shots of the sheeted bodies. . . .

The shot I wanted most was that of firemen bringing the fourth body ashore after it finally was removed.

As I knelt to take this picture, the fire policeman and a dozen members of the crowd surrounded me, waving their hands and blocking my view.

When I attempted to get another angle they followed and I couldn't get the shot off.

I yelled to the state policeman for "police protection," but the same trooper who had waved me off earlier turned around and replied hotly." I wouldn't give you a thing. You don't deserve it." . . .

About that time, the mother of the three dead boys fell on the body of one of her sons. Policemen and firemen by this time were causing such a commotion that she looked up from the body.

When she saw me there with my camera she stood up. Holding her only surviving son—a two-year-old—over her head, she exclaimed hysterically:

"Why don't you take a picture of him? He's all I have left."

That really set the crowd off. A few seconds later the mother fell again across the bodies and I took one more shot.[17]

It is possible to understand the viewpoints of all of the various principals in this vignette. The photographer who wrote the story for *Editor & Publisher* recognized the debatable nature of the case and, as he said, was writing to get the thoughts of "experienced photographers and newsmen on this question of basic newspaper ethics." His candor in recounting the episode was admirable.

Certainly one can empathize, too, with the grief-numbed parents and with the officers at the scene, shaken by the poignant multiple tragedy.

As we contemplate it now, distant in time and space from the event, it seems clear enough that the conflict of professional obligations with humanitarian instincts should have been resolved in favor of the latter. But for the man on the spot, the decision may not always be so apparent.

Others Who Decide

The decisons may not be clear cut, either, for those further along in the journalistic chain, the editors up the line who determine which pictures and which film footage will get through the gates and become available to the reading and viewing public.

Frank Stanton, the head of CBS, once observed that "in reporting . . . violence journalism faces perhaps the greatest philosophical and intellectual challenge in its history."

Those who make the gatekeeper decisions at later stages in the journalistic process, long after the photographs and films have been shot, are of course keenly sensitive to the news values of such pictures. They too know the findings of the readership studies, and as realists they are aware that even the readers and viewers who express shock about the publication of a gory or a grief shot will nevertheless have paid close attention to the picture when it came to their attention. (Just as the readers who complain about too much crime news in the paper will usually have read with fascinated care every lurid detail before turning away to protest.)

Columbia Journalism Review conducted a symposium survey of the views of six experienced journalists as to how they would decide on the publication of a set of actual shots of tragedy, violence, or grief. The six included two newspaper editors, a veteran press photographer, a news magazine picture editor, a TV news director, and a senior network TV producer. All six were asked to look over the set of photographs and indicate whether or not they would have used them, each of course judging in terms of his own medium.

A few excerpts from the survey suggest how diverse were their views, and on what bases they differed.

One of the test pictures was of a Congolese rebel being stomped to death by a soldier. The rebel is on the ground face down, apparently attempting to lift himself on his arms. The soldier's boot is descending and about to strike the neck of the prone man whose face shows his terror. (The picture had been published in the *New York Daily News*, Jan. 11, 1965.)

To the question "Would you have used the picture?" the six responded with 4 yes, 1 no, 1 maybe. One yes response: "Real good picture—well worth using." And the one no vote: "I would not use this. I think it is simply more than our mass television audience, with its large number of youngsters, could accept. Human brutality toward other humans has a nauseating quality."

Another of the test photographs was of Malcolm X, the black leader, just after he had been fatally shot. His bloodstained shirt is open, wounds are visible, persons are bending over him to give him aid. The vote from the panel: 2 yes, 2 no, 2 maybe. A sample yes: "It is not upsetting to the reader. It tells a story of a violent man meeting a violent death." And one no: "Generally speaking, I shy away from close-ups of corpses." (The picture was published in *Life* on Mar. 5, 1965.)

A third test shot was of a father and his two sons, clutching each other in grief, apparently over the death of the wife and mother. Here the vote was 1 yes and 5 no. The lone yes: "Not offensive—obviously points up a real story of tragedy and is a vital part of any news report." And a sample from the majority of no voters: "I would not print this picture—any more than I would stand around and stare at such a scene." And from another: "Human anguish can never be shown decently." (The photograph was distributed by the Associated Press; whether it had been published anywhere the *CJR* article did not indicate.)

And a fourth photograph was one of two dead persons strapped into airplane seats, floating in Boston Harbor after the crash of an airplane attempting to land. The two were floating face up, their features visible. All the panelists voted no on this one. Their reactions were particularly interesting.

From one: "I probably would not print it. BUT it is almost unique because so few air disasters leave anything recognizable. There is great pathos in these passengers still strapped to their seats, looking as if they never knew what happened to them."

And another: "This shot of crash victims closeup in death would tax the emotions of a publication's strongest reader."

And yet another: ". . . not likely to be used because people fly in airplanes all the time and it is too gruesome. Only would be considered for a street edition, not home edition." (The picture had originally been published by the *Boston Globe* in 1960.)[18]

These various instances posed hard decisions for the panel of experienced gatekeepers, and it is revealing that their judgments often varied so widely. The values in such situations are difficult to sort out, and the guidelines that apply—as we have so many times noted in this book—are rarely sharply etched and definitive. The kinds of arguments that seemed to be decisive in the final decisions of the six respondents were in some instances bluntly professional ("Real good picture . . . tells the story of a violent man meeting a violent death . . . a vital part of any news report . . ."); in others they were apparently rooted in concern for the sensibilities of the subjects or the audience (". . . human brutality toward other humans has a nauseating quality. . . . Human anguish can never be shown decently. . . ."); and in still others they seemed to reflect a strained attempt at compromise (". . . would be considered for a street edition, not home edition. . . .")

The mix of viewpoints reflected in the responses quoted in the *Columbia Journalism Review* symposium probably could be considered representative of media gatekeeper approaches to the ethical questions posed by grief and gore pictures. Since such pictures still crop up with frequency, however, it must be assumed that pragmatic professional values outweigh sensitivity more often than not.

Lies, White and Black

Ethical considerations and news values—as well as some other ingredients —are mixed in other kinds of decisions about the use of pictures in the mass media.

The venerable aphorism that "pictures don't lie" probably never did have much validity. But in these days of candid cameras, trick lenses, and darkroom wizardry it has even less.

Often pictures do *not* tell the truth. In some cases only small and relatively harmless "fibs" may be involved. But in others outright distortion is peddled by the camera—or, rather, by those who use the camera or the pictures it takes.

It is the simplest thing in the world, for example, for a skilled photographer to select a picture angle that will create a misleading impression in the viewer's mind.

Once when then President Lyndon B. Johnson was leaving a Washington church after Sunday service, a photographer waited until he paused on the steps directly in front of the clergyman. The picture that resulted showed the President apparently wearing a bishop's mitre and holding the episcopal crook in one hand while grinning broadly at the crowd.

175

No harm done, perhaps, and no real malice involved. But consider another case.

During the years immediately following the assassination of President John F. Kennedy, there was continuing speculation about the future of his widow, Jacqueline. Wherever she went, photographers followed. When she went out to a restaurant or a play, columnists took note of the identity of her escort and speculated about the seriousness of the relationship. On one such occasion a photographer caught a shot of the former First Lady at a party, leaning forward to speak to someone. But he used a lens that foreshortened the scene, so that she appeared to be nuzzling another person, a celebrated Washington figure, who was actually all the way across the room from her. The picture, published with an ambiguous caption, left anyone who saw it with a grossly misleading impression of the reality of the situation.

Take a look at the photograph below.

United Press International Photo

It was taken by a United Press International photographer and sent out to papers around the country accompanied by the following cutlines:

Senator Henry Jackson, of Washington, a candidate for the Democratic nomination for president, stopped in Winter Haven Park, Feb. 9th, to deliver an impromptu talk. An estimated 40–50 persons were on hand to hear his speech.

But when the picture was published in numerous newspapers and newsmagazines, editors revamped the cutlines in various ways, typically by cutting out the last line. The result was to depict Jackson as addressing a "rally" apparently consisting of three persons, one a youngster on a bicycle.

The photographer for the local Winter Haven Park newspaper had taken another picture of the same scene, but from a more distant vantage point, revealing the larger number of persons actually on hand. The UPI photographer, presumably to get a closer shot, had moved up to a point where only the front row of the audience could be seen.

The senator quite understandably protested, and strongly, the way in which the picture and doctored cutlines had been used in various parts of the country and before the national audience of the news magazines. The other picture taken by the local paper's photographer was distributed later, but by then the damage to the senator's campaign had been done; he had been portrayed nationwide as a figure of ridicule, a candidate who went about making his pitch to audiences of three. He had been the victim of unethical journalism, whatever the motivations that may have been behind the mishandling of the picture and cutlines.

An even more blatant ethical violation was reflected in a photograph that one of the wire services awarded a $100 prize and the title of best non-cliché picture of the month.

The photo was of a defendant in a murder trial, a woman charged with killing her husband and sending his body down a cliff inside a burning automobile. In the picture the woman was shown conferring with her attorney, but looking straight at the camera—through a frame consisting of a half-burned tire from the death car. A hand could be seen at the upper part of the picture, steadying the tire.

It was not a cliché photograph, agreed. But consider how many infractions, of how many codes of ethics, had been necessary to bring about the stagey shot. The defendant's attorney had clearly connived at

177

it, since he was part of the picture; it was indefensible for him to permit his client to be depicted framed—literally—by an incriminating piece of evidence. And to get that evidence into the picture the photographer had to enlist the cooperation of some officer of the court, the judge or a bailiff. Neither one had any right to condone the affair. As for the photographer, he had put news values above ethical considerations.

In other instances where photographs seem to have been misused, the evidence is not so clear cut. Still, there's enough to provide the justification for some serious questions.

Judgment, or . . . ?

In a small western city a hot dispute had developed over policies being enforced in the local school system. Factions had formed, and sides had been taken by teachers, parents, school officials—and by the local newspaper. Then came a climactic school board meeting and a heated debate. The next day's paper pictured the leaders of the two opposing factions as they addressed the school board and the audience before a microphone. The spokesman for the side supported by the paper was shown in a thoughtful pose, speaking calmly. The leader of the faction opposed by the paper was depicted with mouth wide open, index finger pointing heavenward, and eyes staring wildly through his heavy-rimmed glasses.

The photographer that night had used a 35 mm. camera, as do most news photographers these days. He had taken a great many shots, again as is customary in such situations. He and the picture editor undoubtedly had many different poses of the two speakers from which to choose. It is possible, of course, that the choice of the sober-citizen pose for the side the paper favored and the angry-shouter shot of the man the paper had argued against editorially was solely a matter of news judgment; it *could* have been that in the opinion of the gatekeepers involved these were the most representative depictions of the two speakers. But a bystander is certainly entitled to some skepticism, and to ask the uncomfortable question as to whether the paper's policy dictated the manner in which the two sides would be personified for the public. Make no mistake, these pictures to some degree conditioned the perception the reader would have of the viewpoints of the speakers. (And it is a pretty safe bet that if the whole file of pictures taken that night had been combed through, poses conveying exactly opposite impressions of the two men could have been found.)

Another questionable case was cited by an editorial in the *Eugene*

(Oreg.) *Register-Guard* during the period early in 1974 when Watergate investigation pressures were mounting:

Pictures Don't Lie?

There is an old saying that pictures don't lie, but the Jan. 28 issue of *Time* magazine disproved the adage. Pictures may not actually lie, but they can fib and distort.

The issue of *Time* on Jan. 28 showed President Nixon in the worst possible way with dark circles apparent under his eyes; his face deeply lined, one eye drooping slightly.

It made the person seeing it think the President was deteriorating and the natural assumption was that it was because of Watergate.

While some members of the White House corps talk among themselves about the incredible pressures which have been brought to bear on Nixon, F. W. Lyon, vice president for newspictures of United Press International, states he has examined more than 100 pictures taken by UPI photographers in the past two months "and they show no discernible change in his (Nixon's) appearance."

Any photographer who shoots 15 or 20 shots of an individual can find one which will show the subject in any one of a number of ways—happy, depressed, tired, alert, well and frail. According to Lyon, in a speech made before the picture appeared in *Time*, it would be relatively easy to "feed the rumors of a deteriorating physical condition by selecting and transmitting those photos which might make the President look older or more tired than he appears in others." Instead, UPI has determined that any photo transmitted of the President must be representative of the majority of all the photos taken at the same time.

Time, obviously, did not show the President the same courtesy.[19]

The photo gatekeepers at the central desks of the two major wire services have considerable leverage, as the editorial noted. The pictures that are selected there to be sent out on the wires as possible illustrations for national or international stories can have a good deal to do with the overall impression that the text-and-picture package will make on the eventual consumer.

For example, when Lt. William L. Calley, Jr., was on trial for the My Lai massacre of Vietnam civilians, a wire service story transmitted one day began thus:

FT. BENNING, GA.—Lt. William L. Calley Jr. admitted today that he directed a mass execution of Vietnamese civilians at an irrigation ditch at My Lai.

Calley, speaking without emotion, of killings at My Lai:

"It was the order of the day."

179

Sent out with the story, and published right next to it in many papers, was a picture of Lt. Calley leaving the courthouse in the company of his civilian attorney. Calley had on his uniform cap and was apparently either laughing or wearing a very broad grin. That happy grin juxtaposed with the grisly admission in the next column left a deep impression on anyone who saw it. Yet was it representative? Was Calley grinning on the witness stand when he made the admission? Was the purpose of sending the light-hearted picture to draw a contrast between the dreadful crime of which he was accused and his own apparent indifference to the gravity of the matter?

There were, it would appear, no questions about the motivation behind the misuse of pictorial material cited by Robert Cirino in his book *Power to Persuade: Mass Media and the News:*

A former producer of New York City's WPIX-TV "Clay Cole" show (a teen-age couples dancing program) testified at a Federal Communications Commission hearing that editing techniques were used to make it look as though there were fewer blacks in the audience than there actually were. He revealed that when this technique didn't work the station would delete live coverage and substitute earlier tapes that depicted the audience as predominantly white.[20]

An Indistinct Line

It is often difficult to make a clean-cut distinction between the manipulation of photographs or film to distort the news and the kind of "reenactment of reality" that in some instances is an integral—if borderline—part of pictorial coverage of a news event.

Certain news developments are predictable and scheduled; others occur without preliminary and in places and contexts where photo coverage would be impracticable or impossible. In the first kind of situation, photographers and cameramen often attempt to stage-manage the situation to whatever degree they can; in the latter, they may attempt to re-create at least a part of a news scene already gone by.

The famed flag-raising photograph at Iwo Jima, which has become for many Americans the symbol of American victory in World War II, was of a reenactment of the original event. In one sense, it was not a depiction of reality; yet in another respect, it told the story faithfully, just as the reporter's quote can honestly represent a speaker's point even if every syllable isn't exactly as the man uttered it.

Some stage-managed photographic or television film coverage, however, exceeds the permissible limits (if it is possible to talk with any certainty of permissible limits). A journalism educator, Ken Macrorie, tells of an instance he witnessed:

Some years ago on the steps outside City Hall in Manhattan, I saw several news photographers loading cameras and other men looking down the street to the right. Pretending to be attached officially to the moment, I witnessed what I now call the *re-enactment of reality.*

As I moved from the curb away from the milling reporters and toward the steps, I noticed Mayor Wagner come out of one of the large front doors of the Hall, look down the street, pop back into the building again. Up the block, a black open limousine pulled around the corner and stopped. On the porch of City Hall, the Mayor stepped out again. He was waiting for a cue. On signal, the car moved slowly toward us and the Mayor started his descent of the long flight of stairs. The Prime Minister of Japan and he met at the curb, the Mayor arriving three seconds before the limousine, to be photographed waiting, graciously greeting. The public was not present for this most public of events. No one had showed except a few policemen and a handful of City Hall's blasé white-collar workers. The swirling cameramen and reporters quickly clustered at the car. One of the self-appointed leaders of the moment, called, "Hey, Mayor! Over here between the flags!" pointing to the front of the limousine where stood tiny American and Japanese flags attached to two chromium staffs rising from the bumper. He pushed the Mayor into position. "Point out the city," he ordered. The Mayor's hand went up, finger extended as if pointing out a particular sight. The Prime Minister assumed the required curious look. He had been shown the city. You could almost hear the TV voice of authority later that evening: "This afternoon, Mayor Wagner welcomed Prime Minister Kishi of Japan at City Hall and showed him the city."[21]

While Macrorie criticized the patent staging of this scene, he acknowledged that there are some news situations where at least some reenactment is necessary if the impression of reality is to be conveyed successfully to the reader or viewer. And he cited as an analogue the lines of poet Archibald MacLeish:

A poem should be equal to:
Not true.

The analogy is an inviting one. A news report, in the literal sense, cannot be "true." If it is "equal to," perhaps that is as much as anyone has a right to expect.

181

But some kinds of pictorial coverage seem to be neither true nor equal to. For example, during the period in the late 1960s and early 1970s when protest demonstrations on college campuses were almost daily occurrences, some television crews used to arrive at the scene where a demonstration was expected to develop equipped with a set of hand-lettered signs with appropriate slogans. These were to be handed out to the demonstrators, should they not have sufficiently pictorial props of their own.

This was more than reenactment; it amounted to the creation of news, and neither poetic nor journalistic license could justify that.

In some other, fortunately rare, instances, cameramen have been heard to urge demonstrators to "throw a few rocks over there" in order to pep up the action of what was turning out to be a tame affair.

It is inevitable that the presence in a news situation of camera crews or even pencil-and-pad reporters will have some influence on subsequent developments. Any one of us will play to the audience, if we sense there is an audience watching; and representatives of the press promise access to the widest of all audiences. But both photographers and reporters have a weighty obligation (as Horst Faas at once sensed at the scene of the Dacca horror) to avoid being a catalytic or precipitating agent in such a scene. Nor should the journalist connive at the fabrication or simulation of a news event, even if it resembles the real thing.

Hillier Krieghbaum recounts an instance of this last:

At times, picture coverage may be created—by more than the conventional professional techniques. On Nov. 1 and 2, 1967, the Columbia Broadcasting System's Chicago station WBBM-TV broadcast a report of a marijuana party held in nearby Evanston, site of Northwestern University. The resulting storm brought hearings by the Federal Communications Commission and a Special Subcommittee on Investigations of the House Committee on Interstate and Foreign Commerce. Deeply involved was John Victor Missett, a 1967 Northwestern graduate and, in the words of the FCC hearing examiner, "a young ambitious reporter" for the station's news staff. The examiner's report held that the pot party broadcast "was prearranged for the benefit of CBS, and that this particular party would never have been held but for Missett's request."[22]

Krieghbaum describes the Missett-staged pot party as beyond the scope of normal reporting procedures. Yet he also notes that it is defensible journalism to depict violations of the law in the process of investigative reporting. Such depictions have occurred often, in print when reporters infiltrated bookie operations to record how they functioned, or on television when documentary crews explored the incidence of illegal abortion or the extent to which prostitution was utilized as an adjunct of business entertaining.

This suggests how indistinct the ethical boundary lines can become. If it really was marijuana being smoked at the Missett party, was the film of the scene "equal to" reality? Or did it constitute the journalistic equivalent of police entrapment, in which a deputy goes into a massage parlor and arrests an operator only after she has finished her ministrations to him? Had the pot party been filmed without the knowledge of the participants, say from behind a mirror-window, would it have been a legitimate venture in investigative journalism rather than a staged, "prearranged" imitation of reality? Or would that have been on a level with the London photographers who used their infrared cameras to catch the British cabinet officer with his pair of prostitutes?

In a memo on "CBS Operating Standards: News and Public Affairs," Frank Stanton, then president of the network, attempted to fix the parameters for television newsmen by citing a memorandum originally written by CBS News president Richard S. Salant in 1963:

There shall be no re-creation, no staging, no production technique which would give the viewer an impression of any fact other than the actual fact, no matter how minor or seemingly inconsequential. The only way there can be certainty is not to let the bars down at all. Anything which gives the viewer an impression of time, place, event, or person other than the actual fact as it is being recorded and broadcast cannot be tolerated.

I recognize that strict application of this policy will result in higher costs or in a less technically perfect or interesting "show" in certain instances. But our field is journalism, not show business.[23]

Mr. Salant's words seem unequivocal and straightforward enough. However, to close this discussion of pictorial journalistic ethics with the note on which it began, let's recall once again that the firmly put precept does not always turn out to be so clear a guideline when journalists face actuality.

The memorandum by CBS News president Salant quoted above was written in 1963, four years before the "prearranged" pot party at Northwestern, and eight years before the CBS network aired "The Selling of the Pentagon."

It is frustrating for the reader, I know, to find the subject we are discussing slipping away elusively just as some sharp, clear benchmarks

183

seem to be emerging. But that is exactly the problem of journalistic ethics, and that is why so extended a discussion is necessary, case by perplexing case. For it is in the instances that come up day by day that ethical principles meet their ultimate tests.

Notes

1Carl E. Lindstrom, *The Fading American Newspaper* (Garden City, N.Y.: Doubleday & Company, Inc., 1960), p. 214.

2Curtis D. MacDougall, *News Pictures Fit to Print ... Or Are They?* (Stillwater, Oklahoma: Journalistic Services, Inc., 1971)

3Hillier Krieghbaum, *Pressures on the Press* (New York: Thomas Y. Crowell Company, 1972).

4Sunday Honolulu *Advertiser-Star-Bulletin*, February 16, 1975, p. B2.

5John Hohenberg, *The News Media: A Journalist Looks at His Profession* (New York: Holt, Rinehart and Winston, Inc., 1968), p. 212.

6Oxie Reichler, "A Fresh, New Look at Newspaper Ethics," *Bulletin of The American Society of Newspaper Editors*, No. 411, August 1, 1958, pp. 13–14.

7Curtis D. MacDougall, *The Press and Its Problems* (Dubuque: William C. Brown Company, Publishers, 1964), p. 343.

8Paul G. Kauper, "The Role of the Press in a Democratic Society," *Editor & Publisher*, CVII, No. 7 (February 16, 1974), 7, 34.

9Anthony Harrigan, "The Surrender of Privacy," *Nieman Reports*, XII, No. 3 (July 1958), 6–8.

10From his column written for publication on July 7, 1974.

11Lindstrom, *The Fading American Newspaper*, p. 214.

12*AP Log*, Jan. 10–16, 1972, p. 1.

13MacDougall, *The Press and Its Problems*, p. 333.

14Joseph Costa, Lloyd B. Walton, and Bruce Roberts, "Get the Picture Or Act the Samaritan?", *Bulletin of The American Society of Newspaper Editors*, No. 465, June 1, 1963, pp. 5–7.

15*Ibid.*, p. 6.

16*Ibid.*, p. 7.

17Arthur W. Geisleman, Jr., "Take Pictures of Tragic Scene or Flee from Irate Onlookers?", *Editor & Publisher*, XCII, No. 33 (August 15, 1959), 13.

18"The Cruel Camera," reprinted from the *Columbia Journalism Review*, IV No. 1 (Spring, 1965), © 5–10.

19Editorial, *Eugene* (Oreg.) *Register-Guard*, February 18, 1974.

20Robert Cirino, *Power to Persuade: Mass Media and the News* (New York: Bantam Books, Inc., 1974), p. 35.

21Ken Macrorie, "Re-enactment of Reality," *Nieman Reports*, XV, No. 2 (April, 1961), 35–37.

22Hillier Krieghbaum, "Cluttering Up the News Picture," *Quill*, LX, No. 2 (February 1972), 8–15.

23Quoted in "What CBS Policy on 'Staging'? Frank Stanton's Memo," reprinted from the *Columbia Journalism Review*, X, No. 4 (November/December 1971) ©, 63.

Abuses of Trust...

"The Brass Check is found in your pay-envelope each week — you who write and print and distribute our newspapers and magazines. The Brass Check is the price of your shame — you who take the fair body of truth and sell it in the market-place, who betray the virgin hopes of mankind into the loathsome brothel of Big Business." — Upton Sinclair[1]

10 It is not practicable to discuss all of the problem areas of modern journalism solely within the context of ethics. Some of these problem areas involve—in various interminglings—practices, motives, or forces that have little to do with codes of behavior, or with decisions made by individuals. Yet, ethical overtones are almost always present to some degree.

It will be the purpose of this chapter and the next to examine some of these multifaceted problem areas, sorting out for analysis the ethical questions involved but not necessarily dealing with the other, intermingled issues, since at least some of them are outside the scope of this book and might better be taken up in an overview of press-government relations, or in an introduction to the economics of the news business.

If you happen to be one who prefers exposition to be developed

185

within neat, narrow categories, the title of this chapter may bother you, since it obviously takes in a wide sweep of territory. But it is the right label for this segment of our exploration of journalistic ethics.

Let's begin by recalling the chief function of journalism in our society: the communication to the public of a reasonably accurate and complete picture of the world around us. We need to have such a picture in order to function, interrelate, survive. Marshall McLuhan, the brilliantly provocative communication interpreter and prophet, has described the mass media as extensions of man's senses—the means by which he can reach beyond his immediate physical surroundings.

Implicit in these depictions of the function of journalism is the assumption that the picture of the world that is brought to us will be a reliable one, that the extensions of our senses will inform us faithfully. That emerges repeatedly in the codes as the central, ruling ethic of journalism—to report the news of the world dependably and honestly.

But this implicit trust is not always honored. The central ethic of journalism is sometimes bent, spindled, even mutilated.

Such abuses of trust are explained away in various ways, rationalized with varying degrees of glibness or conviction as outside the control of individuals, or forced by external circumstances. But even though numerous other factors may have played a part, some ethical shortfall is also involved in almost every instance.

Heirs of Munsey

Among those who abuse the trust of the public and violate the central ethic of journalism are those who look upon the media of communication as did Peter Hamilton: as business ventures owing nothing to society and everything to the stockholders.

All of the media are basically businesses, to be sure: most are Very Big Business, as we have earlier noted. (In mid-1974, the Knight newspaper chain and that owned by Ridder Publications announced plans to merge, and the sum involved was $173.9 million.) But they are far more than businesses, or ought to be. They are invested with special privilege and status by the Constitution because they are expected to serve the public interest by providing that faithful picture of reality without which our system cannot function.

The responsible publisher or broadcast station owner recognizes both obligations—that of operating efficiently enough to survive as an economic entity, and that of fulfilling the public interest by giving honest measure in the news columns and newscast time slots. Such a stance of compromise is both pragmatic and ethical.

But there are some media owners who see their properties through Hamilton's eyes, or through those of Frank Munsey, a sort of Fourth Estate realtor of an earlier era. Munsey bought and sold newspapers like apartment houses, wheeling and dealing with profit as his only objective and, in the process—in the words of William Allen White—turning a once-noble calling into an 8 percent investment. Such media barons have never been much concerned about the public interest aspect of the field; their attention has been fixed on the fat, black figures in the counting house ledgers. (Lord Thomson of Fleet, a contemporary chain owner whose holdings include well over 100 newspaper properties in Britain, Canada, the United States and elsewhere, is bluntly candid about why he keeps gobbling up more every chance he gets—because they make money for him. "I'd be a fool otherwise, wouldn't I?")

Not all present-day proprietors put profits first, by any means. Many are as conscientious about their mission as any of the revered figures of journalistic histories. But there are others, particularly some of the chain and group operators, who resemble Munsey more than Pulitzer in their outlook.

Such types take great pride in the superbly automated production facilities in their newspaper plants ("You can eat off the composing room floor, it's so clean!"), in the efficiency of their central accounting systems, and in the dependability of their circulation staffs.

But ask them about the quality of the news report they supply to their readers and the discussion turns vague. In fact, many such owners put as little as possible into what ought to be the heart of the operation: the gathering and processing of the news. They will cheerfully stuff the columns and pages with whatever can be had most cheaply—wire-service copy, syndicated features by the bundle, comics, bland editorials from the canning factories, recipes to pad out the food ads. Of all the elements of news the most expensive, of course, is local news reported by an able local staff. The cost-conscious publisher, particularly one accountable to a chain headquarters to keep his unit competitively profitable within the group, cuts as many corners as he can in the area of local coverage. The community—and the basic ethic of journalism—suffer as a result.

The counterpart of such a publisher in the broadcast field is the station manager fighting for ratings, jazzing up his news coverage with happy talk, filling the broadcast day with as many ads as can be squeezed in without arousing the Federal Communications Commission, and turning over a few minutes early each Sunday morning to some local clergyman by way of a perfunctory bow to his "public service" obligations.

Such generalized betrayals of the journalistic ethic cannot be anatomized and dissected as simply as the cases we have looked at in earlier chapters, in which individuals faced conflict-of-interest questions or grappled with decisions involving news values at odds with humanitarian considerations. For factors other than personal codes of behavior are indeed involved.

Yet isn't the publisher or the station manager who puts return on equity far higher in priority than journalistic obligations as guilty of an ethical lapse as the reporter who accepts a "freebie"? And aren't the stakes vastly greater here? We are talking now about ethical default on a grand scale, with proportionately large and lasting consequences.

Back in the days of Munsey and the first Hearst, less than 5 percent of the newspapers of the country were owned by chains and groups; now that figure is around 50 percent. In the broadcast field, although individual chains or groups typically include fewer units (because the FCC limits the number of radio or television stations that can be held by a single ownership), the overall tendency for these media to be owned in blocks resembles that in the newspaper field.

Let's note again: by no means are all, or even most, group owner-ships failing to meet their obligations within the central journalistic ethic. Many group newspapers or network-owned broadcast stations are among the best in the nation, in terms of service to the public. And it is certainly true, also, that wide ranges of good and bad performance can be cited in individually owned media properties. Group or chain opera-tion is not automatically suspect, and individually owned properties are not invariably responsibly run.

Yet the fact remains that there are built-in pressures that influence the managers of group-owned media properties (Which publisher in the Jones League Newspapers will win the trip to Greece for showing the greatest profit improvement for the year? Which station manager in Group X has saved the most by automating operations and cutting down the payroll—and thus meriting advancement to a bigger market?). It is easy for the main reason-for-being of the paper or the station to be lost in the shuffle, even when intentions may be good.

The degree to which the basic journalistic obligation is unmet may vary widely, whether we are talking about chain properties or individ-ually owned ones. It may be a gross imbalance—profits put ahead of news to the point that the reader, listener, or viewer simply isn't getting a full, honest picture of the world. More often it may be a less drastic matter of trimming sails slightly, avoiding taking chances with aggressive local reporting for fear of upsetting a comfortable, profitable situation.

Loren Ghiglione, who conducted the survey of New England news-papers cited earlier in this book, commented that on many New England dailies there was clearly evident a "don't rock the boat" attitude. As one publisher told him: "We don't dig under the carpet to any particular extent. We don't go looking for trouble. . . . I take my living out of this city and I figure it's my job to do everything I can for it."[2]

In one of a series of *Wall Street Journal* articles on the press, reporter Dan Rottenberg described a small town editor who usually gave thorough coverage to his community, but who also deliberately soft-pedaled or underplayed stories that were likely to alienate a news source or pain a long-time acquaintance (the editor believed that a local bond issue was an extravagance, but didn't oppose it in the paper because the measure was the brainchild of a friend: ". . . it was close to Bill's heart . . .").[3]

Is there a meaningful difference between the action of a police reporter who conveniently "forgets" to write up an embarrassing incident in order to cover up for a friendly news source down at the station, and an editor's silent acquiescence to an unwise bond issue because it is "close to Bill's heart"? Don't both qualify as ethical lapses? Can the editor's wider responsibilities to keep his paper solvent in a small, close-knit community legitimately be advanced as justification for warping principles to avoid alienating powers-that-be? Or is the fault even greater when a high-level gatekeeper tampers with the flow of the news?

The Home Team

While generalized, institutional ethics-bending has perhaps been more frequently evident in situations involving media economics than anywhere else, there are other reasons why media proprietors sometimes alter the picture of reality a little (or a lot) before putting it before the eyes of the public. Among these reasons has been a spirit of sectionalism or support for the home town—what newspaper publisher Warren Harding, in his pre-presidential days, summed up as a policy of "Boost, don't knock."

In one sense, this represents an extension of the philosophy expressed by the New England editor quoted earlier, who said, "We don't go looking for trouble. . . . I take my living out of this city and I figure it's my job to do everything I can for it." The booster's motivation may not be to keep local advertisers or officials happy; it may instead be a reflection of a spirit of defensiveness or protectiveness with respect to the region or the community. Whatever the motive, however, if the end

189

result is a false picture of reality, the journalistic ethic is not being properly served.

A case in point was traced out by two researchers at Stanford University and later published in a *Columbia Journalism Review* article. The two, David Rubin and Stephen Landers, noted an article that had appeared in the November 1968 issue of *McCall's* magazine under the headline "Drink At Your Own Risk." The article was critical of the quality of water supplies available to the residents of more than 100 cities and presented data indicating that in many of these cities water from the taps was only "provisionally" safe to drink.

Rubin and Landers then systematically checked out how this article in a national magazine had been handled as a news situation at the local level, particularly in those communities adversely described. The two researchers found that there was a widespread tendency for local publications to take a hostile or defensive stance, criticizing the magazine's data and quoting local water board denials rather than undertaking any genuine follow-up investigation to find out what the facts really were.

Clearly the majority of papers erred in giving sole prominence to officials who were actors in the situation, from whom the newspapers had no right to expect disinterested answers. Yet many were content to act as an uncritical conduit. . . . A newspaper editor should remember that to shield his community and readers from outside criticism is a dangerous practice.[4]

It may be a dangerous practice, but it is not uncommon. On many papers it is almost instinctive to pull the wagons into a circle and rally the defenses when some outlander has the temerity to criticize the home town.

And the attitude isn't characteristic only of small-town editors.

In 1973 the magazine *Media & Consumer* coordinated a "national meat test" in which seven metropolitan newspapers and television stations cooperated. Reporters from the papers and station staffs went out to food markets in the seven areas and purchased packages of ground beef. These were then tested in independent laboratories, and the results of these tests were subsequently released through the cooperating media channels and also nationwide. The findings indicated that a third of the ground beef packages purchased contained fecal material, and two-thirds contained high counts of coliform bacteria.

As Francis Pollock, editor of *Media & Consumer*, noted in an article in the *Quill*, the seven cooperating media agencies reported the results fully, even though these results reflected on some local merchants in each instance.[5] But the reactions of some other newspaper and broadcast decision makers were in a different vein, as Mr. Pollock points out:

Some editors agonized over whether to run the stories about the National Meat Test that were moved by the wire services. After all, if they weren't in one of the seven cities covered, what conclusions could be drawn about the hamburger in their own cities. Some, thus, chose not to run the story, among them the New York *Times*. . . .

One New York State editor told us the following:

"Our publisher's view was that since none of the places tested were in New York State, the report's validity in our own area was reduced. In fact, it was thought it might cast an unjustly poor image on our area's supermarkets. It was thought that the New York State inspection system is superior to others in the nation and radically different results might be found here."

So, that editor's readers not only didn't learn that bad meat had been found in other cities, but, since the paper assumed New York's health officials were doing a good job, they would never be likely to find out if meat in their supermarkets was good or bad.[6]

Another, and even more puzzling instance of "home team" psychology developed when the *Dayton* (Ohio) *Journal Herald* got a tip that the two U.S. senators from Indiana were linked in various ways to a so-called "bankruptcy ring" operating in Indianapolis.

The Dayton paper assigned one of its investigative reporters, Keith McKnight, to look into the matter, and later assigned a second reporter as well, Andrew Alexander. The two worked for a year probing into the story, and their findings were eventually published as an 11-part series. The stories appeared to confirm existence of a bankruptcy ring and demonstrated some connection between the operations of the ring and one Indiana senator, as well as a former governor of that state. Then, as an editorial in *Columbia Journalism Review* recorded:

Recognizing that Indiana lay beyond its own circulation territory, the *Journal Herald* took care to see that its series was distributed in that state. Before publication it sent copies to three dailies, in South Bend, Kokomo, and Evansville. It also gave a copy to the Associated Press.

If the *Journal Herald* had thought that these steps would ensure publication in Indiana, it was soon disillusioned. Not one of the three dailies used the series, nor, the *Journal Herald* found, did other papers—despite a detailed summary transmitted on the AP regional wire each day. One radio station—which the *Journal Herald* people dubbed Radio Free Indiana—called Dayton every day for the latest information, which it broadcast; the station was WIBC, Indianapolis. A momentary beam of hope came when the Indianapolis *News* reprinted a *Journal Herald* editorial demanding disclosure by Sen. Bayh; then a court reporter for the *Star* produced a story raising the question of indictments in the case. But the reporter abruptly was removed from his beat, and the Pulliam newspapers resumed their silence . . . .

. . . McKnight says, "Never in my ten years of journalism have I witnessed anything so blatantly and unalterably wrong. Yet my partner and I are powerless to do anything about it. Our objectivity has since become encumbered by outrage but even if it was not, the shouts of two journalists, in Dayton, O., don't carry very far."[7]

Silence in the South

The practice of one newspaper's going into another's territory to cover a breaking story, or an uncovered story, is not exactly commonplace, but it used to happen fairly often in the South not very many years ago.

During the years following the 1954 school integration ruling of the Supreme Court, some Southern newspaper editors and publishers purposely adopted a policy of playing down or suppressing altogether incidents that reflected the growing restiveness of the black population. Their reasoning was that to give attention to the sit-ins, the picketings, and the racial clashes would only make an unstable and potentially dangerous situation worse. The result was a deliberate altering of the picture of the world so far as the readers of these newspapers were permitted to perceive it.

Only when reporters for Northern papers, national magazines, or networks, or more enlightened neighboring Southern papers, came in to report what was actually happening was the falsity of this picture exposed.

One community in which such planned suppression of the news took place was Augusta, Georgia, a town served by a morning-evening newspaper combination, the *Chronicle* and the *Herald.*

As George McMillan, a writer for *Columbia Journalism Review,* evaluated it, "the Augusta story is an astonishing case history in how a local newspaper monopoly can ignore the news it does not like for its own readers and, because of the way news is disseminated, keep it from readers everywhere."[8]

As instances of racial unrest and civil rights protest developed in

Augusta, the local papers either ignored them altogether or buried the reports in obsecure locations.

Two *Chronicle* reporters who tried to break through the blackout of news of racial unrest by sending fuller accounts to the Associated Press and the *Atlanta Constitution* were shortly fired by the *Chronicle* for "willful circumvention of the authority of the city editor and managing editor and contributing news to a competing media."[9]

In the long run, the news-suppression policy in Augusta, as elsewhere in the South, proved to be counterproductive even in terms of the rationale devised for it by the blackout editors. For the people in those communities, uninformed for years about the deep-seated troubles brewing in their midst, were taken by surprise when the lid could no longer be kept on; they were unprepared for the violent and bitter passages that followed as the civil rights movement gathered momentum in the South and throughout the nation. The readers of Augusta had not been well served by their newspapers, nor had the journalistic ethic.

A Scoop or a Life?

There are, however, circumstances in which most editors will agree that news suppression can be justified even within the context of the journalistic ethic. We have already noted in another connection the near-universal policy of suppressing the names of rape victims, and the almost equally widespread practice of withholding the names of juveniles charged with minor, first-offense crimes.

Another situation in which many editors and broadcasting news directors will agree to at least a temporary news blackout is in the case of kidnappings.

A survey of managing editors whose newspapers are members of the Associated Press was conducted shortly after the kidnapping of Patricia Hearst, daughter of the president of the *San Francisco Examiner*. At the time of the kidnapping, San Francisco police and the FBI requested that newspapers, broadcast stations, and wire services in the San Francisco area suppress the news for 12½ hours after the event occurred. The authorities feared that publicity might endanger Miss Hearst's life. All of the media complied with the request, including the Associated Press. The survey of the managing editors was to determine whether they agreed or disagreed with the action taken by the media decision makers in San Francisco. Of 328 editors replying to the survey,

193

260 said they agreed with the blackout decision, 40 disagreed, and 28 were not sure.

Some comments from the respondents:

What we did was the ethical, responsible thing to do. To have rushed out in a life-be-damned headline splurge would have been, in my view, nothing short of irresponsibility on our part.—Louis D. Boccardi, executive editor of AP

The easiest course in all of these cases is just to do what the authorities ask us to do. They say . . . it may endanger a life. We say OK and are comfortable in the thought that we have cooperated for good reason. But must we not ask ourselves each time we make an agreement whether it might just be that the authorities are wrong: that there is actually a greater risk to the victim . . . because of the withholding of the information than if we had not withheld it?— Richard D. Smyser, managing editor of the *Oak Ridge* (Tenn.) *Oak Ridger*

In cases where we know a human life may really be at stake, I would think it irresponsible of the press not to take this into account. Admittedly we never know for sure which path is right, but I would not like it said that for the sake of a news story, I might have been responsible for a human life.— Robert P. Clark, managing editor of the *Louisville Courier-Journal* and *Times*[10]

In other surveys of a similar nature, comparable groups of editors have indicated that they would be inclined *not* to withhold or delay news of an airplane hijacking, racial or civil disturbances, or bomb threats in schools or public buildings. But when the issue is one in which it seems clear that immediate breaking of the story might be fatal to a kidnap victim, most editors appear to agree with one of their number who said "I would rather lose a scoop than a life."

When Power Corrupts

There are times—fortunately not frequent—when news is altered or suppressed not for reasons of boosterism, not to avoid alienating advertisers, not to protect a threatened kidnap victim, but quite simply and nakedly to further the personal aims or vent the individual animosities of the man who runs the only—or almost the only—wheel in town.

A publisher or a broadcaster *can* use his media property as an instrument for personal revenge or promotion. No law prevents him. But in this present day he probably will not get away with it for long if the community he theoretically serves is at all alert, and if the other media in the community are on their toes. There was an era in the first third of this century when press lords could issue and enforce edicts prejudicial to enemies and partial to friends. The first William Randolph Hearst ordered the editors of his newspaper chain not to allow the name of Mae West, a Hollywood rival of Hearst's mistress, to appear in any of the Hearst publications. Col. Robert R. McCormick, the opinionated editor of the *Chicago Tribune*, insisted that his editors further his own anti-British prejudice at every opportunity and never, under any circumstance, use a news item that depicted the British in a favorable light.

These men and their methods have to a very large degree passed from the scene. But some of their spiritual descendants are still very much alive and well, as occasional exposés by forthright press critics uncomfortably remind us.

David Anderson, writing in *Columbia Journalism Review*, has chronicled the tactics of a radio and television broadcaster in Michigan, Harold Gross of Lansing, who used his stations and a cable system to tilt the news in support of his personal interests. In an effort to expand his cable operations, Anderson reported, Gross used a selective news blackout against city council members who opposed him:

Larry Carr, a former cameraman for WJIM-TV [one of the Gross stations], says he first learned of the blackout policy when he was sent to shoot footage of a city council meeting in the summer of 1967. When Carr arrived, he was told by reporter William Applegate . . . not to shoot any long shots of the city council. As Carr relates the story, "All filming of the city council was done with close-ups of guys who turned out to be in favor of giving Gross the franchise. On one particular night, the policy made me too angry to even shoot. I told Applegate I didn't think this was a news operation and left." . . . Carr is not the only cameraman who was told not to film certain city councilmen, but others say they are afraid they will be blacklisted if they come forward.[11]

Anderson also reported that Gross used his stations' news coverage to prod balky advertisers into paying their bills:

A memo sent by Gross to sports director Tim Staudt late in 1972 says: "I heard your story last night at both 6 and 11 on the Tennis Tournament being conducted at the Lansing Tennis Club. These people owe us $1,500 which is a

195

year overdue and are making no effort to pay us. Considering these circumstances, I do not want to give them any publicity on the Club or any of their activities."[12]

Another time, when the manager of a rival cable company was shown on a news show on the Gross station, the news director the next day received a memorandum asking: "Why is it you persist in putting Harold Moore on our six o'clock news when he is our enemy?"

Publisher William Loeb of the *Manchester* (N.H.) *Union Leader* is known around the nation for his vituperative front-page editorials attacking his enemies, political and personal. But he also is known, less widely, to have used his news operation for similar personal ends.[13]

When a man Loeb disliked was named president of the University of New Hampshire, Loeb mounted a campaign that *Newsweek* described as "one of the most brutal newspaper assaults ever directed at a U.S. university official."[14] And on another occasion the New Hampshire publisher directed his editors to withhold from the paper all copy about a prizefight in which Muhammad Ali was to appear, on grounds that Ali's refusal to serve in the armed forces warranted such a response.[15]

An episode involving a paper not far from New Hampshire, the *Boston Herald American*, had some disquieting overtones as it was reported in the *New England Newspaper Survey:*

The ethics of reporting on the paper are also dubious. The *Herald American* ran a series of articles attacking the Metropolitan District Commission, a catchall agency for recreation, parks, highways, water supply, sewerage, and other functions in the Greater Boston area.

On March 31, John Sears, Commissioner of the MDC, held a press conference in which he accused the *Herald American* of running the series as a "vendetta" because of "a disagreement with *Herald American* managing editor Jack McLean."

Sears claimed that in 1970 he was pressured by McLean to hire McLean's son. The son was hired. Sears said in the press conference that a year afterward he was again reached by the managing editor asking that his son be promoted. The commissioner said that the son's superiors did not recommend a promotion and the son was not promoted. Sears attributed the paper's series to that. McLean in response said that he had "never personally contacted" the commissioner.[16]

Instances such as these obviously do violence to the central journalistic ethic that the news shall be reported honestly and comprehensively. They reflect the willingness of persons in possession of great power to employ that power not in the public interest, but for their own ends. A British statesman once warned that power corrupts; he was speaking of and to politicians, but his words might as aptly be applied to those whose hands are at the controls of the mighty megaphones of the media of mass communication.

Heroes and Villains

Reporters and others down in the ranks of the news-gathering and news-processing operation do not have as much leverage as publishers and editors in using the media for personal ends. As we have earlier seen, however, such lower-echelon journalists *do* have numerous opportunities to divert, dilute, or dam up the flow of news on a smaller scale. When they take advantage of these opportunities their motives are often different from those of the press barons who manipulate the media—not always more honorable, perhaps, but different.

To be sure, there are occasional isolated instances such as that of the Philadelphia reporter who blackmailed local businessmen by threatening to run unfavorable news about them unless he was paid off (chapter 3). Personal gain was plainly the motive in that case.

Usually, however, when reporters, cameramen, or desk editors abuse the journalistic ethic by retouching the picture of reality a bit, it is not likely to be for personal gain, or for simple spite. In most cases it results from the journalist's conscious or unconscious attempt to interpret the news so as to bring out the best points of a figure who is currently a media hero, or to reveal the black nature of a current media villain, or to advance a cause seen to be "right," or to unmask a movement perceived to be "wrong."

At this point we are skirting close to a kind of no-man's-land (or, in these enlightened days, a "no-person's-land"), a territory fought over inconclusively in a dozen battles and skirmishes that have gone into the journalism texts as "objectivity vs. interpretation," or "editorializing vs. advocacy," or "new journalism vs. old."

This is a pretty sizable piece of territory, as well as a controversial one. The issues that have been fought over (and are still being fought over) include ones that are by no means exclusively ethical in character, but involve the changing nature of journalism in a period of accelerating change throughout society. A full book would be needed to explore all

197

of these issues informatively—and, in fact, at least half a dozen such have already been written.[17]

For our purposes, it will be enough to note briefly the characteristics of the "new journalism" experimentation and call attention to some of the ways in which such experimentation may strain the central journalistic ethic.

In *Other Voices: The New Journalism in America,* Everette E. Dennis and William L. Rivers categorize the various forms of new journalism that have come on the scene in the last decade or so. They also note the rationale offered by the practitioners of the new journalistic forms:

The best objective report may cover all the surface of an event, the best interpretative report may explain all its meanings, but both are bloodless, a world away from the experience. Color, flavor, atmosphere, the ultimate human meaning—all these, the new journalists contend, are far beyond the reach of conventional journalism. This is one of the central reasons for the emergence of different forms and practices, but there are others.[18]

The new forms and practices, according to the Dennis and Rivers typology, include:

—new nonfiction

—alternative journalism

—journalism reviews

—advocacy journalism

—counterculture journalism

—alternative broadcasting

—precision journalism

With some of these categories of new journalism we do not, in this book, need to be concerned in detail. Precision journalism, for example, is essentially only old journalism—objective journalism—practiced with the efficient new tools of the social scientists: opinion surveys, computers, census figures. Whatever ethical problems are associated with precision journalism are very like those we have been examining in general terms in earlier chapters.

Counterculture journalism—the underground press—is aimed at a specialized audience (usually the young and alienated) and makes no bones about it. If it is concerned with ethics, such concern would be in terms of values and standards far different from those respected by journalists generally.

As for the journalism reviews, we shall be looking into them in a later chapter, since they constitute one of the few quality-control agencies currently functioning.

That leaves us with the new nonfiction, with alternative journalism and alternative broadcasting (they fit together), and with advocacy journalism, to examine at this point.

No Instant Capotes

The new nonfiction practitioners include such writers as Truman Capote, novelist turned new journalist; Gay Talese, a former conventional news reporter; and Tom Wolfe, who evolved through newspapers and magazines into book-length reportage.

Capote and Talese represent one school of the new nonfiction writers, and their approach could best be described as saturational. They burrow into a story at great length and with minute detail, as Capote did when he recounted the saga of two real-life murderers in his book *In Cold Blood*, or as Talese did in *The Kingdom and the Power*, a fascinating backstage look at power struggles within the hierarchy of the *New York Times*.

Their style includes the recreation of conversational exchanges that may not have been overheard by the reporter or anyone else and the depiction of the thoughts and feelings of protagonists in the news situation. The new nonfiction writers defend these practices—which traditional journalists tend to regard as akin to fictionalizing—on the ground that they get so close to the story and to the people about whom they are writing that the reconstructions and the thought reading are as faithful to reality as the straight reporter's boiled-down but representative quote.

When such a thesis is advanced by a Truman Capote or a Gay Talese, who spend quite literally months or years working on a single book-length report, it has considerable plausibility. The trouble begins, and the journalistic ethic is endangered, when less experienced writers with far less time at their disposal attempt to emulate the masters.

There are no instant Capotes, and no shortcuts to the kind of non-fiction reportage that he and Talese have developed. When other journalists working against short deadlines try to pull off the trick, they are obliged to resort to expedients that can't pass the journalistic test, new *or* old.

Such an expedient is the "composite character," someone who doesn't exist as such but is presented in an interpretive account as an actual person. The attributes of the composite character may all be true of several other people, and the things that purportedly happen to the composite character may actually have happened to a number of other persons. But the character to which the reader is introduced in the story is in essence fictional, although the reader is not told this.

Writers who make use of composite characters as a device of the new nonfiction insist that they are representative and thus "equal to," in the poet's language used earlier in this book.

But once the reporter begins dipping into the novelist's paint pots, how true will his colors remain to the journalistic ethic? How is the reader to know which "facts" are reality and which semifiction?

And when the followers of Capote and Talese on the staffs of daily newspapers begin reconstructing the thoughts and motives of the figures in the news, what assurance has the reader that this reconstruction reflects painstaking, time-consuming homework, rather than hurried, ill-informed guesswork?

Tom Wolfe and his followers try for the "color, flavor, atmosphere" of the news in a different fashion. Wolfe evolved a style characterized by a cavalier disregard for conventional punctuation, rhetoric, or usage. He invented new words, freely indulged in what used to be called editorializing, and conveyed the *feeling* of situations or characters by stylistic means.

Wolfe handled these tools with a sure and colorful touch. The result certainly was not conventional journalism. Whether it was closer to reality, to *experience* as Dennis and Rivers put it, than was the old journalism, is arguable. What is not arguable is that copycat efforts by writers without Wolfe's exceptional talents, and without the time to spend weeks developing a single feature—as Wolfe did—fell woefully short in most instances of either journalism *or* experience.

The new nonfiction may be a short-lived adjunct to journalism, or it may turn out to be one, at least, of the waves of the future. But it calls for literary abilities of a very high order and for deadline freedom that is so costly that mass media managers think it is unrealistic.

Back-Swinging Pendulum

The advocacy journalists, many of them columnists or political writers, reject the "old" journalism because in their eyes a long-standing imbalance needs to be redressed.

It is their contention that traditional, objective reporting automatically favors the status quo (for example, by letting "official sources" shape the news, by operating within established value contexts). It is high time, the advocates contend, that journalism use its vast leverage to spur improvement in society. They want newspapers, broadcasting stations, and magazines to stop being mirrors of what now is, or sterile conduits for the reiteration of conventional wisdom, and to become instead instruments of change.

The journalists of advocacy don't want to be simply observers; they want to be up on the stage, with a piece of the action. They want to be involved, not dispassionate; they want to be allowed to let their own opinions show through in their reportage.

Not surprisingly, the advocacy journalism thesis has met with varying degrees of dismay and outrage by those steeped in traditional practices. The traditionalists see in the new movement nothing more than a fashionable label for an old abuse—distortion and editorializing in the news columns.

Eric Sevareid, a veteran and respected television commentator, well expressed that school of thought:

Militant young men and women, in both newspapers and broadcasting, argue that even the *quest* for objectivity is a myth, that the prime purpose of the press is not to report the world but to reform it, and in the direction of their ideas. We have all read the learned articles that tell us objective news accounts deceive the reader or hearer, obscure inner truths that the reporter perceives. He must therefore personalize the news, infuse it with his own truth. They would not leave this to the editorial writer, columnist and commentary writer, whose work is clearly marked away from the hard news. They believe that this will give a true integrity to news columns and news broadcasts. I believe it will ruin them.[19]

When journalists take on the additional mantle of advocacy they put their credibility as reporters of news in jeopardy. They may do this

201

knowingly, justifying the risk on the grounds that the ends to be served are urgent and just. Or they may be unaware of either their partisanship or the consequent hazard to their journalistic standing.

For example, when the Ervin Committee, the select committee set up to investigate the Watergate scandals, was meeting in daily televised sessions in 1973, the network commentators who were covering the scene were inevitably drawn into the absorbing melodrama. When television reporters would be brought on camera during committee recesses to sum up testimony or report backstage developments, they often would wonder aloud to the audience of 40 million why this or that line of inquiry hadn't been pursued by the committee counsel. And, sure enough, a bit later in the hearing day the suggested questions would come up; the television reporters had, in effect, signed on as assistants to the investigating staff.

A few years earlier, a celebrated trial generated a similar involvement by reporters ostensibly assigned to write from the sidelines. The trial was that of a New Orleans businessman, Clay L. Shaw, who had been charged by the then district attorney, James Garrison, with having conspired in the assassination of President John F. Kennedy. Months of sensational charges and countercharges had preceded the trial itself, and the press corps on hand numbered 175 when the sessions began. Before long, the reporters started to take sides in corridor debates, and eventually some began to take even more active roles.

Two writers for *Columbia Journalism Review*, Roger M. Williams and Michael Parks, described how several of the reporters evolved into participants rather than observers, passing on tips and advice to defense attorneys.[20]

One of the reporters who became thus drawn into the story he was supposed to be covering later said that in his 20 years in the business he had "never gotten involved in any story like I did in this one." And the two *Review* writers concluded:

. . . it is a long step from criticizing an official and his actions to helping blunt them through actions of one's own. It is a step a journalist can ill afford to take—while he still professes to be a journalist.[21]

Theodore H. White, author of several books on presidential campaigns, recorded another aspect of advocacy journalism in action:

I did the movie version of *The Making of the President 1968*. We had two crews on the road all the time. They were young and wonderful cameramen.

I was busy writing my book and reporting and I couldn't direct the film crews, so about nine months later when I finally got to Hollywood to put the film together, I found that these young people absolutely adored Eugene McCarthy and Robert Kennedy, and there was not a bad shot of either Gene McCarthy or Bobby Kennedy in the thousands and thousands of feet that we took. The images were glowing. On the other hand, these people who worked with me did not bring back one human shot of Hubert Humphrey. Everything that was taken looked sinister.[22]

Ever since advocacy or activist journalism came on the scene, there has been a tendency for such reporters to foster the fortunes of their heroes of the moment and repeatedly focus on the bad profile of their pet villains. John F. Kennedy benefited from a friendly press corps during his presidency, while Lyndon Johnson had ups and downs in both bad-guy and good-guy roles, and Richard Nixon became the longest-playing villain in the history of press-politician relationships. (More on that in the next chapter.)

Henry Kissinger, through a good part of his career as presidential foreign policy adviser and later as Secretary of State, was a notably successful media hero. After President Nixon's forced resignation and the accession of President Gerald Ford, Kissinger's treatment by the press reverted to normal, but during a period of about four years it appeared that he could do no wong in the eyes of the media.

His mixture of overpowering scholarship, deep-voiced authority, and canny cultivation of press people—and the fact that he was just about the only consistently accessible high official in the Nixon administration—combined to assure him almost unprecedentedly favorable treatment by the diplomatic reporting corps. As *Time* observed:

Indisputably, a kind of special relationship has developed between a usually admiring press and a courting Kissinger over the years since he unpacked his books in the White House basement in 1969. . . . At times reporters seem even more preoccupied with Kissinger's image than he is. All it took was a few well-publicized dates with such Hollywood lovelies as Marlo Thomas and Samantha Eggar to establish Kissinger as a "secret swinger." When Kissinger's role is less engaging, newsmen tend to look the other way. The press scarcely dwelt on Kissinger's embarrassing 1973 interview with Italian journalist Oriana Fallaci, in which he saw himself as a "cowboy—alone astride his horse."[23]

The envied reporters who regularly flew with Kissinger on his celebrated missions in search of peace in Vietnam and a cease-fire in the Middle East became not only the best-informed journalists in the world at the time ("We know more than most U.S. ambassadors in the places we visit," said one) but also, in effect, part of the Kissinger apparatus or staff. Here is a revealing comment from one analysis of the Kissinger-press relationship, particularly with respect to the airborne entourage:

All of this can affect the way a journalist sees his colleagues as well as his own mission. "Have you got anything coming up that'll embarrass us?" one investigative reporter recalls being asked by a worried diplomatic reporter who was about to depart on a Kissinger trip. "It was the 'us' that really killed me," the reporter added.[24]

The spirit of "us" is perhaps the most insidious aspect of advocacy journalism if one is viewing the new development within a context of the journalistic ethic.

Max M. Kampleman, campaign advisor to Senator Hubert Humphrey in the 1972 presidential primary campaign, observed at that time:

I sense that the tendency toward advocacy journalism is there—both on the air and in the print media. And even though frequently the advocacy happens to be on my side, I think it's a disservice to our democratic institutions. I don't like it.[25]

And Nicholas von Hoffman, nationally syndicated columnist who was regarded as one of the first and most successful of the advocacy journalists, once wrote of some of his counterparts:

Some of the leading figures in U.S. journalism are throwing off the old clothes of skepticism and are putting on uniforms and enlisting in a variety of causes. This is usually called the new journalism, and it is usually justified by saying that times are so bad, the issues so crucial that the old norms are a luxury we can't afford. The new journalists are impervious to the counter-argument that it is exactly in the worst of times when partisanship is most irrational and unseeing that we most need persons speaking and writing who are free of its claims.

When a newspaperman joins up with the cause, he risks serving higher loyalties than his work and his own opinions; he is in danger of becoming a spokesman, a person who no longer conceives of his duty to tell all there is to tell but to make his side look good, to emphasize what's alluring and skip over what's hard to explain.[26]

The Alternatives

Those who fall into the Dennis-Rivers category of "alternative" journalists, both print and broadcast, to some degree share with the exponents of advocacy the conviction that established journalism has too long and too consistently supported things as they are and thus, in effect, resisted change and reform.

But the alternative journalists do not depart from the basic standards of the craft as they have been acknowledged through recent decades; they do not "put on uniforms" or "join up" to become partisan advocates.

They are exemplified by such newspapers as the *San Francisco Bay Guardian*, and such broadcast operations as KQED-TV in the same city. Their approach is to use relatively conventional reporting methods, but to zero in on areas of coverage that the traditional media have neglected or soft-pedaled. The *Guardian*, for example, devotes whole issues to examining in close and unflattering detail the activities of some Bay Area utilities that have usually had only cursory attention from the major media.

In other words, the alternative journalists slant or tilt the news only in the sense that they concentrate on certain types of news, in the effort to correct what they consider to be the sins of omission of the "old" journalists.

They do not pose ethical problems in the strict sense. Their activities do, however, raise a possibility that was explored by J. Russell Wiggins, former editor of the *Washington Post* in an article in the *Quill*. Wiggins recalled the fact that American journalism evolved from the fragmented, strongly partisan press of the early nineteenth century into a nonparty journalism of general circulation, suitable to the age of consensus in which we have been living through most of the present century. But, he went on:

Now I think it takes no seer to perceive that the age of consensus is ending or certainly will be ending in the '70s. I do not say that the characteristic daily newspaper will end with it; but I do say that it is going to be increasingly difficult to retain the confidence of a reader audience of infinitely more diverse views. The more that society divides into irreconcilable fragments, the more difficult it will be to maintain that universal credibility necessary both to general reader distribution and to advertising profitability in newspapers of general circulation. . . . I think it likely that one of two things will happen. I prefer to believe that they [newspapers of general circulation] will meet the challenge of such an era. . . . I think, however, that it is not utterly impossible that a fragmented polity will lead us back to the equivalent of the 18th century party press in which the absence of impartiality will be redeemed by candor of confessed partisanship at a calamitous cost in terms of comprehensive coverage and professional standards.[27]

The alternative journalists presumably have no wish to return to the days of the party press. Yet as more specialized channels arise to provide corrective coverage, to swing the pendulum in the other direction, to displace the medium of general circulation, the closer will the journalistic scene of today come to resemble that of 150 years ago. There might be both good and bad in that prospect; whether you prefer to see the cup half-full or half-empty depends to a considerable degree on how you choose to define Establishment and Alternative Journalism.

In the next chapter we'll take a look at one further area in which abuses of the central journalistic ethic have taken place—and an area in which other, nonethical issues of great significance also have been at stake.

Notes

[1]Upton Sinclair, *The Brass Check: A Study of American Journalism* (Pasadena, California: published by the author, 1920), p. 436.

[2]Loren Ghiglione, ed., *Evaluating the Press: The New England Newspaper Survey* (Southbridge, Mass.: published by the editor, 1973), p. 4.

[3]See Dan Rottenberg, "E. J. Van Nostrand: Easygoing Editor," in *The Press: A Critical Look from the Inside.*, ed. A. Kent MacDougall (Princeton: Dow Jones Books, 1972), pp. 34–41.

[4]David M. Rubin and Stephen Landers, "National Exposure and Local Cover-up: A Case Study," *Columbia Journalism Review*, XIII, No. 2 (Summer, 1969), 17–22.

[5]The seven cooperating media: WBZ-TV, Boston; WTTW-TV, Chicago; *Dayton* (Ohio) *Daily News*, Louisville (Ky.) *Courier-Journal*; *Philadelphia Bulletin*; *St. Petersburg* (Fla.) *Times*; and *The Bay Guardian*, San Francisco.

[6]Francis Pollock, "Getting the Goods on Ground Beef," *Quill*, LXI, No. 12 (December 1973), 17–19.

[7]"Indiana Papers, Please Copy," reprinted from the *Columbia Journalism Review*, XI, No. 3 (September/October 1972), © 5–6.

8George McMillan, "Georgia Unchronicled," *Columbia Journalism Review*, I, No. 2 (Summer, 1962), © 39–42.

9*Ibid.*, p. 40.

10Joe Shoquist, "Editors Back AP Decision to Delay Kidnapping Story," *Associated Press Managing Editor News*, No. 72 (April 1974), pp. 1, 4–5.

11David Anderson, "Blackout in Lansing," reprinted from the *Columbia Journalism Review*, XII, No. 6 (March/April 1974) ©, 26–29.

12*Ibid.*, p. 28.

13See Albert R. Hunt, "William Loeb: Lrascible Publisher," in *The Press: A Critical Look from the Inside*, A. Kent MacDougall, ed. (Princeton: Dow Jones Books, 1972), 42–49.

14Quoted in Jules Witcover, "William Loeb and the New Hampshire Primary: A Question of Ethics," reprinted from the *Columbia Journalism Review*, XI, No. 1 (May/June 1972), © 14–25.

15*Ibid.*

16Loren Ghiglione, *Evaluating the Press*, p. 166.

17Among them: Everette E. Dennis and William L. Rivers, *Other Voices: The New Journalism in America* (San Francisco: Canfield Press, 1974); Thomas Wolfe, *The New Journalism* (New York: Harper & Row, Publishers, Inc., 1973); and Robert Glessing, *The Underground Press in America* (Bloomington: Indiana University Press, 1970).

18Dennis and Rivers, *Other Voices: The New Journalism in America*, pp. 4–5.

19Eric Sevareid, "The Quest for Objectivity," *Nieman Reports*, XXIV, No. 4 (December 1970), 13.

20Roger M. Williams and Michael Parks, "The Clay Shaw Trial: Reporter-participants," *Columbia Journalism Review*, VIII, No. 1 (Spring, 1969), 38–41.

21*Ibid.*, p. 41.

22Theodore H. White, "America's Two Cultures," *Columbia Journalism Review*, VIII, No. 4 (Winter, 1969–70), 8–13.

23"A Too-Special Relationship," *Time*, CIII, No. 25 (June 24, 1974), 52.

24Roger Morris, "Henry Kissinger and the Media: A Separate Peace," *Columbia Journalism Review*, XIII, No. 1 (May/June 1974), 14–25.

25"The Press in the 1972 Campaign," a symposium, *Nieman Reports*, XXVII, No. 3 (Fall, 1973), 3–9.

26Nicholas von Hoffman, "The Unnatural Job and a Desire to Keep It So," *Quill*, LIX, No. 11 (November 1971), 14–15.

27James Russell Wiggins, "The Press in an Age of Controversy," *Quill*, LVII, No. 4 (April 1969), 8–14.

The Press in Politics... "A reasonable hypothesis is that the most powerful effect of the mass media on public knowledge . . . is the ability of the media to focus public attention on certain problems, persons, or issues at a given time."

—Wilbur Schramm[1]

11 When press critics draw up their indictments against the media of mass communication they invariably include a count or two citing bias and distortion in the handling of news of politics. They sometimes label the offenses as violations of journalistic ethics.

And the politicians themselves, from Washington to Ford, rarely have been satisfied with the way in which the press of their day has presented them to the public; somehow their numerous virtues are never adequately emphasized, while their missteps—both public and private—are noted in much more detail than the politicians would prefer. This, the aggrieved politicians frequently assert, demonstrates the lack of ethical standards in the press.

As with the kinds of situations we were examining in the last chapter, the area of political reportage is one in which the journalist's ethical values do indeed have to withstand some tough testing. But it is also an area in which other, broader questions are involved as well. Sorting out which matters to include in a discussion of press ethics isn't a simple task, since there is a good deal of complex intermingling.

For example, underlying all press coverage of political news is the concept of the adversary relationship between press and government. The terms "fourth estate" and "the fourth branch of government" are not empty labels; the press does indeed function as an indispensable element of our system by keeping the business of politics under close scrutiny on behalf of the public. In this role, reporters and editors necessarily have to adopt a critical, aggressive, and inquisitive stance toward those in office, of whatever party. Of their own volition, officeholders can't be expected to call attention to any but their good works; in their place, any of us would likely also want to put the best foot forward. But the voters need to see both feet, and to know whether there is any clay in the composition. It is understandable that the officeholder, eager to maintain a sufficiently attractive public image so that he can be elected next time around, would find the journalist's adversary stance troublesome, even dangerous to his survival. But that doesn't mean that it is an unethical stance.

Let's note again, for clarity's sake: There *are* instances of unethical political journalism to be cited; but some of the complaints by politicians involve activities that don't deserve such citation.

Consider one complaint that has been current for generations. Democratic party candidates, particularly at the national level, have pointed to the tendency of newspapers to endorse the Republican candidate, whoever he happened to be at the time, as evidence that the press was biased against Democrats.

Franklin D. Roosevelt was opposed by the editors of most of the country's papers (but he won the presidency four times nonetheless). Harry Truman campaigned as much against the press as against the 80th Congress. Adlai Stevenson coined the phrase "one-party press" to describe the united front of media opposition he encountered as his party's standard-bearer in 1952 and 1956. Among Democratic presidential candidates, only Lyndon B. Johnson, in his 1964 race against the conservative Barry Goldwater, was supported by any substantial segment of press leadership.

Yet this long record, and the complaint of bias based upon it, must be looked at closely if we are to evaluate them in terms of ethical violations. For the support so regularly extended to the Republican candidates in recent decades has been primarily in the form of *editorial page* endorsement. The editorial page is the plainly labeled section in which the opinion of the paper's ownership is expressed, along with other views. It is scarcely surprising, nor should it be considered unethical, that newspaper ownership would express its preference for the political party that has traditionally advanced conservative economic policies; similar expressions have been made in various ways by many other owners of substantial properties.

Insofar as the political preferences of media ownership have been expressed through the editorial function—and only through that avenue —there can be little basis for complaint about violation of the journalistic ethic.

Where ethical questions legitimately arise—and where the critics' and the politicians' charges bite—are in those instances where newspapers or other media have employed the *news* function as well as the editorial function to further the political fortunes of their favorites.

A candidate who gets a fair break in news coverage has an opportunity to make his case with the voters, and if they are impressed by that case he can win even though every editorial writer, columnist, and commentator in the business has formally announced support for the opposition. It may not be easy, but it can be done.

Franklin Roosevelt was undismayed by the lack of editorial page support for his many candidacies because he well knew that he was getting plenty of coverage on page one and elsewhere in the news sections. Truman's 1948 whistle-stop campaign was fully reported by the news pages even though the editorial writers kept speculating about which luminaries would be picked for the cabinet of President Dewey. The news of Truman's underdog campaign got through to the voters and they sent him back to the White House (and Thomas E. Dewey back to the top of the wedding cake, from which, an unkind contemporary critic had said, he always appeared to have just stepped down).

Deck-Stacking

But a candidate has ample cause to complain if the news operations are being stacked against him. If he is the victim of unbalanced coverage (vastly greater space to his opponent's campaign activities) or of slanted, distorted news coverage, he may well lose when he might have won in a fair fight.

Such deck-stacking has been evident in American journalism in varying degrees throughout its history. In the days of the Partisan Press, during the first half-century or so of the nation's existence, it was the rule rather than the exception for newspapers to use an all-out, no-holds-barred approach in politics. They were openly party organs in those days and made little pretense of balance or fairness in coverage; the whole of the paper was, in effect, an editorial expression. Yet, as William Rivers and Wilbur Schramm point out in *Responsibility in Mass Communication,* this was not considered *in those times* to be out of line, unethical, or in any sense a violation of the concept of press freedom protected by the Constitution.

Consider: The guarantee in the Bill of Rights makes it unnecessary for a newspaper or magazine owned by a devout Democrat, or a devout Republican, *even to mention the names* of the opposition party's candidates for President, Congress, the city council, the school board, and other offices, much less to present their platforms, policies, and programs. The vast range of other political concerns can be treated according to a publisher's whim, or not at all. This is one of the measures of the freedom granted by the U.S. Constitution and embedded in the libertarian idea.[2]

Over the years, and particularly with the evolution of the concepts of social responsibility and objective reporting, the kind of blatant bias evident in the days of the partisan press has to a considerable degree disappeared from the scene. As the journalistic ethic is now generally understood, political candidates should receive fair and equal treatment in the news columns; what the editors do about expressing their opinions on the editorial page should be a wholly unrelated matter.

As Rivers and Schramm observe:

As much as by any other factor, the change has been influenced by the journalist's ethic. Taught from the beginning to seek out and report fact, the young journalist takes it as an article of faith that he is not to slant news toward private, personal, or group interest. This ethic pervades the news operation, touching those who are in its orbit—including owners—as well as those who have been schooled in its tradition. It is almost unimaginable today that a publisher or broadcaster would try to order his employees to present news in a way that squares with his own political leanings. This springs in part from the pervasive journalist's ethic, in part from the growing belief among the owners and managers of the mass media that their right to reach great publics implies an obligation.[3]

This assessment is no doubt a valid one so far as most journalists are concerned in most situations. While publishers may still be united in their editorial page endorsements, the great majority of present-day editors and reporters try their best to play the news of politics straight in the rest of the paper, balancing space equitably and sorting out news values without regard to partisanship.

There are, however, exceptions.

There are still some publishers who try to use *all* of the leverage of their newspapers or magazines, news as well as editorial, for political purposes, and there are still writers who go along with this abuse of the journalistic ethic. They have counterparts in the broadcast media as well.

It should be underlined once again that the exceptions are aberrations, departures from a norm that is generally responsible. But since departures do exist, let's look at a few examples.

Time's Tactics

Time has been singled out by numerous press critics and journalism scholars as a vehicle for bias and distortion in reporting political news. The magazine's editors and writers have through the years acquired a widespread reputation for their adroit blending of fact and opinion in what is still advertised as "The weekly *news*magazine."

Several analysts have noted the techniques used by *Time* to stack the deck against those it has opposed politically, and to build up those it has favored. References to the magazine's heroes are usually flattering, any mention of a villain of the moment is likely to be denigrating. Constant repetition of such themes over a period of time can build up stereotypical impressions in the reader's mind and condition the way in which he will perceive the personages referred to. As communication researchers have emphasized, the greatest impact the media have on the formation or change of public opinion is in terms of impressions built up over a long period. John C. Merrill, a professor of journalism at the University of Missouri who studied the way in which *Time* had handled political reporting through three presidencies, concluded that the magazine regularly editorialized in its "news" columns and made use of a "whole series of tricks to bias the stories and to lead the reader's thinking."[4]

Those *Time* is promoting speak out "warmly" or "with a happy grin," while those out of favor respond "curtly" or "flushed with anger." While such evaluative terms may fit the situation some of the time, the pattern of good-guy and bad-guy in *Time's* characterizations is too consistent to be explained away in terms of news values or reporters' judgments.

213

Even one former editor of the magazine, T. S. Matthews, acknowledged the validity of the criticism leveled by Merrill and others:

In 1952, when it sniffed victory in the air at long last, there was no holding *Time*. The distortions, suppositions and slanting of its political "news" seemed to me to pass the bounds of politics and to commit an offense against the ethics of journalism.[5]

Time's loyalties and its targets have changed over the years, but the tactics have remained familiar. Until late in Lyndon Johnson's administration, the magazine was a stout supporter of the Vietnam involvement by American forces ("It's the right war in the right place at the right time," said one editor); later the magazine changed its opinion, but used its same, familiar stacked-deck tactics in opposing continued American fighting. Republicans usually were *Time* favorites, but in the post-Watergate period the magazine became one of Richard Nixon's most vicious and vindictive pursuers.

Henry Luce and other editors of *Time* repeatedly contended that, since they had never professed to be objective in their charter manifesto or in other statements of policy, their slanting of the news in the magazine was no more unethical than the newspaper editor expressing his views in the editorial column.

Yet there is that line in the advertising: "The weekly *news*magazine." And there is little doubt that many readers view *Time's* reports as unmanaged news; in fact, as Professor Merrill's study pointed out, the writers go to great pains to establish an impression of verisimilitude for all the copy in the publication. Certainly insofar as political news is concerned, *Time* bends the journalistic ethic out of recognizable shape.

Back Home in Indiana . . .

Time has no monopoly on deck-stacking tactics, however, as a detailed case study of the handling of a presidential primary compaign by two of Indiana's leading newspapers emphasized several years ago.

Jules Witcover, then with Newhouse National News Service and later to join the *Los Angeles Times* staff, traveled on the 1968 Democratic presidential primary trail and in the process got a close-up view of political coverage as practiced by the *Indianapolis Star* and *News*.

In the primary that year the candidates were Robert F. Kennedy, Eugene J. McCarthy, and Roger D. Branigin. Kennedy and McCarthy, both senators and both strong contenders, were in the race to move their national campaigns along. Branigin, then governor of Indiana, was running as a favorite son, without national stature or legitimate hopes—but with the staunch support of the two Pulliam newspapers in Indianapolis.

Before the campaign was over, Kennedy was to describe the papers publicly as "the worst newspapers in the country," and his press secretary, Pierre Salinger, was to charge them with "outrageous and callous disregard for fairness" in covering the campaign.

In response, Eugene C. Pulliam, publisher of both Indianapolis papers, issued a statement from Phoenix, where he owns the *Arizona Republic:*

Bobby Kennedy is like all spoiled children. When he doesn't get what he wants, he bellyaches about it. The facts are Kennedy and his entourage received more space in *The Indianapolis Star* and *The Indianapolis News* than any other candidate, largely for the reason he brought his whole family, including his mother, to Indianapolis and they made news and we printed the news and pictures.

Of course we are opposed to his candidacy because we don't believe men who spend millions of dollars in a primary campaign should be given the nomination for the highest office in our government. Editorially, we have tried to make it clear that Indiana, at least, is not for sale. But in our news columns we have given Kennedy a far better break than he has given any of his opponents.[6]

Where was the truth? Had there been "outrageous and callous" violation of the journalistic ethic? Or was this another case in which the politician complains only because he hasn't been the beneficiary of a kind of publicity-agent coverage by the press?

As Witcover sorted it all out in a detailed *Columbia Journalism Review* article, there apparently had indeed been some lapse from ethical practices.

For example, Witcover examined Pulliam's assertion that Kennedy had received more space in the Indianapolis papers than had the other candidates:

From March 28 through May 7, the survey showed, Branigin had received 664 column-inches of staff copy in the *Star*, compared with 459 for Kennedy and 382 for McCarthy. In the *News*, the breakdown was Branigin, 384 column-inches; Kennedy, 253; McCarthy, 202.

Sheer volume of space, of course, does not in itself prove editorial bias. The flow of news is uneven; in a political campaign, one candidate often is more active than another, says more, or creates more public interest. Among out-of-state reporters who covered all three candidates, that candidate in the Indiana primary clearly was Kennedy. His crowds dwarfed those of the other two, and in fact the campaign rapidly began to revolve around him as a personality. Kennedy himself—the outsider, the big spender, the Bobby-come-lately—became the dominant issue. Yet in the forty days surveyed he made page one in the *Star* only eleven times and in the *News* only six times in the editions kept in the papers' own rag files. Branigin stories were on page one of the *Star* seventeen mornings (sometimes two or three stories on the same day) and on page one of the *News* fourteen evenings. McCarthy, who was treated offhandedly until the late stages, made page one of the *Star* three days, and two days in the *News*, in the editions checked.[7]

Witcover also noted the *Star*'s deliberate doctoring of an editorial quoted from the *New York Times*. The editorial appeared on page one of the *Star* under the headline: **"Is Indiana for Sale? Asks the New York Times."**

One paragraph in the quoted editorial, as printed in the *Star*, read as follows:

In the three-cornered struggle now nearing a climax in Indiana, the power of money works in favor of Senator Robert F. Kennedy, who can draw upon the resources of a huge family fortune. Governor Roger D. Branigin, the "favorite son" candidate, is the leader of a state party organization.
Senator McCarthy, without a personal fortune . . .

But as the editorial appeared in the *Times*, it had included additional material, which the *Star* editors had deleted without any indication to their readers. The original *Times* wording, with the portion deleted by the *Star* italicized:

In the three-cornered struggle now nearing a climax in Indiana, the power of money works in favor of Senator Robert F. Kennedy, who can draw upon the resources of a huge family fortune. Governor Roger D. Branigin, the "favorite son" candidate, is the leader of the state party organization *which controls thousands of patronage jobs and which still engages in the ancient and disreputable practice of levying a 2 per cent party tax on the salaries of state employees.* Senator McCarthy, without a personal fortune . . .[8]

That was deck-stacking with a vengeance, a solidly documented instance of shady journalistic ethics.

Witcover concluded his analysis thus:

The use of editorials and cartoons to project a newspaper's point of view is, of course, a tradition of American journalism, and a strength when exercised straightforwardly and responsibly. . . . But when the line between a newspaper's editorial view and its reportage of the news becomes so blurred that the average reader no longer can be expected reasonably to discern where fact ends and opinion and propaganda take over, the community—and the integrity of the news business—are ill-served.[9]

Mr. Loeb Again

Four years later there was another Democratic presidential primary, and that same Jules Witcover was on hand to witness another instance of dubious ethical performance by a newspaper. This time the scene was New Hampshire, and the cast of characters included Senator Edmund S. Muskie of Maine, Mayor Sam Yorty of Los Angeles, and William Loeb, publisher of the *Manchester* (N.H.) *Union Leader*, a man we met in chapter 10.

Loeb, a bluntly outspoken conservative, had for years caught national attention from time to time with his vitriolic editorial characterization of persons in political life whose policies he disliked. He called Dwight D. Eisenhower "Dopey Dwight" and "that stinking hypocrite." John F. Kennedy was "the Number One threat to America." Eleanor Roosevelt was, to Loeb, "Ellie and her belly-crawling liberal friends." And Eugene J. McCarthy was, succinctly, "skunk."

Most of Loeb's barbs were hurled via his editorial column, which he would move to the front page for special occasions or to take aim at special targets. But he didn't always stay within even those expanded editorial boundaries.

In the 1972 primary, the leading candidate for the Democratic nomination, and at that time considered to be an almost unbeatable front-runner, was Senator Muskie. But Muskie was not at all popular with Mr. Loeb, so Loeb undertook to import a more suitable candidate. This turned out to be the mayor of Los Angeles, Sam Yorty, who was little known outside his own state and not a figure of stature even there. But he was a hawk on the Vietnam war issue, and that was what Loeb wanted. So Yorty went on the New Hampshire primary ballot as the darkest of dark horses, but assured of VIP treatment in the *Union Leader,* the state's most powerful news medium.

Witcover made a quantitative analysis of the news coverage of the primary candidates in the *Union Leader* during a five-week campaign period and found the same sort of evidence of imbalance that he had observed in Indiana four years earlier. The totals: Yorty, 870 column-inches; Muskie, 420 column-inches; Senator George McGovern of South Dakota, 262 column-inches; Senator Vance Hartke of Indiana, 241 column-inches; and Representative Wilbur D. Mills of Arkansas, a write-in candidate, 144 column-inches. As Witcover summed it up:

> . . . the spectacle of Yorty receiving more than twice as much space as Muskie, and well more than the other four Democratic candidates combined, is indefensible on its face. Yorty, unlike Muskie and McGovern, never was a serious candidate, except in Loeb's eyes. Nor did Yorty ever say or do anything during the campaign that would have merited major news play under standard journalistic yardsticks.[10]

Witcover painstakingly details the angry, hammering attacks on Muskie that the paper kept up throughout the primary, both through Loeb's editorials ("Senator Flip-Flop Muskie") and in manipulated or blown-up news stories.

The most celebrated instances were two that came late in the campaign. One was the publication by the *Union Leader* of a letter that Loeb had purportedly received from a young man in Florida. The letter writer said he had overheard a Muskie assistant say at a drug rehabilitation center in Fort Lauderdale that Maine did not have many blacks, "but we have Canucks" (a derogatory term for the Franco-American population component in Maine and New Hampshire). Muskie, the letter writer said, found the comment "amusing."

Muskie promptly denied that the statement had been made and challenged the authenticity of the letter. Not then nor later was Loeb able to substantiate the letter or its contents, but he never disavowed it and in fact wrote several editorials referring to the letter and how without it "no one in New Hampshire would know of the derogatory remarks emanating from the Muskie camp about the Franco-Americans in New Hampshire and Maine—remarks which the senator found amusing."

About the same time, the *Union Leader* reprinted on its editorial page a short, gossipy item from *Newsweek,* condensed from an article that had appeared in *Women's Wear Daily.* The original article had been an account of a campaign bus trip with Mrs. Muskie, in highly informal style. The boiled-down version in *Newsweek* consisted chiefly of quotes of Mrs. Muskie's comments to the women reporters on the bus with her ("Pass me my purse—I haven't had my morning cigarette yet" and "Let's tell dirty jokes").

The two episodes, close together, broke through Muskie's earlier determination not to get into a cat-and-dog fight with Loeb. He determined to go to the *Union Leader* office in Manchester and denounce Loeb's tactics. Let's pick up Witcover's account:

On Saturday morning, as planned, Muskie went to the paper, stood on the back of a flatbed truck, and amid falling snow denounced Loeb as a "liar" and a "gutless coward." Muskie produced the director of the Fort Lauderdale drug rehabilitation center to attest that no remarks such as the Morrison letter had described had been made, and New Hampshirites of French-Canadian origin defended the Senator against the "Canucks" charge. But Muskie, in his anger, broke down. Of Loeb's reference to Mrs. Muskie, he said: "This man doesn't walk, he crawls. . . . He's talking about my wife. . . . It's fortunate for him he's not on this platform beside me!" For a moment, Muskie could not go on. Reporters at the scene said tears ran down his face and some heard him say, "A good woman . . ." and then stop, unable to continue.[11]

In those few minutes that snowy morning, Edmund Muskie's campaign for the presidency was mortally injured. The image of the candidate breaking down, weeping, unable to speak, spread out into the public consciousness, not only in New Hampshire but throughout the country. Within weeks the former front-runner was to all intents and purposes out of the race. Loeb's goading attacks had worked far better than perhaps he had ever hoped.

The publisher's responses to reporters who interviewed him three days after the episode were revealing:

Q: Would you agree, Mr. Loeb, if this letter [the "Canuck" letter] does turn out to be a fraud, or it's from a young schoolboy, that it would be a very wrong thing to have done to publish this letter without checking the authenticity?
A: No, I really wouldn't. . . . What you have overlooked entirely is that the situation has gone far beyond the authenticity of the letter, or lack of authenticity. Mr. Muskie is not going to lose votes in New Hampshire on the basis of the authenticity or lack of authenticity of the letter. Mr. Muskie is going to lose votes in New Hampshire because he acted like a silly damn

fool in front of the *Union Leader* building. That's the reason why he's going to lose votes. . . .

Q: Mr. Loeb, I would just like to pursue this for a couple of minutes, in the realm of journalistic ethics. I presume that—

A: Now I'm a very gentle person. I get along nicely with people, but I'm not interested in discussing with you the question of journalistic ethics. If you pass beyond that point you can get the hell out of here right now, it's as simple as that.[12]

There is no point in adding anything more to the Loeb story.

The Piranha Fish

A final case involving ethics and political reportage has to do, ironically, with one phase of the coverage of the Watergate scandals. "Ironically" because, as has been noted in an earlier chapter, some aspects of Watergate showed the press in its finest hours.

There is a story (probably apocryphal) told about evangelist Billy Graham addressing a large public meeting in London. He called on all those who wanted to go to heaven to stand up. Everyone rose except one man in the front row. "What's the matter with you?" asked Billy, "Don't you want to go to heaven?"

For a moment there was silence. Then the man answered, "Not immediately."

In a very similar position, persons in and of the press who are faced with the question: "Aren't you proud of the role of the media in Watergate?" have to pause, too, if they are honest, and then respond: "Not completely."

We have already noted the remarkable achievements of the two young *Washington Post* reporters, Woodward and Bernstein, in uncovering by dogged investigative reporting one of the major scandals of American political history. The prizes and honors that have come to them have been deserved.

We also noted earlier, however, that the role of some of the rest of the press during the first phase of Watergate coverage was not so admirable. There was a business-as-usual aproach on the part of most of the press, a comfortable reliance on the "official sources" and their assurances that Watergate was no big thing. For much of the American press, during that first phase of the Watergate affair, no particular plaudits were due.

And it has been pointed out in an earlier discussion of anonymous sources (chapter 6) that in the later, catch-up stage of press coverage of Watergate many newsmen were far more careless than Bernstein and Woodward had been in relying on anonymous accusers and faceless sources. Misinformation with lasting, damaging consequences was peddled recklessly by reporters and columnists who finally realized that they had earlier missed the boat on Watergate and were trying to make up for lost time and lost opportunities by grabbing at anything that came along, whether it checked out or not.

These were some of the less savory facets of the press treatment of Watergate, and reason for an impartial press analyst to resist throwing his hat in the air automatically whenever "Watergate" is mentioned.

But there were other reasons as well.

During the final, climactic phases of the Watergate affair, when impeachment evidence was being assembled by the House Judiciary Committee, and when leaks of evidence from that source, from the Senate Watergate Committee, and from various grand juries were trickling out almost daily, some elements of the press seemed to be caught up in what has been called variously the "wolf-pack syndrome" or the "piranha approach." (Ben J. Wattenberg, adviser to Senator Henry M. Jackson in the 1972 presidential primary campaign, commented on the phenomenon in that period: "We saw it first with Muskie, when they built him up and then tore him down, and then with McGovern, when they built him up and tore him down; they have the bias of the piranha fish—they will go after anything that bleeds.")[13]

In the late stages of the Watergate episode, Richard M. Nixon and his presidency were losing blood fast. And the approach being taken by some of the press, notably the major TV networks and the two major news magazines, *Time* and *Newsweek,* was such as to cause even Howard Simons, the *Washington Post*'s managing editor, to wonder about the eagerness of some elements of the press to "rush in to get a bite of that bleeding body in the water."

To a considerable degree, the press had by then acquired a vested interest in seeing the President's ultimate downfall. Through the long months of the Ervin Committee hearings, the trials, the warming up of the impeachment machinery, the press had been maintaining a kind of drumroll of increasing intensity, leading to the climactic moment when the blade would fall on the scaffold. In one sense, the President *had* to be destroyed, or the long buildup by the columnists the commentators, and the news magazines would end in frustration.

Now let's pause a moment to clarify one point. It was very much the responsibility of the press through the two years of Watergate exposure and investigation to keep the story alive, to prevent it from just dwindling away. Nothing would have pleased the group around Nixon more than to have Watergate fizzle out because the public lost interest, or the press turned to other things. So the insistence by the media on keeping public attention focused on the various stages of the investigations, trials, and hearings was entirely defensible and in all respects in accord with the central journalistic ethic.

There is a difference, however, and one with ethical overtones, between keeping a stern and unyielding spotlight on a major national issue, and taking a vindictive pleasure in twisting the knife in a squirming victim. (Howard Simons, on the day word came to the *Post* newsroom that Haldeman, Ehrlichman, and Dean had resigned, wisely cautioned his exulting colleagues: "Don't gloat. We can't afford to gloat.")

But some journalists during this period found the chance to release an animosity that had been long repressed for reasons of professionalism or prudence. And the chance was too tempting to pass up.

One reporter, James M. Perry of the *National Observer*, acknowledged in a column in that paper:

... Nixon's supporters are largely right about us—we do not like their man and we never have ... some journalists have enjoyed telling the American people about Nixon and Watergate. Some journalists always have believed that Nixon was the kind of man Watergate seems to prove he is: devious, slippery, deeply suspicious of people who don't belong to the 'team,' isolated, introverted, unprincipled, tricky. Look, some of us might want to say, if we could: this is the man we've been telling you about all these years. Tricky Dick! Dick *is* Tricky.[14]

This notion, that the press generally had always hated him, was one that President Nixon and those around him called attention to repeatedly. And they tried to make that the basis for depicting the whole of the Watergate affair as a press extravaganza, something blown out of all proportion by irresponsible newsmen.

With Malice for One . . .

That last was obviously insupportable. The press didn't create the Watergate scandals; it merely reported them—and somewhat belatedly, at that.

But the *manner* in which at least some of the reportage and commentary was handled, particularly in the late stages of the drama, and the motivation that showed plainly behind that manner, did leave some elements of the press open to criticism.

For example, Edwin Diamond, a commentator on the *Washington Post* TV station, cited critically what he described as a "form of mass non-communication that can only be called psychojournalism," directed at the President and designed to depict him as one about to break down mentally.

The psychojournalistic style is characterized by blind items, innuendo, murky attribution and the shifting of the burden of discussion onto others. The overall tone raises apprehensions without explicitly confronting them.[15]

Time and *Newsweek* were the chief offenders, according to Diamond. Their reports described the President as listless, passive, when he spoke without gestures. When he was animated on the podium, they described him as kinetic, jerky, unnatural.

... the language is euphemistic, the confrontation with reality never direct. Apparently, the press is scattering clues–it has some suspicions about Richard Nixon's mental capacities—but it doesn't have the courage or the knowledge to say so. The stories of these episodes hung in mid air, feeding the public fears that something may be wrong.[16]

Another instance of hanging a negative impression in mid-air was the practice of one major network (ABC) of using a standard backdrop for its news anchormen whenever a Watergate-related story was being aired. The backdrop was a replica of the Presidential seal, with what appeared to be an enormous rubber stamp reading "IMPEACHMENT" superimposed on it. Viewers take from a television program as much information from the visuals as they get from the words spoken on the show; how much conditioning of the public mind was accomplished by the nightly appearance of the rubber-stamped seal?

It was left to a British writer, however, to give the most viciously outspoken expression to the anti-Nixon feeling of many newsmen. Tom Driberg, a columnist for *The New Statesman*, commented on Nixon's televised resignation speech thus:

As we saw—for, I hoped, the last time—that nasty, snarling little withdrawal of lip from teeth which passed for a Nixon smile, I felt that the only appropriate and more or less creditable exit for him would be suicide.[17]

These and various other instances of what appeared to be an unseemly eagerness on the part of some elements of the press to skewer Nixon on any pretext drew sharp reactions from both within and without the journalistic fraternity.

Some samples:

From Franklin B. Smith, editor of the editorial page of the *Burlington* (Vt.) *Free Press:*

As a veteran newspaperman dedicated to the principles of objective and fair reporting without fear or favor, I find repugnant the vast coverage of the Watergate affair. Much of this coverage by the press—and here I include newspapers, television, radio, and magazines—has been blatantly abusive both of our traditional American sense of justice and of the First Amendment's guarantee of press freedom.

There have been countless instances of clear distortion or curious neglect on the part of the press in the coverage of this unhappy affair. . . . [Mr. Smith went on to cite 12 specific instances in detail, then concluded:]

. . . most certainly this period will be remembered, with more sadness than outrage, as the darkest chapter in the long history of American press freedom.

As a veteran newspaperman of principled dedication, I grieve for my profession.[18]

From a letter sent to *Time* magazine by Clare Boothe Luce, widow of the founder of the magazine:

Sir: Harry Reasoner recently took *Time* to task on ABC-TV for certain instances of its obsessional and below-the-belt reporting on Watergate, which he said had betrayed the canons of both objective and ethical journalism.

It was predictable that sooner or later *Time* would begin to pay the price for its editorial overinvestment in the destruction of the President. That price, as Reasoner noted, is the loss of journalistic prestige and credibility. How ironic, and how fitting, that a distinguished media colleague and certified Nixon critic like Reasoner should blow the whistle on *Time* for its phobic Watergate reporting![19]

From columnist Art Hoppe of the *San Francisco Chronicle:*

The White House press has been wryly critical in private of every President since FDR. Cynicism is issued with their pencils and notebooks. But never have they been so openly and fearlessly hostile, never have their jokes been so vicious nor delivered with such relish. . . .
And you can't help feeling in this atmosphere of viciousness, vindictiveness and jubilant relish that if the President is driven from office in disgrace, it will not be so much for any high crimes or misdemeanors, but simply because this town hates his guts. . . .[20]

Finally, from New York University professor Irving Kristol, a frequent press critic:

Journalists today are extremely "idealistic" in the same sense that many college students in the '60s were "idealistic"; they are not much interested in money, only in power. And "power," for the media, means the power to discredit and destroy—it is through such successes that they acquire visible signs of grace. After Watergate, the media are in a state of mind that can only be described as manic. They feverishly seek new victims, prominent ones if possible, obscure ones if necessary. There is the smell of blood in the air, and of fire and brimstone, too.[21]

There is hyperbole in all four of these comments, of course, but substance as well.

It was unfortunate and needless, the overkill that some elements of the press indulged in during the late stages of the Watergate episode. Their excesses led to a tarring of the motivation of the press as a whole and blemished what had been a signal triumph of investigative reporting and of the historic adversary role of the press in our representative democratic system. That aspect of Watergate should stand as a lasting warning to newsmen that the serving of personal spites or personal favoritism in the coverage of the news is the sort of ethical lapse that can bring the credibility of the entire field into question in the public mind.

Notes

[1]Wilbur Schramm, *Men, Messages, and Media* (New York: Harper & Row, Publishers, Inc., 1973), p. 261.

2William L. Rivers and Wilbur Schramm, *Responsibility in Mass Communication* (New York: Harper & Row, Publishers, Inc., 1969), p. 48.

3*Ibid.*, p. 49.

4John C. Merrill, "How Time Stereotyped Three U.S. Presidents," *Journalism Quarterly*, XLII, No. 4 (Autumn, 1965), 563–70.

5T.S. Matthews, *Name and Address* (New York: Simon and Schuster, 1960), p. 274.

6Jules Witcover, "The Indiana Primary and the Indianapolis Newspapers—A Report in Detail," reprinted from the *Columbia Journalism Review*, VII, No. 2 (Summer, 1968) © 11–17.

7*Ibid.*, p. 12.

8*Ibid.*, p. 14.

9*Ibid.*, p. 17.

10Jules Witcover, "William Loeb and the New Hampshire Primary: A Question of Ethics," reprinted from the *Columbia Journalism Review*, XI, No. 1 (May/June 1972), © 14–25.

11*Ibid.*, p. 21.

12*Ibid.*, p. 22.

13"The Press in the 1972 Campaign," a symposium, *Nieman Reports*, XXVII, No. 3 (Fall, 1973), 3–9.

14James M. Perry, "The Media and Nixon," *National Observer*, XII, No. 27 (week ending July 7, 1973), p. 5.

15Edwin Diamond, "Psychojournalism: Nixon on the Couch," *Columbia Journalism Review*, XII, No. 6 (March/April 1974), 7–11.

16*Ibid.*, p. 9.

17Tom Driberg, "London Diary," *New Statesman*, August 16, 1974, p. 218.

18Franklin B. Smith, "Fear and Loathing in Vermont," *New York Times*, April 7, 1974, Op-Ed page.

19*Time*, CIII, No. 14 (April 8, 1974), 5–6.

20*San Francisco Chronicle*, May 19, 1974, Sunday Punch section, p. 1.

21Irving Kristol, "Political Pollution in Washington," *Wall Street Journal*, October 17, 1974, p. 18.

And Now What?... "As a matter of fact,

even to speak of the 'profession' of
journalism today is to indulge in flattering
exaggeration. Journalism has not, as yet,
acquired the simplest external signs of a
profession."—Irving Kristol [1]

12 That scornful dismissal above from Mr. Kristol is demonstrably undeserved.

Admittedly, the news gathering and disseminating business does not have the "external signs," the attributes of a profession as set out in dictionary definitions; there is no body of knowledge peculiar to the field which must be mastered by those wanting to practice; there is no licensing hurdle to get over, there are no policing bodies to ensure responsible performance.

But the men and women in the media of mass communication—or a great many of them, at any rate—do indeed *behave* like professionals. They respond—again, many of them—to ethical principles; they regard themselves as committed to serving the public interest; they resist—most of the time—omnipresent temptations to abuse vast power for personal ends.

The fact that so many of the journalists of the nation *do* behave in a professional way even though they are not subject to the prescriptive overview characteristic of the recognized professions gives them an even stronger claim to the status than would be the case if they were supervised by licensing and policing boards. Mr. Kristol's indictment is thus simplistic and overdrawn.

Some readers may find these comments in defense of the professionalism of journalists incongruous, a kind of non sequitur, coming as they do in the concluding chapter of a book devoted largely to an examination of cases involving ethical shortfalls of one degree or another.

But the incongruity is more apparent than real.

It was pointed out in the opening chapter that the ethical challenges that confront journalists are daily, not exceptional, occurrences. It was also noted that most of the challenges are responsibly met; some, it was acknowledged, are not. The purpose of this book has been to illustrate, case by case, the wide range of problems and decisions the journalist is expected to face and resolve within the urgent deadline limits of the working day.

Of necessity, then, we have been concentrating on the unmet challenges, the missteps, the wrong judgments, the individual failures. We haven't paused with each citation to make the balancing observation that dozens of similar challenges were met responsibly elsewhere in the world of journalism on the day this or that particular lapse took place.

This has indeed been—quite deliberately—a long look at the unlovely aspects of journalism, at the warts up close. For it is exactly from the missteps that the practical implications of generalized ethical principles can be understood. And perhaps out of that understanding can come an upgrading of a standard of performance that is already creditable, already professional—but which *could* be improved.

The very fact that it has been possible to assemble so many cases to consider suggests that there is room for improvement. And the Gallup, Roper, and other polls that have in recent years showed substantial public disenchantment with the media of mass communication underline the need for getting on with that improvement with all deliberate speed.

The questions left for us to consider are how this improvement is to be accomplished, and by whom, or what?

The Role of the Codes

The codes, of course, are a help. We reviewed them, and the ways in which they were developed, early in this discussion.

But how much leverage, as a practical matter, do journalistic codes have?

They cannot be compared with legal or medical codes, since in those fields ethical principles are enforced by licensing agencies and policing bodies. It is also the case that the medical and legal codes are more specific and rigid than those that have been developed in the field of journalism.

It was at one time believed that if only journalists could agree on a set of principles comparable to those in the recognized professions such as law and medicine, the problem of press ethics could be solved in a stroke.

Casper Yost, editor of the *St. Louis Globe-Democrat* in the 1920s, told the then-fledgling American Society of Newspaper Editors:

The ethics of journalism must be somehow expressed in definite form, and somehow established as the rule of practice of an influential number of journalists, before we can have professional recognition. Individual standards will always remain individual, and continue to be as varied as individual nature, until the profession of journalism, through collective consideration and action, establishes a code of professional ethics by which all journalistic conduct may be measured.[2]

Yost's advocacy was instrumental in the development of the ASNE Canons of Ethics that we examined back in chapter 2, along with excerpts from numerous other codes.

But a code of principles in a field that is unpoliced by any supervisory agency can accomplish only so much. H. L. Mencken, editor then of the *American Mercury*, once wrote:

Every now and then the newspapers make it known that some state editorial association in an obscure and backward state or some convention of teachers of journalism—i.e., incompetent journalists who have given up the struggle— has met to formulate a code of journalistic ethics. Nothing more, of course, is ever heard of the matter. If, as sometimes happens, a sonorous and pious code is actually drawn up and signed in blood, it becomes as much a dead letter the day afterward as the Seventh Commandment or the Eighteenth Amendment. No American newspaper, so far as I am aware, has ever made any serious attempt to carry out the terms of any such code. The day one does so I shall be prepared to hear that the governors of the New York Stock Exchange have passed a resolution requiring stockbrokers to observe the Beatitudes.[3]

If one filters out Mr. Mencken's celebrated bombast, there is a valid point to be found in his observation. How influential is a code of conduct for which there is no enforcement machinery?

Not many years after the ASNE Canons of Ethics were adopted, that organization was faced with the problem of a member who had grossly violated the provisions of the canons. Would the group muster up the gumption to discipline the offender by the only means the association's rules permitted—that is, by expelling him from membership? The editors hemmed and hawed and equivocated, but never acted.

In the episode involving the Indianapolis newspapers in the 1968 primary campaign (cited in chapter 11), Robert Kennedy's press secretary, Pierre Salinger, filed a protest with that same ASNE and requested an investigation. The response from Vincent S. Jones, then ASNE president: "We don't have any authority like that. We don't police our members and we don't investigate our members."[4]

The National Conference of Editorial Writers, which has a code of principles, has specifically refused to set up any sort of machinery for enforcing that code or even for receiving complaints from readers.

The hard fact is that codes without teeth, without an agency to enforce them, tend to be most influential with those who are *already* behaving responsibly and ethically; they often have little effect on the ones who need the guidance most (such as Mr. Loeb, for example).

But please don't misunderstand the point; this is not to say that there is no value in the codes and canons. It is essential, as we noted early in this discussion, that agreement be reached somehow within a society—or within a professional field in that society—as to what is generally accepted as right conduct and what is outside the pale for that society and that time. Even if the codes we fashion are broad and generalized in nature (certainly the case with the journalistic codes) they are nonetheless useful. Those who do desire to respond to a sense of ethics have at least some precepts by which to be guided.

The danger lies in assuming that once a code has been drawn up, the matter has then been settled. So far as journalism is concerned, that is not the case. As William Rivers and Wilbur Schramm point out:

Social responsibility is defined by various publishers and journalistic groups; it certainly is relative, and sometimes nebulous; and no solution that would be widely agreed upon and enforced can ever be reached. In fact, the whole point of social responsibility is that it is defined by journalists and enforced not at all. If it were defined and enforced by government, it would be nothing more than an authoritarian system in disguise.[5]

To what point have we come so far?

We have seen that generally understood ethical principles do exist in the field of journalism, some embodied in formal codes, some accepted as craft attitudes, some implied by the responsibility society places on the journalistic function.

We have seen that the performance of the media under the influence of this generalized ethic or code is reasonably good, but uneven and clearly capable of improvement. In the absence of any enforcement agency, however, the ethic or code, just by itself, doesn't offer much hope of accomplishing the desired improvement.

To turn the enforcement task over to government—through an agency comparable to, say, the Federal Communications Commission or the Federal Trade Commission—would be to abridge the First Amendment and invite the advent of a police state (consider to what unthinkable ends the Watergate affair might have gone had the media been under the federal thumb at the time).

Existing internal press organizations, such as the ASNE, have not proved to be very effective in enforcement of the ethical codes, except insofar as they may be a restraining influence to some degree and a source of support to those journalists who do tend to behave ethically in the first place.

Is there, then, no realistic prospect of any additional upgrading of the performance of the mass media?

(Before going on to frame some answers to that question, I should offer the reader a warning that from this point on most of the concluding passages of this chapter will represent simply the author's personal viewpoint; they should be read in that light and discounted to whatever degree may seem appropriate.)

There are, it seems to me, various ways in which efforts are likely to be made in the years to come to improve the standards of performance of the journalistic media. Some of these ways appear promising and productive, while others have some built-in hazards that must be avoided; some are already being explored, others are at the drawing-board stage. On balance, there are more reasons for hope than for dismay so far as the prospect for upgrading the ethical values and the performance of the press is concerned.

The Sideline Critics

One impressively hopeful development has been the emergence of professional reviews of the media of mass communication—regular critiques of journalists, mostly by their fellows.

231

There have, of course, almost always been individual press critics on the scene, from Upton Sinclair through the late A. J. Liebling, to the contemporary Ben H. Bagdikian. Their work provided a now-and-then goad to press performance; but the efforts of individual critics did not have the sustained influence of the reviews.

Nieman Reports, a limited-circulation quarterly published by the Nieman Foundation of Harvard, was first in the field, back in the 1940s. For a time, it was just about the only voice offering informed appraisal of the performance of the press on a regular basis.

Then in the early 1960s *Columbia Journalism Review*, published by the Pulitzer Graduate School of Journalism, was launched. Through the years, with the help of foundation money, it has built up a circulation vastly larger than that of *Nieman Reports* and has become the most influential of the critical reviews. The numerous citations of *CJR* articles studded throughout this book like raisins in a pudding attest to the vigor and persistence with which the *Review* has been keeping an unsparing eye on the performance of all of the media of mass communication. It is evident that a case book such as this one would have been all but impossible to put together without generous reliance on such inhouse monitors as *Nieman Reports* and *Columbia Journalism Review*.

And they aren't the only avenues now open for informed appraisal of media performance. In the aftermath of the 1968 Democratic Convention at Chicago, when local newsmen were disappointed in the standard of coverage given to the street disturbances by the media, a local press critique came into being. *Chicago Journalism Review* focused on the shortcomings, as its writers saw them, of the media in that city. It was imitated in numerous other cities and regions around the country. While many of these reviews have been short-lived or ineffectual (some were little more than ill-tempered gripe sheets), others have weathered the first struggling months to become solidly established. The most effective have been *(More)* in New York and the *Chicago Journalism Review*.

None of these journals—except Columbia's—has a substantial circulation. But they do reach the people who count, the media circles in their communities and to some extent around the nation. And they are read at the schools of journalism, where future generations of journalists are forming their impressions of the profession.

The various philanthropic foundations of the country could make no better investment in the future of American journalism than to give aid to the best of the reviews, particularly to those at Harvard, Columbia, and some few other educational institutions where the idea has also caught on. Here, as the frequent citations in this book effectively attest, is one avenue through which the often nebulous ethical codes of the profession are being interpreted and emphasized, given practical meaning and impact.

Much larger audiences are being reached by other efforts at appraisal of media performance by some of the media elements themselves.

The *Wall Street Journal* and its associated publication *The National Observer* regularly publish detailed and perceptive analyses of the activities of print and broadcast media. Some of these have been collected in book form.[6]

The news magazines, too, deal with the press on a departmental basis, though chiefly on a reportorial rather than a critical level, and occasional attention is given to the various media by other mass-circulation magazines and broadcast outlets. These tend to be sporadic and uneven, however, compared with the output of the reviews.

At the Academy

There is hope for upgrading of the standards of the press also in the work of the schools and departments of journalism, despite Mr. Mencken's snide brushoff of the educators ("incompetent journalists who have given up the struggle").

In every journalism curriculum there is at least some attention—and usually a good deal—given to the concept of journalistic ethics—and the applications of that concept. Journalism educators, who are typically qualified in both scholarly and professional experience, have been responsible for virtually all of the philosophic overviews of journalistic ethics. Among the most comprehensive and thoughtful of these now in print are *Responsibility in Mass Communication* by William L. Rivers and Wilbur Schramm, J. Edward Gerald's *The Social Responsibility of the Press*, and John C. Merrill's *The Imperative of Freedom*, all three of which have been cited several times in this book. There are many others, most of them listed in the bibliography that follows this chapter.

The schools and departments, and the thoughtful explorations of ethical concepts produced by the educators and researchers in those schools, are having and will have a ripple effect on the performance of the mass media through the years as student generations move up through the ranks of newspaper, magazine, and broadcast hierarchies.

Some ripples—though whether they can be credited to the influence of the schools may be arguable—are already evident in some of the media.

In one sense, the local reviews in Chicago and elsewhere represent one such ripple, one that spilled out over the edges a bit. But there are others as well to be noted.

Scandinavian Import

One is the development of a concern by some media managers that there be some kind of built-in agency of critical appraisal on each individual publication, a not-so-still voice of conscience to keep everyone ethically aware.

A concept has been borrowed from the Scandinavian countries, that of the "ombudsman," an official appointed to represent the little man with a complaint against the bureaucratic establishment. Some newspapers have set up such offices, among them the *Louisville Courier-Journal*, the *St. Louis Post-Dispatch*, and the *Washington Post*. Ben H. Bagdikian, perhaps the ablest and most articulate of the contemporary press critics, filled the role on the *Post* for a number of months, before his outspoken critiques of the paper's errors precipitated a showdown with top management and his return to free-lance criticism. But the *Post* continued the office, and filled it with a worthy successor to Bagdikian.

At the *Post* and at other papers that have experimented with the idea, the ombudsman not only acts as a conduit for reader complaints about bad treatment or fact errors, ensuring that such complaints are promptly dealt with, but also serves as a monitor of staff performance generally. Regular reports from the ombudsman to the readers are printed in the paper, explaining how a particular problem stemmed from a craft condition, or correcting an error if a correction was due. After some years of experimentation, the *Post* published a book made up of such reports, as well as internal memos showing how the ombudsman office functioned to improve the performance and the ethical sensitivity of the paper's entire staff, from reporters to editors.[7]

A survey conducted by the American Newspaper Publishers Association News Research Foundation in 1973 indicated that at that time about 9 percent of newspapers in the responding sample were experimenting with the ombudsman approach in one form or another. (Not many use the term "ombudsman," however, since readers seem to have difficulty with it; the *Courier-Journal*, for example, keeps getting letters addressed to "The Omnibusman" or to "Dear Omnipotent.")[8]

The same ANPA study also revealed that a good many papers that had not yet tried the ombudsman device had nevertheless been making an effort to better relations with readers by various other means. Some had tried the press council approach (discussed later in this chapter);

others had set up advisory committees of community leaders and convened these groups regularly to discuss press practices and problems; still others were publishing regular columns, typically written by the managing editor, to provide readers with explanations of the mechanics of gathering and processing the news.

The attitude reflected by these various gestures is one that is new to many editors and publishers, who a decade or more earlier would have held that there was little point in courting the understanding and support of the reading public in this fashion. Now they are concerned, and rightly so. They have become aware that there is a deep distrust among large numbers of the consumers of media products.

The media of mass communication appear to the individual readers and viewers as vast, overpowering, and often arrogant agencies. Anything that helps to reduce the relationship to less frightening proportions—ombudsmen, press councils, editors' columns, or advisory committees—may help to enhance the regard of the consumer for the media, as well as to keep the staff responsive to the rights and sensibilities of the reading, listening, or viewing public.

The Right of Access

A variation on the ombudsman approach has been advanced in quite another context, and one with some disquieting overtones. In order to ensure that readers have an opportunity for redress on all papers, not just those that may have tried the ombudsman idea, it has been suggested that there be established for the print media a kind of equivalent of the fairness and equal-time doctrines under which the broadcasters must function. Under these doctrines, promulgated by the Federal Communications Commission, a radio or television broadcaster whose station carries an attack on some individual or organization must provide to the party attacked an opportunity to respond. (The equal-time rule, which applies primarily to political candidates, specifies that if a station gives or sells time to one candidate for office, it must provide equal time on the same terms to all other candidates for that office.)

Jerome A. Barron, a law professor at George Washington University, has proposed that the First Amendment be reinterpreted to embrace a doctrine of right of access in all the media of communication, a kind of universally applied combination of the equal time and fairness doctrines. In other words, someone who has been unfairly dealt with in a newspaper or magazine should be given space to publish his response, just as the broadcaster must provide air time in a like situation.[9]

This is a beguiling and, on the surface, a reasonable proposal. But, more closely examined, it also has ominous implications.

As a practical matter, any newspaper could be inundated with right-of-access responses from legions of readers with real or fancied grievances if such a concept were actually put into effect. Virtually any news story contains something that someone might take exception to or think ought to be rebutted.

More significantly, such a right-of-access system would inevitably require some sort of government arbiter to ensure that the equal-space allotments actually were made as requested. And that would bring us face to face again with the specter of a government-controlled press.

John C. Merrill asks in *The Imperative of Freedom:*

How will decisions be made about what shall or shall not be printed under a Barron-type system? What would be a fair and rational manner of making such determinations if we are to take them out of the hands of individual editors and publishers? A federal press court of some type? A national *ombudsman*? An FPA (Federal Press Agency) organized along the lines of the Federal Communications Commission?[10]

Merrill's concerns have already been realized in at least one instance. In Florida a political candidate found an ancient statute on the books embodying in almost so many words Barron's right-of-access thesis. So when the *Miami Herald* criticized him editorially he trotted down to the paper's office next day with a long rebuttal statement and demanded that the paper print it verbatim or face being sued under the long-forgotten but still extant law. The paper refused, and the candidate went to court. In fact, he eventually went all the way to Washington, where on June 25, 1974, the Supreme Court of the United States handed down a ruling: the Florida law was unconstitutional.

Said Chief Justice Burger in his opinion (which reflected a unanimous decision, incidentally):

The choice of material to go into a newspaper and the decisions made as to limitations on the size of the paper, and content, and treatment of public issues and public officials—whether fair or unfair—constitutes the exercise of editorial control and judgment. It has yet to be demonstrated how governmental regulations of this crucial process can be exercised consistent with First Amendment guarantees of a free press as they have evolved to this time.[11]

The court's uncompromising and unanimous opinion seems to suggest that for the medium-range future, at least, the right-of-access approach is not likely to be pursued. And that is just as well; despite its attractive ring, the phrase conceals a very real threat to the independence of the press.

At the Council Table

One other approach toward the goal of improving the standards and performance of the media—the press council—has fewer booby traps than the Barron access plan. But its effectiveness appears to be uneven.

The press council idea, like the ombudsman, is an import, but from Great Britain this time rather than Scandinavia.[12] Since 1963 a British press council has functioned, made up largely of persons in the news business or formerly in it, but including as well a small complement of laymen. Its purpose is to receive and examine complaints of unfair or deficient press performance, most of them emanating from the public. If the council finds that the publication accused has indeed been guilty of lax performance, it issues findings to that effect. These findings do not constitute any kind of sentence or penalty on the offending editor or publication, but they are given distribution and presumably have the impact of a public reprimand. It is of course difficult to determine with accuracy how much effect the activities of the Council have had on the standards and performance of the British press; most analysts agree that it has been a force for good, and the initial hostility and opposition to the council that were manifest in the British press leadership have largely dissipated. Most British editors now support the Council, and as press analyst William L. Rivers notes:

The British journalists' applause is not the result of their being treated favorably by the Council. Of the 446 complaints adjudicated during the past six years, the Council upheld the reader and criticized the newspaper in 247 cases. Although the Council has no legal power, it has succeeded because it has used wisely a weapon the press has learned to respect: publicity:[13]

There have been several experiments with the press council idea in this country, most of them on a local or state basis. But within the last several years a national press council has been established under the auspices of the Twentieth Century Fund and is now open for business.

The American version of the national council differs from the British approach in that in this country most of the council members represent the public rather than the news media. However, in its first years, the American council was given the same sort of reception by the U.S. press as its British counterpart had received many years earlier. Most American editors and publishers opposed the national council concept; even the estimable *New York Times* announced that it would refuse to cooperate with council investigations of complaint cases. Those editors and others who resisted the council idea typically justified their position on the grounds that the press should be left to police itself and that any outside agency would inevitably represent an encroachment on the freedom of the media.

The American national press council was originally limited by its charter to consideration of complaints dealing with "national" news media (meaning the wire services, the broadcast networks, and the news magazines). However, in its second annual meeting in December, 1974, the Council voted to recommend to the Twentieth Century Fund, its financial sponsor, that its purview be extended to accept "legitimate complaints about press and broadcast performance from any citizen anywhere in the United States."

The American council has no more legal enforcement powers than does the British version.

After a rather slow start, the new American council began to receive cases and to publish decisions, including the one involving columnist Victor Lasky that was discussed in Chapter 3. Optimistic observers such as William L. Rivers predict a useful future for the council; its critics remain skeptical, and some among them view the council as a deceptive forerunner to some kind of government overview of press functioning.

Press councils at the local level in this country have been effective to varying degrees. In *Backtalk*, two educators who conducted local press council experiments, William L. Rivers and William B. Blankenburg, reported that a year's trial run of the idea in two western small towns resulted in improved understanding by the public of the newspapers' problems, and a heightened sensitivity on the part of the editors with respect to the concerns and attitudes of their subscribers.[14]

The two experiments described in *Backtalk* were sponsored by a foundation, the Mellett Fund for a Free and Responsible Press, which also underwrote similar but less successful ventures in two midwestern towns.

Regional councils have also been established in Minnesota and Hawaii in this country, and in Canadian provinces.

In fact, the case for the press council idea was put most forcefully by a Canadian, William Heine, writing in the *Bulletin of the American Society of Newspaper Editors:*

North America's print media are unwise to continue indefinitely as the only major elements of democratic society from whose decisions there is no appeal.

A President can be impeached.

A Prime Minister can be defeated in Parliament.

Lawyers can be disbarred.

Doctors can be denied the right to practice.

Labor union leaders can be voted out by members and controlled by law.

Corporate officers can be removed by boards of directors.

Corporations can be reconstituted by law, specifically by trust law.

The list is endless, and includes broadcast outlets, which can lose their license by decisions of regulatory boards in both Canada and the United States.

The print media, however, by common law, tradition and precedent in Canada, and by the First Amendment to the Constitution of the United States, are answerable to no one—and certainly not to any legislative body, for unethical or improper conduct. It can be argued that the reader, by his impact on circulation, is the ultimate control over the print media. That argument is invalidated by the reality that most North American cities have one newspaper, which is almost incapable of going out of business and unlikely to be driven out of business.[15]

Implicit in Mr. Heine's argument is the assumption that the press council would constitute an adequate agency of appeal from the actions and decisions of the mass media. And therein lies the weakness.

For the press councils, at whatever level, have a limited leverage simply because they do not have enforcement powers. They can publicly reprimand an offender, which has some impact, certainly; in Britain it has been a restraining influence on a substantial proportion of the press. But the worst offenders against ethical standards are the very ones least likely to pay attention to reprimands, public or not, unless the reprimanding agency is also in a position to wield some more substantial sanctions.

239

It would seem that the greatest impact of the press councils is likely to be on the responsible editors, publishers, and broadcasters who for the most part were already attempting to behave ethically. An additional value of the councils may be the mutual understanding that grows out of the exchange across the council table between the members of the public and the managers of the media. These values should not be dismissed as insignificant, of course. But neither should too much be expected of them.

One Good Man

That brings us, finally, to the one factor that has for most of the history of journalism been the chief guarantee of integrity—the character and conscience of the men and women who own and work in the media of mass communication.

Among the many lures and motivations that draw men and women into the business of journalism (ego-gratification, love of writing, wanting to be where the action is) one that has consistently influenced at least a majority of journalists is the desire to contribute something of value to the public welfare. The central journalistic ethic of making a faithful picture of reality on which the public can act has been, to these men and women, a compelling ideal.

Please don't misread this point; I don't mean to confer halo and sainthood on all the legions of the Fourth Estate. There are plenty of time-servers in this field as in any other, plenty who are only doing a job and taking home a paycheck, and even some—as we have seen—who are scoundrels in the making or in full flower.

But a fact that anyone who has spent any time in the mass media of communication will attest to is that there are a very great many persons who *do* respond to the journalistic ethic, who *do* regard themselves in a public service role as much as any doctor or teacher may be, and who consciously choose an occupation that offers fewer material rewards for their talents than they could command elsewhere because they believe that occupation to be a singular and important one.

In discussing the strains of journalistic philosophy that actuate many of the best persons in the field, John C. Merrill underlines the indispensability of a sense of personal commitment:

The concept of duty to principle . . . anchors freedom and fulfills rationality: It keeps the journalist from being blown back and forth by the winds of social pressure and personal expediency. It protects him against the morality of utilitarianism. The journalist pursues truth because he would will that all journalists pursue truth; he has an obligation to pursue and present truth, not out of some conviction that "truth will make for better government" or out of some other hoped-for benefit, but simply because he has a duty to the maxim that *journalists must present the truth.*[16]

The American people are luckier than most of them realize that a sense of public service and commitment to principle has been as prevalent as it has among individual journalists, both those who gather and write the news and those who own and control the media.

Where both owners and staff members share the same degree of commitment to the journalistic ethic, the public is well and honestly served. It takes a Frank Stanton, head of CBS, to give a forum to a Walter Cronkite or an Eric Sevareid, or a stable of Spectrum commentators. It takes an Arthur H. Sulzberger to assemble so brilliant a constellation as the one that presided over the *New York Times* (of Sulzberger, the *Wall Street Journal* observed in his obituary, ". . . no newspaper can be greater than the vision and integrity of the man who makes the ultimate decisions.")

That is the ideal combination—leadership imbued with a sense of responsibility to the public and a staff conscientiously attempting to put into practical effect the generalized codes and principles of the field.

Where ownership and staff do not see alike the journalistic ethic—and the public—inevitably must suffer. A good staff obliged to work under an owner or publisher whose goals are money and power rather than public service may have some limited room to maneuver, some ability to practice sound journalism despite the polices set from above. But, as Ben H. Bagdikian has pointed out:

Whatever his title, the chief editorial executive selects his subordinates and transmits his values through them. New visitors to newsrooms are usually surprised by the lack of constant communication among staff workers and the apparent casualness of decision-making on the news. In reality, the organization is suffused with the values of the executive, producing a unanimity, or near-unanimity, enforced not only by the punishment-and-reward system but also by the iron demand of smoothly processing information in a limited period of time.[17]

In other words, whether ethical considerations will be respected in the practice of journalism depends on the presence of personal integrity both in the front office and at every desk in the newsroom, or behind every microphone and camera in the studios.

There must be a sense of calling and commitment, an individual response to the concept of journalism as a form of public service. And let me note again that despite the cynics' sneers, large numbers of journalists through the years have made that response. Not *all* journalists, *all* of the time, admittedly. But much of the time, and on most occasions when the hard decisions had to be made.

How do we stand today with respect to this ingredient of personal integrity in journalism—both at the top and in the ranks—and what are the prospects that it will continue to serve as a force to uplift the standards of performance in years to come?

The appeal of the public service ethic undeniably still is there; swelling enrollments in journalism schools at a time when overall college populations have been either static or declining attest to the persistence of the lure. This field and that of law have been "in" for several years, for some of the same reasons—young people see in them a means of working some good in society, of bringing about improvement.

The emergence of a "journalists' movement," a sort of revolt in the newsroom by staff members who would like a share in the decision making that determines the character of a print or broadcast property, suggests that the public service ideal exists among present staff members as well as those entering the preparatory pipelines.[18] These are all hopeful and encouraging signs.

But there are some disheartening considerations as well. We have earlier noted the steady trend toward concentration of ownership of the media, the growth of the chains and groups. In such situations the interaction between ownership and staff is buffered and diluted, and properties slip out of individual hands and into those of corporations, boards of directors, even hydra-headed conglomerates. The incalculable influence of the strong, ethical individual at the helm, with a Sulzberger's "vision and integrity," is lost in the corporate maze of automation, balance sheets, and stock options.

Bagdikian poses the ultimate question:

On the other hand, more and more news media companies are being absorbed in chains and conglomerates that not only increase impersonality but also raise the problem of journalism becoming a subsidiary or by-product to much larger non-journalistic activity of the parent company. If a non-journalistic corporation is considered justified, as it is, in trying to positively influence media treatment of its activities, what happens when the same corporation owns the news medium it wishes to influence?[19]

There seems no early end to this trend, although there was at least a flicker of hope in mid-1974 when Justice Department antitrust lawyers

242

began a long-planned effort to break up cross-media ownerships (that is, ownership situations such as in Bluefield, West Virginia, in which one family owns newspaper, radio, and televison properties, giving it a head-lock on the flow of information in that community).

We can be grateful that many individually owned papers still hold out, in large cities and small. Katherine Graham and her *Washington Post*, which was built to greatness by her father and her husband and maintained in that spirit under her direction, serve the nation's capital with journalism of distinction. The *New York Times* continues in a splendid tradition, and the *Los Angeles Times*, though now almost a con-glomerate by itself, still operates under the individual direction of an owner who turned it from a fat but undistinguished metropolitan giant into one of the world's fine newspapers, with one of the ablest staffs any-where. The *Louisville Courier-Journal* and *Times*, now in the hands of the third generation of the Bingham family, are rightly described by the *Wall Street Journal* as the "Messrs. Clean of the newspaper industry . . . no small distinction at a time when the ethics and credibility of the American press are undergoing their closest scrutiny in recent memory."[20]

But the trend toward concentration of ownership seems inexorable. When I first came to the state of Oregon, 20 years ago, only one of the state's daily newspapers was owned by a non-Oregon interest. Now 53 percent of the state's dailies are in the hands of out-of-state chains or groups, and of the remaining all but two are in home-grown groups formed within the state. (One of the two individually owned holdouts, the *Eugene Register-Guard* is one of the finest, most responsible news-papers of any size in the nation.) The same pattern of concentration is evident across the country.

The Wired World

But if these currently visible trends are disturbing, there may be others even more alarming in the making.

If we are to believe the prophets of communications-to-come, the Marshall McLuhans and others who foresee a "global village" intercon-nected by television, and a "wired world" in which cable systems will bring anywhere from 50 to 200 two-way channels into every home, the concerns we may have now about the ethics of journalism may be as nothing compared to the worries that will be with us then (or with those of us still around to worry).

In that future time (guesses run from the year 2,000 by Ben H.

243

Bagdikian, author of *The Information Machines*,[21] to a much closer date, such as 1984), the citizenry will be able, by pushing the buttons on their home consoles, to call up almost unlimited quantities of news and entertainment. Representations of newspaper and magazine pages will be projected on wall-size screens, to be read at the user's convenience; an attached printout device will provide permanent copies of any item that looks worth saving for the bureau drawer or desk file. Books, newspapers, magazines, as we know them, will be things of the past, only museum relics, and information will be kept in central data banks to be dispensed through the ubiquitous cable.

Many kinds of business and allied activities will be conducted by means of the two-way cable, according to the prophets' vision of the future. Housewives and husbands will be able to shop by cable, bankers will shift funds around electronically, doctors will diagnose by television. And virtually all education will be possible in the home, in front of that glowing screen. The lucky mothers of that future era will have their little ones with them 365 days a year (which ought to popularize greatly the zero population growth movement). It is possible to picture the inhabitants of that distant day evolving gradually into pear-shaped blobs, well cushioned for long sitting, with overdeveloped index fingers for pushing the console buttons that activate the cable system, and with bulging, thick-lensed eyes to keep focused on the all-giving screen.

It is an appalling prospect, simply from an aesthetic point of view. If one contemplates as well the problem of sustaining ethical standards in a world where, to all intents and purposes, there will be a single medium of communication—very likely under some form of government control—the view is even bleaker. Orwell may have been conservative.

Fortunately for us, all of this is very probably many years away. Bagdikian's estimate of the twenty-first century appears sounder than those of the alarmists (or optimists, depending on your point of view) who think in terms of the 1980s or 1990s.

So, for the moment, let's put the wired world and its problems aside for another author to deal with at another time.

What Color Cover?

For a final thought about the present situation of the press, and the concern of this book with the maintenance and uplift of the ethical standards of the journalism we are living with today, let me note again the signs that in my judgment are reason for encouragement and optimism.

The reviews, the analyses provided by the academy, the in-house ombudsmen, and above all the stubborn persistence of the appeal of the central ethic of serving the public by getting and disseminating the news as fully and honestly as possible—these add up to a strong basis for faith in the continuation and the upgrading of the performance of the media of mass communication we depend upon for the flickering pictures of the world beyond our immediate circle.

Perhaps some small help, too, can come from such a compilation as this book provides of ethical challenges and problems. For ethics is not a disparate topic in journalism; ethical questions infuse every aspect of the media fields, and should be considered within the contexts of all of those fields, as these pages have been attempting to suggest.

Harold Innis recalls the discussion by a group of university graduates in which the subject of literature was mentioned. One said, "Literature? Sure; we took it in the senior year. It had a green cover."[22]

I have no idea at this writing what color the publisher will decide to put on this book (perhaps a multicolor plaid would be appropriate?).[23] But I earnestly hope that the subject matter won't be remembered by future journalists who may dip into it as something separate, something to be brought to mind briefly on Sundays. For there is nothing more central, nothing more elusive, nothing more pervasive in the fields of journalism than the topic on which the foregoing pages have centered.

In fact, it may well be that if journalism loses touch with ethical values, it will at that same moment cease to be of use to society, and cease to have any real reason for being.

But that, for the sake of us all, must never be allowed to happen.

And, for my part, I am confident that it never will.

Notes

[1] Irving Kristol, "Crisis for Journalism: The Missing Elite," in *Press, Politics and Popular Government*, ed. George F. Will (Washington: American Enterprise Institute for Public Policy Research, 1972), p. 43.

[2] Quoted in Leon Nelson Flint, *The Conscience of the Newspaper* (New York: D. Appleton and Company, 1925), p. 386.

[3] *Ibid.*, pp. 388–89.

[4] Jules Witcover, "The Indiana Primary and the Indianapolis Newspapers—A Report in Detail," reprinted from the *Columbia Journalism Review*, VII, No. 2 (Summer, 1968), © 11–17.

[5] William L. Rivers and Wilbur Schramm, *Responsibility in Mass Communication* (New York: Harper & Row, Publishers, Inc., 1969), p. 50.

6A. Kent MacDougall, ed., reprinted from *The Press: A Critical Look from the Inside* (Princeton: Dow Jones Books, 1972). © Dow Jones Books, 1967.

7Laura Longley Babb, ed., *Of the press, by the press, and for the press (And others, too)* (Washington: The Washington Post Company, 1974).

8Findings of the ANPA survey were published in Keith P. Sanders, "What Are Daily Newspapers Doing To Be Responsive To Readers' Criticisms?" *News Research Bulletin, No. 9,* November 30, 1973, published by the American Newspaper Publishers Association.

9Professor Barron's thesis is discussed in detail in his book *Freedom of the Press for Whom?: The Rise of Access to Mass Media* (Bloomington: University of Indiana Press, 1973).

10John C. Merrill, *The Imperative of Freedom: A Philosophy of Journalistic Autonomy* (New York: Hastings House, Publishers, Inc., 1974), p. 114. Copyright © 1974 by John Calhoun Merrill, excerpted by permission of Hastings House, Publishers, Inc.

1142 *United States Law Week* 5103 (1974).

12Actually, the concept of a press council had been advanced in the United States a good many years before the British version was established. The Hutchins Commission on a Free and Responsible Press discussed the possibility in its 1947 report. Former Senator William Benton of Connecticut proposed a similar council for radio and television in 1951. Individual editors, among them Raymond Spangler of the *Redwood City* (Calif.) *Tribune* and William Townes of the *Santa Rosa* (Calif.) *Press-Democrat,* conducted short-lived experiments between 1946 and 1950. But the first systematic approaches in this country came later, after the British council had been functioning for many years.

13William L. Rivers, "How to Kill a Watchdog," *The Progressive,* XXXVII, No. 2 (February 1973), 44–48.

14William L. Rivers *et al., Backtalk: Press Councils in America* (San Francisco: Canfield Press, 1972).

15William Heine, "In Canada: A Provincial Council," *Bulletin of The American Society of Newspaper Editors,* No. 574, January 1974, pp. 12–14.

16Merrill, from *The Imperative of Freedom,* p. 199. Copyright © 1974 by John Calhoun Merrill, by permission of Hastings House Publishers.

17Ben H. Bagdikian, "Professional Personnel and Organizational Structure in the Mass Media," in *Mass Communication Research: Major Issues and Future Directions,* ed. W. Phillips Davison and Frederick T. C. Yu (New York: Praeger Publishers, Inc., 1974) pp. 122–42.

18Several articles on this topic were published in the Summer, 1970, issue of *Columbia Journalism Review,* and there have been recurring references to the progress of the journalists' movement in many *CJR* issues since.

19Ben H. Bagdikian, "Professional Personnel and Organizational Structure in the Mass Media," p. 124.

20David P. Garino, "Louisville Newspapers Cherish Independence, Guard it Jealously," *Wall Street Journal,* July 11, 1974, p. 1.

21Ben H. Bagdikian, *The Information Machines: Their Impact on Men and the Media* (New York: Harper & Row, Publishers, Inc., 1971).

22Harold A. Innis, *The Bias of Communication* (Toronto: University of Toronto Press, 1951), p. 194.

23At the time I was reading the final page proofs on this chapter, an article appeared in *The National Observer* for the week ending July 26, 1975, with a headline that suggested yet another cover possibility: "Journalistic Ethics: Not Black, Not White, But . . . A Rainbow of Gray."

A Selected, Annotated Bibliography

Associated Press Managing Editors Association. *Guidelines.* New York: Associated Press Managing Editors Association, 1969. A collection of newsroom, reporting, and publishing policies and procedures.

⸻. *1970 Supplement—APME Guidelines.* New York: Associated Press Managing Editors Association, 1970.

BABB, LAURA LONGLEY, ed. *Of the press, by the press, for the press (And others, too).* Washington: The Washington Post Company, 1974. Editorials, ombudsman columns, office memos, all from the *Washington Post* and dealing with a variety of policy, procedural, and ethical questions.

BAGDIKIAN, BEN H. *The Information Machines, Their Impact on Men and the Media.* New York: Harper & Row, Publishers, Inc., 1971. A perceptive, detailed look at the future of the mass media, particularly the newspaper press.

⸻. *The Effete Conspiracy and Other Crimes by the Press.* New York: Harper & Row, Publishers, Inc., 1972. A representative collection of Bagdikian's critical appraisals of the press during the 1960s, most of them from *Columbia Journalism Review* issues ranging from 1962 to 1971.

BARRON, JEROME A. *Freedom of the Press for Whom?: The Rise of Access to Mass Media.* Bloomington: University of Indiana Press, 1973. An elaboration of Barron's "right of access" interpretation of the First Amendment.

BERNSTEIN, CARL, AND BOB WOODWARD. *All the President's Men.* New York: Simon & Schuster, Inc., 1974. The detailed story of how the *Post's wunderkinder* did in Nixon and Company.

BRINTON, CRANE. *A History of Western Morals.* New York: Harcourt, Brace and Company, 1959.

CATER, DOUGLASS. *The Fourth Branch of Government.* Boston: Houghton Mifflin, Company 1959. An examination of the nature and role of the Washington correspondents' corps.

CIRINO, ROBERT. *Don't Blame the People: How the News Media Use Bias, Distortion and Censorship to Manipulate Public Opinion.* New York: Random House, Inc., 1971. Angry citations of cases, some well documented, others somewhat sketchy.

————. *Power to Persuade: Mass Media and the News.* New York: Bantam Books, Inc., 1974. In the same vein as *Don't Blame the People.*

COHEN, STANLEY, AND JOCK YOUNG, eds. *The Manufacture of News. A Reader.* Beverly Hills, California: Sage Publications, 1973. The following chapters are of particular interest: "Bias through selection and omission: automobile safety, smoking," by Robert Cirino; "News as eternal recurrence," by Paul Rock; "Political deviance: the press presentation of a militant mass demonstration," by Graham Murdock.

Commission on Freedom of the Press (The Hutchins Commission). *A Free and Responsible Press.* Chicago: University of Chicago Press, 1947.

CRAWFORD, NELSON A. *The Ethics of Journalism.* New York: Alfred A. Knopf, 1924. An early ethics text composed to a large degree of quotes from press association codes of ethics.

CROUSE, TIMOTHY. *The Boys on the Bus.* New York: Random House, Inc., 1973. Press correspondents and how they covered the 1972 presidential campaign; heroes, villains, craft attitudes, deadline pressures.

DAVISON, W. PHILLIPS, AND FREDERICK T. C. YU, eds. *Mass Communication Research: Major Issues and Future Directions.* New York: Praeger Publishers, Inc., 1974.

DENNIS, EVERETTE E., AND WILLIAM L. RIVERS. *Other Voices: The New Journalism in America.* San Francisco: Canfield Press, 1974. A survey of the various branches of New Journalism, with samples of each.

EMERY, MICHAEL C., AND TED CURTIS SMYTHE, eds. *readings in mass communication: concepts and issues in the mass media* (2nd ed.) Dubuque: William C. Brown Company, Publishers, 1974. A useful selection of readings drawn from journals of press appraisal and criticism.

EPSTEIN, EDWARD JAY. *News from Nowhere: Television and the News.* New York: Random House, Inc., 1973. One man's analysis of how television news is shaped by institutional and other forces.

FLINT, LEON NELSON. *The Conscience of the Newspaper.* New York: D. Appleton and Company, 1925. An early approach to journalistic ethics.

FRIENDLY, FRED W. *Due to Circumstances Beyond Our Control.* New York:

Random House, Inc., 1967. A former network newsman and producer describes pressures on TV news from advertisers and others.

GERALD, J. EDWARD. *The Social Responsibility of the Press.* Minneapolis: The University of Minnesota Press, 1963. One of the most thoughtful and literate discussions in print on the subject of press ethics.

GHIGLIONE, LOREN, ed. *Evaluating the Press: The New England Daily Newspaper Survey.* Southbridge, Mass.: Loren F. Ghiglione, 1973. A paper-by-paper anatomizing of the New England daily press, with praise and criticism for each publication.

GLESSING, ROBERT. *The Underground Press in America.* Blomington: Indiana University Press, 1970.

GRIFFITH, THOMAS. *How True: A Skeptic's Guide to Believing the News.* Boston: Atlantic-Little Brown & Co., 1974. Pungent and critical comments about all the media from a former *Time-Life editor.*

HASELDEN, KYLE. *Morality and the Mass Media.* Nashville, Tenn.: Broadman Press, 1968. A churchman who is also an articulate journalist looks at press ethics from the viewpoint of morality. Philosophical and thought-provoking.

HENNING, ALBERT F. *Ethics and Practices in Journalism.* New York: Farrar & Rinehart, Inc., 1932. Another early and not particularly searching view.

HOGGART, RICHARD. *On Culture and Communication.* Oxford: Oxford University Press, 1972. Lectures by a perceptive British observer, not dealing with ethics directly but touching occasionally on related topics.

HOHENBERG, JOHN. *The News Media: A Journalist Looks at His Profession.* New York: Holt, Rinehart and Winston, Inc., 1968. An experienced newsman's appraisal of the good and bad in his field.

INNIS, HAROLD A. *The Bias of Communication.* Toronto: University of Toronto Press, 1951. McLuhan's foreruner; less showy, less entertaining, but in some respects more understandable.

KATZ, JOSEPH, PHILIP NOCHLIN, AND ROBERT STOVER, eds. *Writers on Ethics.* Princeton: D. Van Nostrand Company, Inc., 1962. A sampling of philosophers, statesmen, economists, and moralists through the centuries.

KRIEGHBAUM, HILLIER. *Pressures on the Press.* New York: Thomas Y. Crowell Company, 1972. An exploration of various kinds of problems confronting the press today, including ethical ones.

LEROY, DAVID J., AND CHRISTOPHER H. STERLING, eds. *Mass News: Practices, Controversies, and Alternatives.* Englewood Cliffs, N.J.: Prentice-Hall, Inc., 1973. This reader contains several useful articles dealing with press ethics.

LIEBLING, A. J. *The Press.* New York: Ballantine Books, Inc., 1964. A collection of columns by the reigning and unsparing press critic of the 1940s and 1950s.

LINDSTROM, CARL E. *The Fading American Newspaper.* Garden City, N.Y.:

249

Doubleday & Company, Inc., 1960. A former Gannett editor's sorrowing appraisal of the problems and the prospects of the newspaper field.

LIPPMANN, WALTER. *A Preface to Morals*. New York: The Macmillan Company, 1929. One of the classics.

MACDOUGALL, A. KENT, ed. *The Press*. Princeton: Dow Jones Books, 1972. A collection of articles on the press that originally appeared in the *Wall Street Journal*, all carefully written and documented. Several deal specifically with ethics.

MACDOUGALL, CURTIS D. *News Pictures Fit to Print . . . Or Are They?* Stillwater, Okla.: Journalistic Services, Inc., 1971.

————. *The Press and Its Problems*. Dubuque: William C. Brown Company, Publishers, 1964. A text on newsroom policies that deals extensively with questions involving ethics.

MATTHEWS, T. S. *Name and Address*. New York: Simon and Schuster, 1960. Another former *Time* editor's autobiographical commentary.

MCGINNIS, JOE. *The Selling of the President, 1968*. New York: Trident Press, 1969. Public relations at work in the 1968 campaign of Richard M. Nixon.

MCLUHAN, MARSHALL. *Understanding Media: The Extensions of Man*. New York: McGraw-Hill Book Company, 1964.

MERRILL, JOHN C., AND RALPH L. LOWENSTEIN. *Media, Messages, and Men*. New York: David McKay Co., Inc., 1971. An introductory text, with a thoughtful section on media ethics.

MERRILL, JOHN C., *The Imperative of Freedom: A Philosophy of Journalistic Autonomy*. New York: Hastings House, Publishers, Inc., 1974. A searching and provocative exploration of the philosophical roots of journalistic ethics; the author's dedication to individualism and integrity in journalism comes through strongly.

RIVERS, WILLIAM L., *The Opinionmakers: The Washington Press Corps*. Boston: Beacon Press, 1965.

————, and Wilbur Schramm. *Responsibility in Mass Communication*. New York: Harper & Row, Publishers, Inc., 1969. An updating of Schramm's original and landmark treatment of the role of the press in society. Excellent case studies of ethical problems.

————, et al. *Backtalk: Press Councils in America*. San Francisco: Canfield Press, 1972.

ROWSE, ARTHUR E. *Slanted News*. Boston: Beacon Press, 1957. A case study of bias in news placement and headline treatment in a presidential campaign.

SCHRAMM, WILBUR. *Men, Messages, and Media*. New York: Harper & Row, Publishers, Inc., 1973. An introductory text that covers the field with grace and clarity, and includes ethical questions in its embrace.

SIEBERT, FRED S., THEODORE PETERSON, AND WILBUR SCHRAMM. *Four Theories of the Press.* Urbana, Ill.: University of Illinois Press, 1956. The classic categorization of operational press theories.

SINCLAIR, UPTON. *The Brass Check: A Study of American Journalism.* One of the earliest—and angriest—of the press critics.

SMALL, WILLIAM. *Political Power and the Press.* New York: Hastings House, Publishers, Inc., 1972. The author is a former CBS network executive.

WILL, GEORGE F., ed. *Press, Politics, and Popular Government.* Washington: American Enterprise Institute for Public Policy Research, 1972.

WOLFE, TOM. *The New Journalism.* New York: Harper & Row, Publishers, Inc., 1973. One of the New Journalists discusses his own and others' contributions.

251

Index